GENDER, CIVIC CULTURE
AND CONSUMERISM

MANCHESTER
UNIVERSITY PRESS

GENDER, CIVIC CULTURE AND CONSUMERISM

MIDDLE-CLASS IDENTITY IN BRITAIN, 1800–1940

edited by

ALAN KIDD AND DAVID NICHOLLS

Manchester University Press

Manchester and New York

distributed exclusively in the USA by St. Martin's Press

Copyright © Manchester Univeristy Press 1999

While copyright in the volume as a whole is vested in Manchester University Press, copyright in individual chapters belongs to their respective authors, and no chapter may be reproduced wholly or in part without the express permission in writing of both author and publisher.

Published by Manchester University Press
Oxford Road, Manchester M13 9NR, UK
and Room 400, 175 Fifth Avenue, New York, NY 10010, USA
http://www.man.ac.uk/mup

Distributed exclusively in the USA by
St. Martin's Press, Inc., 175 Fifth Avenue, New York,
NW 10010, USA

Distributed exclusively in Canada by
UBC Press, University of British Columbia, 6344 Memorial Road,
Vancouver, BC, Canada V6T 1Z2

British Library Cataloguing-in-Publication Data
A catalogue record for this book is available from the British Libarary

Library of Congress Cataloging-in-Publication Data applied for

ISBN 0 7190 5267 X *hardback*
     0 7190 5676 4 *paperback*

First published 1999

06   05   04   03   02   01   00   99   10   9   8   7   6   5   4   3   2   1

Typeset by
Action Publishing Technology Ltd, Gloucester
Printed in Great Britain by
Biddles Ltd, Guildford and King's Lynn

CONTENTS

PART TWO   **GENDER, IDENTITY AND CONSUMER CULTURE**

ILLUSTRATIONS

NOTES ON CONTRIBUTORS

Jill Greenfield completed her doctorate on 'Gender, technology and the boot and shoe industry 1850–1911' in 1998. Her thesis was based at the University of Warwick, where she had previously completed an MA on women's magazines in the 1930s. Her work on consumer magazines has been published in *Media History* and *Twentieth Century British History*.

Simon Gunn is Principal Lecturer in History in the School of Cultural Studies, Leeds Metropolitan University. He is currently writing a book on the middle class in nineteenth-century England, *Rites of Power: Bourgeois Culture and the Industrial City, 1840–1900*, for Manchester University Press.

A. James Hammerton, Reader in History at La Trobe University, Melbourne, Australia, is the author of *Cruelty and Companionship: Conflict in Nineteenth Century Married Life* (Routledge, 1992, 1995) and *Emigrant Gentlewomen: Genteel Poverty and Female Emigration, 1830–1914* (Croom Helm, 1979). His chapter in this volume forms part of a larger study on lower-middle-class marriage and masculinity.

Kate Hill is Lecturer in History at the University of Lincolnshire and Humberside. She was awarded her Ph.D. in 1997 at the University of Lancaster for a thesis on Victorian municipal museums.

Christopher P. Hosgood is Associate Professor and Chair of the Department of History, University of Lethbridge, Canada. His published work includes studies of the Victorian petite bourgeoisie, including articles on shop life, shop-keepers and commercial travellers. He is currently working on a study of shopping and shop culture in *fin de siècle* London.

Alan Kidd is Reader in History at the Manchester Metropolitan University. His publications include *Manchester* (in the 'Town and City Histories' series, Keele University Press, 2nd edn, 1996); *The Making of the British Middle Class? Studies of Cultural and Regional Diversity since 1750*, edited with David Nicholls (Sutton Publishing, 1998); *State, Society and the Poor in Nineteenth-Century England* (Macmillan, 1999).

John Lowerson is Reader in History at the University of Sussex. He works largely on the social and economic history of modern British leisure patterns. His last book was *Sport and the English Middle Classes, 1870–1914* (Manchester University Press, 1993). He is completing a substantial book on the social and cultural history of the amateur operatic movement, also for Manchester University Press.

Dianne Sachko Macleod is Professor of Art History at the University of California at Davis and is also a faculty member in Davis's international summer programme at the Université de Nice. She was born and educated in Canada and worked in art galleries and at the California Arts Commission for several years before obtaining her Ph.D. in the History of Art from the University of California at Berkeley. Her book, *Art and the Victorian Middle Class : Money and the Making of Cultural Identity* (Cambridge University Press, 1996), was awarded the Jacques Barzun Prize in Cultural History for 1997 by the American Philosophical Society. She is currently writing a book about women collectors in Great Britain, France and the United States.

David Nicholls is Professor of History and Head of the Department of History and Economic History at the Manchester Metropolitan University. He is the author of the *Lost Prime Minister: A Life of Sir Charles Dilke* (Hambledon Press, 1995) and co-editor with Alan Kidd of *The Making of the British Middle Class? Studies of Cultural and Regional Diversity since 1750* (Sutton Publishing, 1998).

Sean O'Connell is a Lecturer in History at the University of Ulster. His book, *The Car in British Society: Gender, Class and Motoring* was published by Manchester University Press in 1998. He is the co-author, with Dilwyn Porter and Richard Coopey, of *Mail Order Retailing in the UK: A Business and Social History* (Oxford University Press, forthcoming).

Louise Purbrick is Lecturer in the History of Art and Design at the University of Brighton. She has published articles on nineteenth-century cultural institutions and is currently editing a collection of essays on the catalogues of the Great Exhibition of 1851. Her work on civic portraiture was supported with a Paul Mellon Research Fellowship at the University of Manchester.

Chris Reid is Senior Lecturer in the Department of Economics at the University of Portsmouth. His research on the history of consumer magazines has been published in *Media History* and *Twentieth Century British History*.

Alison Twells is Lecturer in Social and Cultural History at Sheffield Hallam University. She has recently completed a Ph.D. at the University of York entitled 'The heathen at home and overseas: the middle class and the civilising mission, 1790–1843'. She has published articles in *Women's History Review and Women's Studies International Forum*, and an essay in *Radical Femininity: Women's Self Representation in the Public Sphere*, edited by Eileen Yeo (Manchester University Press, 1998)

Arline Wilson is a member of the History Department at the University of Liverpool. Current research interests remain focused on the cultural development of Liverpool and the town's merchant elite.

Craig Young is Senior Lecturer in Geography in the Department of Environmental and Geographical Sciences, Manchester Metropolitan University. He completed a B.Sc. in Geography and a Ph.D. in Geography and Economic and Social History at the University of Edinburgh. His Ph.D. was entitled 'The social, economic and geographical aspects of small craft businesses in rural Scotland, c. 1750–c. 1950'.

ACKNOWLEDGEMENTS

Most of the chapters in this volume had a previous existence as short papers delivered to the conference, 'Aspects of the History of the British Middle Classes since 1750', held at the Manchester Metropolitan University in September 1996. The conference attracted over forty speakers and more than 100 delegates. We would like to express our appreciation to all those who either gave papers or contributed to the discussion especially Geoffrey Crossick and Keith Nield for leading and stimulating debate at the plenary sessions. The papers selected for inclusion here have been reworked and extended by their authors.

1

INTRODUCTION: HISTORY, CULTURE AND THE MIDDLE CLASSES

Alan Kidd and David Nicholls

'Class' was once the unassailed territory of the social historians. From the 1960s to the 1980s, various versions of modern British history pivoted on the concept of class. Some of the theorising was self-consciously Marxist in which class conflict appeared as the 'motor' of historical change, but even for many non-Marxists class remained a central organising concept. In the 1990s class is rarely the predominant analytical tool reached for by the historian. Moreover, the questions have changed and the very basis of social history has been challenged along with the categorical and analytical assumptions of 'History' itself. Under the various influences of feminist historiography, the new cultural history, French critical theory and the 'linguistic turn', the place of 'class' in historical writing, quite literally, has been 'de-centred'.

Where does this leave the study of the British middle classes? This is a doubly pertinent question. On the one hand, it requires us to attend to the social history 'discontents' as they have been disparagingly called.[1] But also it requires us to acknowledge the lack of a tradition of writing on the social history of the middle classes. As students of modern British history know, the social historians of the 1960s through the 1980s were obsessed with the working class (accorded the leading role in the Marxist narrative) and by comparison neglected the middle classes. Since the mid-1980s social historians have set out to redress this imbalance and the essays in this volume are part of this trend in historiography. They mostly originated as papers delivered to a conference on the history of the British middle classes since 1750 held at Manchester Metropolitan University in September 1996. During the plenary session of that conference, Geoffrey Crossick remarked that the social history of the middle classes was in its infancy compared to the more established historiography of the working classes; it was in this relatively undeveloped state that it was faced with the challenges of deconstruction and the 'linguistic turn'. The babe was being smothered in the cradle. However, it is important not to overstate the situation. While the study of working-class and labour history may possess a more ancient pedigree, despite its tender years the infant study of the middle classes does have its own history; although admittedly, the major contributions have come from the pens and word processors of economic or political historians and only comparatively recently have social and cultural histories of the middle classes become more plentiful.

I

Compared with well-worn narratives of the 'making' and 'remaking' of the working class in the nineteenth century and the impact of Fordist and post-Fordist production methods on class structures and institutions in the twentieth century, there are fewer histories about the middle classes. However, there are some key narrative elements, which until the early 1980s possessed a compelling power. It was broadly accepted that the 'middle class' of the late eighteenth and early nineteenth centuries was a new social formation, the chief beneficiary of an 'industrial revolution' which had transformed Britain's economy, society and culture. This new social grouping was characterised as the 'industrial and commercial middle class' and its history was chiefly located in the industrial towns of the Midlands and the North. Moreover, it was portrayed as the victor in a political revolution embodied in the 1832 Reform Bill and symbolised in the dominance of liberal ideology in the Victorian period.

However, the conventional account of the early trajectory of the middle classes was to be undermined partly by the deconstruction of the concept of an industrial revolution itself and partly by theoretical concerns arising from the impact of postmodernism. In the former case, historical understanding of British economic development has undergone a revision in which altered perceptions of the longevity and unevenness of industrialisation have opened up new questions and debates about social structures. Far from industrialisation being conceived as a national event of seismic proportions transforming British society (a 'revolution'), historians no longer regard the process as either a nationally or temporally uniform phenomenon.[2] This has affected the way historians feel able to talk about the issue of class formation. Whilst, as recently as 1990, R. J. Morris could publish a monograph describing itself in the sub-title as a study of the 'Making of the British Middle Class', by 1995 Dror Wahrman assumed that his own study, 'Imagining the Middle Class', 'explains why such a book cannot be written'.[3] Part of the explanation for this change lies also in a loss of faith in the scientific nature of historical enquiry. In particular, historical explanations which depend on the credibility of overarching and progressive models of historical change (such as Marxism and its free-market counterpart, 'modernisation') are rejected as 'grand' or 'meta' narratives.

The uncertainty about 'grand narratives' prevalent amongst the current generation of social historians undermines the use of concepts such as class and brings into doubt projects which purport to examine the history of particular classes such as the middle class. The whole notion of class as a valuable concept for the understanding of something called British society has been questioned by the work of those historians most influenced by critical theory and the 'linguistic turn'.[4] The chief target of British academics has been the concept of the 'working class'.[5] In their critiques, they have drawn attention to the 'constituting' nature of language, arguing that language alone, understood as discourse, constitutes our knowledge of the world and rejecting the assumption that words (the 'signifiers') reflect something 'real' (the 'signified'). This is to subvert the idea central to historical materialism (and indeed the *Annales* school) that there exists an underlying social or material structure upon which the 'rest' (culture, language, politics, class consciousness) is based. Thus, in the new formulation the proper study for the historian becomes discourse: human culture is understood as a system of symbolic 'signs' to be read as 'texts'.[6]

The 'text' analogy of the post-structuralists and cultural anthropologists challenges the structuralist assumptions of much history writing; historicises these assumptions (explains their intellectual 'archaeology' to borrow Foucault's terminology) and casts all structures as cultural constructs, structured in discourse rather than being themselves the structuring foundations of life. Thus, for example, 'economics' does not precede or determine so-called 'super-structural' elements such as religion, politics and culture, but is itself (like all else) a discursive code. In this sense, everything is a text and in the (in)famous words of Jacques Derrida, 'there is nothing beyond the text', that is, there is no knowable real world, there are no determining historical structures. This is not generally meant to imply that social, political and economic factors do not exist, but simply that our knowledge of them is limited by the language we use to describe them.[7] Moreover, since there are only texts it follows that there are only the stories related in those texts. Post-structuralism challenges the possibility of all notions of objective knowledge. Under the influence of Derrida, it is assumed that there can never be a knowable unity of meaning between signifier and signified. Instead there is an infinite variety of potential meanings or 'readings', between which it is not possible to prioritise (except perhaps on political or moral grounds?). Thus, it is argued that historical narratives do not describe the real world for they could not do so. 'What really happened' is beyond our knowledge and even the assumption that there can be a 'History' to recover is misleading since, given the innumerable perspectives represented in the 'traces' we call original or primary sources, there are many different equally 'real' pasts to write about. If such thinking is followed through, the implications for the work of the historian and for the nature of historical enquiry are dramatic to say the least. All coherence goes from the notion of historical truth. All that is left is invention. Some theorists, therefore, liken the writing of history to that of literature. Each employs a series of rhetorical devices and, in the words of Hayden White, 'historical narratives are verbal fictions, the contents of which are as much invented as found'.[8]

However, this does not mean there are no histories to write. Historians are invited to continue to construct their narratives, as long as they accept that they are not describing some 'real world' (the 'social' of social history) outside or behind the texts they write. Moreover, we are also asked to acknowledge the full implications of a proposition with an ancient pedigree, that each historical narrative represents a 'position': a political stance or an intellectual viewpoint. Many historians would accept that historical writing is never completely disinterested, but argue that presumptions and hypotheses may change in the face of the evidence. But in the light of postmodernist relativism this becomes a realist illusion. Instead, we are encouraged both to be more self-conscious about our own political and intellectual positions and to address more explicitly in what we write the question of how our texts might be read. To ask less what is history? and more whom is history for?

But all this leaves historians with problems of identity. If the intellectual

interest or political position of historical constructions may be all that matters
about them, why continue to write history or consider it superior to say journalism? Moreover, why continue to employ historical methodologies if we are
only agents of a fictive imagining, employing certain narrative tropes and other
rhetorical devices? But we go on with the show despite our knowledge of the
deconstruction of the production. Why do we do it? The 'linguistic turn'
teaches that there is no immanent truth in history awaiting discovery. Attempts
to construct coherent grand narratives no longer appear tenable. Socio-
economic determinism has lost its credibility. History is discourse and its
meaning is not unambiguous.

However, all this need not imply that the historical method has no
credence. Post-structuralist historians themselves still use archives, still
acknowledge their sources and adopt all the usual scholarly apparatus.[9] Indeed,
even if history writing is a literary exercise, history is different from literature.
Literary invention is restrained only by the limits of language and the conventions of genre. History writing is subject to further fundamental constraints.
Although there is no all-knowing vantage point available to the mortal mind and
the truth about the past is by definition unrecoverable, we are not entirely in the
dark. The past is not completely unknowable. The writing of history, whether
influenced by post-structuralism or not, presupposes a relationship with the
'real world' however indirect and mediated, however unaccountable to any
notions of absolute truth. In the practice of the research and writing of history
there is always a dialogic relationship, not between historians and the (non-
recoverable) past, but between historians and the traces of the past they utilise
in their constructions. No one writing history should mistake these 'traces' for
'the past' itself but without them there can be no narrative constructions. They
provide the limits of the possible.

In addition, there are further dialogues between the historian and the traditions of historiography and between the historian and the collective community
of scholars looking over their shoulder as they write. These are relevant for the
concept of historical truth. Of course, historians employ some invention,
provide a plot, but the scale of the invention is limited, partly by the availability
and character of the primary sources, but chiefly by the requirement to be subject
to a relativist (not absolute) set of criteria. These include notions of reliability
and plausibility. Arbitrary invention or falsification is not allowed. Reliability
and plausibility are determined by the community of historians active in their
respective 'historiographical clusters'. Historians do not expect to discover
inalienable truths and they are now more than ever aware of the linguistic and
semiotic complexities of what they do, but there is an expected approximation to
truth, however transient and pluralistic that 'truth' is understood to be. Without
a notion of 'truth' history is redundant.[10] Post-structuralism has not made
historical writing redundant, although it has not left it unchanged.

One impact of these broadly postmodernist ideas has been to focus attention on the process of history writing itself and upon the various
historiographical 'clusters' around particular narratives. The history of the
British middle class is one such historiographical cluster. It is a historiograph-
ically significant one since it is closely related to one of the so-called 'grand

narratives'. The Marxist theory of history is an example of a grand narrative, claiming all-encompassing or universal explanatory power. Since the Second World War, historical writing on class in general and the middle class in particular, has, in part, derived from the influence of Marxist historians over the agenda of social history. The totalising ambitions of historical materialism found an echo in the aspirations of social history in the 1960s and 1970s to provide a 'total' history of society on the assumption that the concept of the 'social' encompassed everything. There were other influences on the 'social history paradigm', chiefly that of social science and social theory; the main impact here was the idea that social history could analyse structures.[11] One of the structures to be analysed was the British class system recognised by Marxists and others as a central element in explaining Britain's economic rise in the nineteenth century and its decline in the twentieth.[12] The grand narrative of modern British society (since about 1750) involved some stories about the origins, formation, structure and history of the British middle class(es). Thus the history of the middle classes, relatively undeveloped as it was compared to its sister narrative about the working classes, 'the forward march of labour', is nonetheless a constituent element in one of the grand narratives of modern British history. As such it is one of the potential victims of post-modernist history. This is what Crossick meant about babes and cradles.

It would be misleading to suggest that post-structuralist thinking has transformed the writing of history. Nonetheless, historians are clearly more uneasy than they were a decade ago about Marxist approaches (although Gramscian ideas still hold a certain authority), the possibilities of structural analysis and the attractions of meta or grand narratives. Most would follow Wahrman on the impossibility of writing a grand narrative of the 'making of the middle class', at least in the sense that Edward Thompson had in mind when he set out to accomplish the task for the history of the working class in the early 1960s.[13] Yet historians continue to write about the middle classes. In putting together a conference on the history of the British middle classes, we were interested to discover 'the state of play' among historians working on the subject (the historiographical cluster). Thus we adopted an open agenda and expected (with some justification as it turned out) that there would be a diversity of approaches. Nonetheless, we did have certain broad questions in mind. How did historians of the middle classes perceive their topic? Why did it still attract them in the postmodernist 1990s? Given their interest, what were the foci of their work? What were the priorities of established scholars? What new questions and approaches were attracting younger academics? In the event, certain unifying themes and approaches emerged in several of the papers at the conference. Chief among them was an interest in the question of culture, especially issues of identity and a focal point was the role of gender. A number of these contributions appear as the essays in this book.[14]

One of the key trends in scholarship is a turning away from structuralist analysis towards a variety of culturalist approaches. There is little evidence any longer of research which attempts to determine the economic and occupational *structures* of the middle classes. A decade or so ago it was deemed unwise, to say the least, for historians to examine the culture of the middle classes without

some clear reference to the assumed underpinning economic and social foundations. This is not to suggest that 'modernist' historiography lacked a culturalist
emphasis. The work of Edward Thompson in the 1960s belies that misconcep-
tion and the role of production and reproduction in the formation of cultures
was a key feature of post-1960s Marxist analysis.[15] Moreover, culture itself was
granted 'material' status by the concept of 'relative autonomy' in the literary criticism of Raymond Williams and others.[16] However, rather than exploring
relationships between the 'social' and the 'cultural', work in the 1990s is
inclined to view 'culture' as the pivotal, all-encompassing concept. 'Culture' in
this context is generally understood as a field of symbolic meanings rather than
as aesthetic practice, although it is treated in both senses in some of the contributions to this volume. Sometimes the analysis is supported by reference to
notions of discourse, often the theoretical position is more vague. Either way
the drift is to culture.

An interest in the new cultural history is accompanied by a concern to
explore the concept of 'identity'. Whereas the Marxist agenda of yore encouraged a focus upon notions of class consciousness rooted in the relations of
production, the post-structuralist-influenced agenda of the 1990s revolves
around a different conception of consciousness, that of 'identity'. This embodies
the extent to which class has been decentred as a focus for analysis, but also the
trend away from the meta narrative. With regard to the former point, social identity is now understood to be a cultural construction in which class is one of a
constellation of meanings, standing alongside gender, race, nation, generation,
place, custom and so on. The game is no longer to prioritise among such influences but to become more sensitive to the plurality, difference and contradiction
inherent in an historical issue; to be more open to close contextualisation and
historical contingency; and to be suspicious of modernist notions of linear
progress. There are various influences encouraging such an approach, not all of
them explicitly post-structuralist, and again it is worth emphasising the extent to
which the 'modernist' agenda should not be caricatured as lacking a culturalist
emphasis expressed, for example, in the rise of feminist historiography since the
1960s. However, the 'linguistic turn' since the 1980s has resulted in a new attention to discourse as the locus of our knowledge of ourselves as animals possessing
culture. Hence the interest in past representations of society and self.

II

The chapters which comprise this volume share a number of concerns and
explore a series of inter-related themes, focusing especially upon gender, civic
culture and consumerism. Eschewing analysis of class structure and formal politics, they are dealing with what could broadly be described as cultural history.
However, this is not regarded as it might be in anthropological terms. There is
little in the way of 'thick culture' as envisaged in the work of Clifford Geertz and
problematised in 'the new cultural history'.[17] Instead, culture is conceived in
broadly discursive terms in some of the essays, whilst others are more traditional
but nonetheless 'culturalist' in their concerns. Thus, for example, gender iden-

tity is considered as a cultural construct replete with political and economic connotations. Equally, the very architectural and spatial patterns of urban living are seen to carry distinct layers of cultural meaning. Perhaps most significantly, the contributors here generally treat the subject of the history of the middle classes as a cultural field on which a range of inter-related questions can be discussed. Concern with 'identities' recurs and is conceived in terms of the mutually constitutive and historically contingent roles of class, gender and place. Interest in the idea of 'modernity' itself is represented in the socio-spatial relations of urban culture and the emergence of gender-laden conceptions of the modern suburban culture of domesticity and consumerism. The detailed cultural aesthetic of the middle classes is explored from the learned societies of the late eighteenth century to the amateur operatic societies of the twentieth-century suburbs. Art and art patronage are dissected as cultural motifs suggestive both of gender and rank. The contradictions and anxieties of, and the transformations within, the 'middle-class view of the world' are a recurrent context, as is the extent to which the construction of cultural meanings is seen to be negotiated in the context of social forces. This is an important point. It suggests the limits to the spread of post-structuralism even among cultural historians alert to its implications, and it implies the persistence of a realm of the 'social', less reductionist than former conceptions but nonetheless 'real'. As Kate Hill puts it: 'the analysis of discourse, rhetoric and narrative needs to be situated within an examination of the way in which discourse was used, and the way in which control of the arenas of discourse limited its use'.[18]

Most of the contributors link gender explicitly to class and see them as inseparable concepts in the meanings attributed to the term 'middle class'. The historical study of gender and gender categories is a development from the longer tradition of women's history. The contribution of feminism to historical scholarship is considerable, not least the insight that power over others is exerted not only in institutional terms (politics, economics and so on), but equally in the everyday life of interpersonal relationships. However, an effect of this has been that gender history is often understood as women's history. By contrast, the influence of post-structuralist thought in the 1980s, especially the work of Michel Foucault, encouraged a broader conceptualisation of the subject.[19] Thus the work of some of the feminist historians was melded with insights about gender as a social construction and the role of sexual difference across time. The culturalist approach that this implied accepts that notions of masculinity and of femininity are not permanent and singular but transient and subject to variable redefinition. Gender inter-relates with other loci of social identity to contribute to the particular and permeable patterns of knowing and meaning which prevail in any given historical moment. Thus the study of gender can throw light on other categories of analysis such as class and vice versa. Gender, therefore, should not be read simply as 'woman'. The focus on gender in this volume is very much concerned with concepts of masculinity and the representation of masculine identity in relation to that of class. It is well known that Leonore Davidoff and Catherine Hall have treated gender as central to an understanding of the cultural formation of the nineteenth-century middle class.[20] Recent work on masculinity has taken the issue further. The extent to which middle-class identity was gendered 'male' now interests a number of scholars and this interest is well represented in the essays included here. The issue of masculine identity and male culture is explored most explicitly in the contributions from Dianne Macleod; James Hammerton; Jill Greenfield, Sean O'Connell and Chris Reid. However, the concern with gender and social iden-tity permeates most of the contributions in this volume.

The book is organised into sections. This chapter, and that which imme-diately follows by Simon Gunn, are conceived as introductory and scene-setting in nature. The concern is to highlight some of the key intellectual and historio-graphical issues which provide part of the context for the more discrete discussions which ensue, although the arguments in Gunn's chapter may be seen also as a broader contribution to the developing historiography of the middle class dealing especially with the notions of a liberal public sphere, urban moder-nity and consumption. The rest of the book is divided into two parts arranged conceptually and chronologically. Both Part One and Part Two are each preceded by a brief 'Prelude' written by the editors, introducing the chapters and providing an overview of their contents. Additionally, at the end of the volume is a selection of further reading, divided according to the two parts, designed less as a bibliography to the chapters as such, and more as a guide to where the interested reader might turn next to understand or extend discussion of the issues raised by the authors in their individual contributions. The first group of chapters is entitled 'Gender, identity and civic culture' and falls within the period 1800–80. The chapters which appear in Part Two under the heading 'Gender, identity and consumer culture' have a different focus and are located within a later time frame, each one of them taking us into the twentieth century. This division within the book is chiefly a reflection of the extent to which the conceptual concerns of those scholars studying the early to mid-nineteenth century – in which the focus is the provincial city, its urban elites and civic culture – differ from those concerned with the later nineteenth and early twentieth centuries, where the chief point of interest is the development of national suburban cultures (especially consumer culture) amongst the broader middle classes.

Several of the chapters in Part One demonstrate a continuing interest in the middle-class elites of the northern industrial cities which itself is an asser-tion of the enduring historical significance of these places beyond the first half of the nineteenth century. However, it is important to stress the novelty of this attention since it does not replicate the concerns of an older historiographical tradition which overemphasised the pace and geographical distribution of industrialisation. It also constitutes a reaction to another well-established inter-pretation in which the national importance of the northern 'manufacturing interest' is considered subordinate to the continuing (or revived) influence of land, finance and 'gentlemanly capitalism'. In both these approaches, the mid-century is picked out as the high-water mark of northern industrial influence and the pivotal moment at which its subordinate status was assumed. However, this has tended to obscure the spatial modernity of the industrial city as it devel-oped throughout the nineteenth century and the connection with both the middle-class elite and the broader suburban classes.[21] In these new histories of the northern middle class it is issues of public ritual, civic culture and urban identity which provide the focus. Thus, several of the chapters focus upon particular locales: Liverpool (Wilson and Hill), Manchester (Purbrick and Gunn), Sheffield (Twells), Preston and Birmingham (Hill).

A key element in Part Two is the development of cultural identities and a culture of consumption associated initially with the lower middle class. By contrast to the attention given over the years to the northern elites of the early industrial era, the history of the lower middle class in the later nineteenth century and first half of the twentieth century has been comparatively neglected. Studies since the 1970s have started to rectify this omission from the historiography.[22] However, most historians of the lower middle class have been concerned with class formation and occupational structures and there has been less attention given to domestic culture or gender divisions and identities. It is in this regard that several of the essays here make original contributions to the study of the middle classes and indeed the history of national culture.

In sum, the chapters in this volume provide an insight into the current concerns and approaches of historians writing about the culture of the 'middle' in Britain between the end of the eighteenth century and the fourth decade of the twentieth century. They suggest a turning away from structuralist analysis but only a partial absorption of the 'linguistic turn'. There is a noticeable reluctance in several of them to abandon completely notions of a 'social' which acts upon language rather than being entirely constituted by it, as discourse. Nonetheless, these historians of the middle classes write in the wake of debates engendered by post-structuralist interventions occurring chiefly in the field of working-class history. As a result, the relatively late development of the social history of the middle classes has involved a turn to 'culture' and to cultural theory in the light of battles over 'class' fought elsewhere. However, the chapters in this volume do not suggest the demise of 'class' as a focus of interest, but do imply a reworking of the concept. Indeed, they demonstrate the continued validity of class identities as a means of understanding British cultures since the eighteenth century as long as they are seen as interactive with other sites of cultural construction such as gender and place. Although it is difficult to justify reductionist arguments (focusing upon either class or gender), there is no need for historians to abandon notions of 'class'. It is worth bearing in mind the extent to which it is implicit in several of these studies that we should see class and gender, not as separate or autonomous, but as *mutually* constitutive of social identity.

NOTES

1 See D. Mayfield and S. Thorne, 'Social history and its discontents: Gareth Stedman Jones and the politics of language', *Social History*, 17 (1992), 167–88, and the subsequent debate in the pages of the same journal.

2 There has been a wealth of writing and debate since M. Fores, 'The myth of the British Industrial Revolution', *History*, 66 (1981), 181–98. For overviews with varying biases see N. F. R. Crafts, *British Economic Growth During the Industrial Revolution* (Oxford, Oxford University Press, 1985); P. Mathias, 'The Industrial Revolution: concept and

reality', in P. Mathias and J. A. Davis (eds), *The First Industrial Revolutions* (Oxford, Oxford Univeristy Press, 1990), pp.1–24; P. K. O'Brien, 'Modern conceptions of the Industrial Revolution', in P. K. O'Brien and R. Quinault (eds), *The Industrial Revolution and British Society* (Cambridge, Cambridge University Press), 1993, pp.1–30

3 R. J. Morris, *Class, Sect and Party: The Making of the British Middle Class, Leeds 1820–50* (Manchester, Manchester University Press, 1990); D. Wahrman, *Imagining the Middle Class: The Political Representation of Class in Britain, c. 1780–1840* (Cambridge, Cambridge University Press, 1995). In using the construction, 'The Making of the Middle Class', in an earlier volume of essays from the same conference we added a crucial question mark to the title to suggest the controversy which surrounds the subject. See A. J. Kidd and D. Nicholls (eds), *The Making of the British Middle Class? Studies in Cultural and Regional Diversity Since the Eighteenth Century* (Stroud, Sutton, 1998).

4 See, especially, G. Stedman Jones, *Languages of Class: Studies in English Working Class History, 1832–1983* (Cambridge, Cambridge University Press, 1983); P. Joyce, *Visions of the People: Industrial England and the Question of Class, 1840–1914* (Cambridge, Cambridge University Press, 1991), and *Democratic Subjects: The Self and the Social in Nineteenth-century England* (Cambridge, Cambridge University Press, 1994); J. Vernon, *Politics and the People: A Study in English Political Culture, c. 1815–1867* (Cambridge, Cambridge University Press, 1993).

5 US scholars, by comparison, have been less obsessed with class, and their panoply of theoretical influences has been broader, including notably that of symbolic or cultural anthropology as well as critical theory and feminism; see the work of Joan Scott, Natalie Davis and Lynne Hunt for example

6 K. Jenkins, *Re-Thinking History* (London, Routledge, 1991) is an accessible introduction to the impact of such thinking on the writing of history. See also the debates over post-modernism and history in the pages of *Social History* and *Past and Present*. A selection of extracts can be found in K. Jenkins, *The Postmodern History Reader* (London, Routledge, 1997).

7 This is not to impute a form of 'linguistic determinism' as some critics have complained, rather the notion of a sort of 'discursive determinism', that is, language itself is seen as part of a broader discursive code which represents forms of power. However, Stedman Jones has objected to such reductionism, which he finds especially marked in Foucault's impact on the 'linguistic turn' in history and sociology. See Gareth Stedman Jones, 'The determinist fix: some obstacles to the further development of the linguistic approach to history in the 1990s', *History Workshop Journal*, 42 (Autumn 1996), 19–35.

8 H. White, *Tropics of Discourse* (Baltimore Md., and London, Johns Hopkins University Press, 1978), p. 82

9 However, accepting the 'fictive' character of narratives can allow alternatives; see for example B. Simon, 'Narrating a Southern tragedy: historical facts and historical fictions', *Rethinking History*, 1:2 (1997), 165–87.

10 For arguments which treat the challenge of postmodernism seriously while arriving at a revised notion of historical truth, see J. Appleby, L. Hunt and M. Jacob, *Telling the Truth about History* (London, W. W. Norton, 1994), esp. Part III; G. I. Iggers, *Historiography in the Twentieth Century: From Scientific Objectivity to Postmodern Challenge* (London, Wesleyan University Press, 1997), esp. Part III.

11 For an overview and assessment of modern social history see A. Wilson, 'A critical portrait of social history', in A. Wilson (ed.), *Rethinking Social History: English Society 1570–1920 and Its Interpretation* (Manchester, Manchester University Press, 1993).

12 The literature on this is voluminous. Among the most original and influential contributions have been: P. Anderson, 'The origins of the present crisis', *New Left Review*, 23 (1964), 26–56; M. J. Wiener, *English Culture and the Decline of the Industrial Spirit 1850–1980* (Cambridge, Cambridge University Press, 1981); W. D. Rubinstein, *Men of Property: The Very Wealthy in Britain Since the Industrial Revolution* (London, Croom Helm, 1981); P. Cain and A. G. Hopkins, *British Imperialism: Innovation and Expansion, 1688–1914* (Harlow, Longman, 1993).

13 E. P. Thompson, *The Making of the English Working Class* (Harmondsworth, Penguin, 1968).

14 The contributions from Macleod and Hosgood and Gunn's first essay were not read at the conference. The rest began as conference papers. A further selection of the papers from this conference is to be found in Kidd and Nicholls, eds, *Making of the British Middle Class?* For full details see note 3 opposite.

15 For defences of the experience–consciousness dialectic of Thompsonian cultural materialism see N. Kirk, 'History, language, ideas and postmodernism: a materialist view', *Social History*, 19 (1994), 221–40; M. W. Steinberg, 'Culturally speaking: finding a commons between post-structuralism and the Thompsonian perspective', *Social History*, 21 (1996), 193–214; M. Hewitt, *The Emergence of Stability in the Industrial City: Manchester, 1832–67* (Aldershot, Scolar, 1996), pp.1–22.

16 For historical studies influenced by Raymond Williams see A. J. Kidd and K. W. Roberts (eds), *City, Class and Culture: Cultural Production and Social Policy in Victorian Manchester* (Manchester, Manchester University Press, 1985).

17 See L. Hunt, 'Introduction: history, culture and text' and A. Biersack, 'Local knowledge, local history: Geertz and beyond', in L. Hunt (ed.), *The New Cultural History* (Berkeley and London, University of California Press, 1989).

18 See p. 99 below.

19 M. Foucault, *The History of Sexuality*, vol. I: *An Introduction*, trans., R. Hurley, (Harmondsworth, Penguin, 1979).

20 L. Davidoff and C. Hall, *Family Fortunes: Men and Women of the English Middle Class 1780–1850* (London, Hutchinson, 1987).

21 See Gunn's essay, ch. 8. below.

22 For discussions of the historiography of the lower middle classes see the essays by Hosgood (ch. 10) and Hammerton (ch. 11).

2

THE PUBLIC SPHERE, MODERNITY AND CONSUMPTION: NEW PERSPECTIVES ON THE HISTORY OF THE ENGLISH MIDDLE CLASS
Simon Gunn

The history of the English middle class has been dominated by two related narratives. Classically, the historical emergence of the middle class was associated with the growth of mercantile and, especially, industrial capitalism; it was capitalism which brought an urban middle class of merchants, industrialists and allied professionals into being, and this class, in turn, acted as the principal agent of subsequent capitalist development. Alternatively, the middle class was portrayed as a 'class of movements'; it was the series of campaigns for political and fiscal reform between 1780 and 1846 which gave the English middle class a distinct political identity and 'consciousness'.[1] During the 1980s these conventional economic and political narratives, organised in different ways around the idea of the progressive 'rise' of the middle class, were disrupted by a series of important new interpretations. The work of W. D. Rubinstein, Martin Wiener and others critically questioned the socio-economic unity of the nineteenth-century middle class, and its capacity to challenge the cultural and political dominance of an older landed elite. Meanwhile, feminist scholars pointed not only to the absence of women in existing accounts, but also to the specific ordering of gender relations on which the 'rise' of the middle class was predicated from the later eighteenth century, and which substantially contributed to its social and ideological definition.[2] While these new studies did not wholly displace the older narratives, they did problematise what had previously been a relatively uncontested area of social history. For the first time, the middle class became a significant object of historical debate.[3]

Over the last decade a new range of theoretical influences has come to inform historical writing on English culture and society, often replacing the liberal, Marxist or Weberian perspectives which underpinned earlier accounts. They have derived from diverse sources, including social and cultural theory, post-structuralism and the 'linguistic turn'.[4] These new perspectives have had a general, if contested, impact across the whole field of modern social history. In this chapter, however, I shall focus on a number of concepts and theories which have had a specific bearing on the recent historiography of the middle class, and in particular on questions of gender, culture and identity. These inform, directly or indirectly, many of the chapters in this volume. In the first section, the concept of the 'liberal public sphere', elaborated by the German social theorist Jürgen Habermas, is critically evaluated in the light of research on the middle class, politics and urban culture in the period between 1750 and 1850.

Habermas's account has limitations, but it is important in pointing to the historical construction of the notion of the 'public' and the articulation of the middle class with an emergent public sphere. In the second section the idea of 'urban modernity' is examined, as applied by sociologists and cultural critics to the great metropolitan and provincial cities of the later nineteenth and early twentieth centuries. Here the focus shifts to questions of middle-class identity, and, specifically, to how identities of class and gender were sustained in the depersonalised and fluid conditions of modern urban life. In the third section, the association between the middle class and consumerism in the period between 1880 and 1939 is explored. This is related to a growing theoretical and historical literature which has emphasised the gradual supersession of identities based on production and capitalist ownership by class and status divisions centred on modes of consumption and styles of life.

These various perspectives represent tendencies in recent historical writing rather than any coherent position or trajectory. The purpose of the chapter, then, is to review some of the theoretical impulses which have come to inform otherwise largely empirical studies of the middle class. Recent theoretical orientations, I shall argue, serve to problematise the concept of the 'middle class' as a consistent sociological and historical entity and to question the possibility of constructing a continuous narrative of the 'middle class' across different historical periods. In conclusion I shall draw out some of these implications for current historiography.

I

The concepts of the 'public' and 'public opinion' have been used by historians and political scientists to denote the collectivity of citizens in society and their generic views on political and other issues. The terms are notably vague: precisely who is included in the 'public' at any given point is unclear. Historically, the idea of the 'public' has been associated with the middle class, despite the implication of a wider inclusivity: Marx, for example, famously denounced the notion of 'public opinion' as a mask for bourgeois class interests.[5] The translation into English of Jürgen Habermas's *The Structural Transformation of the Public Sphere: An Inquiry into a Category of Bourgeois Society* in 1989 was therefore significant in reviving interest among Anglo-American scholars in the diffuse, and even discredited, ideas identified with the concept of the 'public'.[6] Originally published in Germany in 1961, the book was an attempt to provide an historical and theoretical analysis of the emergence and decline of the 'liberal public sphere' between the late seventeenth and the mid-twentieth centuries. As a critical theorist, Habermas had a normative aim: to outline the democratic possiblities for what he termed 'rational-critical' debate in contemporary western societies. For historians, however, the main interest lies in his account of the development of a distinctive public sphere in the eighteenth and nineteenth centuries, in which England acts as an exemplar.

Noting the confused cluster of meanings associated with the idea of the 'public', Habermas defined the public sphere as a realm existing between state and society, which mediated between them. In its 'liberal' or 'bourgeois' form, it represented a 'sphere of private people come together as a public' to engage in rational discussion of the rules governing political, economic and cultural life.[7] As it emerged in the late seventeenth and early eighteenth centuries, the liberal public sphere was defined in opposition to royal or absolutist authority. In the latter case, the concept of public authority was embodied exclusively in the monarch and the court: 'they represented their lordship not for but "before" the people'.[8] This type of 'representative publicness' was gradually replaced in the eighteenth century by the idea of a 'rational-critical public', entry to which was nominally accessible to all, but which in practice was limited to educated, propertied men. Within this specific conception of the public sphere, 'reason' not status determined the outcome of public discussions which spanned the full range of topics from literature and art to politics and trade. The participant in the 'public' combined the role of property-owner and '(hu)man', conflating a class- and gender-specific identity with the impulse to universalism inherent, according to Habermas, in the concept of the liberal public sphere from its inception.[9]

How, then, did this liberal public sphere come into being? Significantly, Habermas locates its origins in the bourgeois household, or what he terms the 'patriarchal conjugal family'. From the late seventeenth century the bourgeois family developed as a private sphere in a double sense: while it rested on the private ownership of property it was also constructed as an 'intimate sphere', nurturing simultaneously an individualised subjectivity and an 'audience-oriented' sociality centred on family and friends. The creation of new literary forms, especially the novel, had an important role both in fostering the idea of individual interiority and in serving as the focus of audience-oriented discussion.[10] In Habermas's account, therefore, the private and the public were linked spheres: the emergence of new kinds of subjectivity was concomitant with the growth of a range of social and cultural institutions which came to characterise the liberal public sphere from the early eighteenth century. They included the press, literary and art criticism, coffee houses, concerts and, to a lesser extent in England, the theatre. If the public for such activities was restricted to the educated, it was of sufficient scale for culture to be commodified and to begin to develop as an autonomous realm.[11]

The world of culture thus underpinned the public sphere of politics. Both domains were governed by similar principles. Matters of political interest, like questions of taste, were best resolved by rational discussion between formal equals based on education and property. As a forum for rational-critical debate, however, the liberal public sphere necessarily developed in opposition to the monarchy and the state in the eighteenth and early nineteenth centuries, in so far as these were identified with arbitrary rule. Politics itself 'took the form of a permanent controversy between government and opposition'; parliament successively attempted to restrict the powers of the press, reaching its high point in the Wilkesite agitations of the 1760s and 1770s; and from the late eighteenth century the weight of 'public opinion' was repeatedly invoked to force the government into political concessions. The resolution of this lengthy confrontation only occurred with the 1832 Reform Act which, for the first time, encompassed 'public opinion' within parliament – from 'the target of critical comment by public opinion', parliament was now transformed 'into the very organ of this opinion'.[12] Just as the market was envisaged as a sphere of transactions between private persons based on property, so politics was construed as a public process of rational communication between private persons, based on education. These principles underscored the ideal of the 'liberal constitutional state' which, as Habermas ironically puts it, achieved fruition 'only for one blissful moment in the long history of capitalist development', in mid-nineteenth-century Britain.[13]

This summary inevitably simplifies complex and detailed arguments, but its purpose is to facilitate an evaluation of Habermas's analysis and its significance for an understanding of the middle class in the period between 1750 and 1850. Habermas's account has been widely registered by historians, though it has not always been received sympathetically.[14] Critics have pointed to two main areas of weakness. First, Habermas ignored the extent to which the exclusion of women from the public sphere was not incidental but fundamental to its constitution. The growth of the public sphere from the mid-eighteenth century occurred at a moment of ideological transformation in gender relations in which masculinity was identified with the public sphere of 'reason' while women were confined by 'nature' to the home. The new figure of the 'public man' was predicated on a series of oppositions to women and femininity which increasingly served to order middle-class social life as well as political discourse. The liberal public sphere was thus not a neutral space but one which was profoundly gendered from the outset.[15] Secondly, as Geoff Eley has argued, the emergence of the bourgeois public sphere is described by Habermas primarily in its relation to traditional authority. The account overlooks the ways it might have been forged in conflict with popular pressures from below, especially in the radicalised political climate from the 1760s. Instead of a single, all-embracing public sphere, Eley argues, it is more appropriate to think of the existence of competing publics, plebeian as well as bourgeois.[16]

Despite these weaknesses, Habermas's study offers considerable insight into the foundations of a public bourgeois culture. As Eley notes in his perceptive critique, 'the value of Habermas's perspective has been fundamentally borne out by recent social history in a variety of fields'.[17] This includes the extensive research on urban and literary cultures, on consumption, and on parliamentary and extra-parliamentary politics in eighteenth-century Britain carried out over the last two decades.[18] In each field the growth of an emergent 'public' has been identified, based loosely though not exclusively on the 'middling sort', and defined in relation to culture, consumption and political debate. Much of the radical, oppositional impulse of this public culture from the 1770s onwards, however, came from provincial, propertied Dissent. It was this group, overlooked by Habermas, which in England contributed key elements to the development of a liberal, universalist ideology: a narrative of progress, focused on the expansion of commerce, manufactures and the town, and given a political cutting edge by the drive for 'civil and religious liberty'.[19]

It is, indeed, in the expanding industrial and commercial centres of Britain in the decades after 1800 that the construction of a bourgeois public sphere is most in evidence. It is apparent in the range of social and cultural institutions established: literary and philosophical societies, subscription libraries, art institutions, clubs, museums and musical associations. Together with the various improvement societies, these formed a dense network of voluntary organisations to be found in almost all the major provincial cities as well as in many smaller towns by the 1830s. Such institutions were not public in the sense that they were open to all: entry was by subscription so that in practice they were confined to educated, propertied men. But unlike the institutions of church, chapel and local government, admission was not dependent on political or religious affiliation. Here what was advocated was rational discussion of art, natural science, political economy, and of the 'laws' which governed each.[20] In the early nineteenth century, this notion of the 'public' often stood in opposition to the 'popular', the model of a liberal public sphere being used (largely unsuccessfully) as a means to regulate the labouring population via 'improving' institutions such as mechanics' institutes, established under the aegis of elite bodies. At the same time, while the 1832 Reform Act institutionalised 'public opinion' within parliament, the 1835 Municipal Reform Act gave formal endorsement to the identity of the bourgeois public sphere with the town and its government. As the *Leeds Mercury* put it, the result of the Act was to enable the new Corporations to take on 'the character of public institutions, in the enlarged and legitimate sense of that term'.[21]

In his detailed study of Leeds between 1820 and 1850 R. J. Morris argued that it was the network of voluntary associations which gave coherence to a 'middle class' deeply fragmented by politics, religion and status: 'Only the voluntary society as a social form allowed that variety of patterns of association, participation and action which was essential if a fractured and divided socio-economic group was to act as a class.'[22] Morris's account of 'middle-class' formation bears strong similarities to that of Habermas; both emphasise the centrality of a range of social and cultural institutions in creating a public space in civil society through which new types of rationality and social interaction were forged. Yet the thrust of their arguments is significantly different: while for Morris it was an emergent middle class which was the agent of the powerful voluntary network, for Habermas the development of the middle class was secondary to the creation of a liberal public sphere. The presence of merchants, manufacturers and professional men in the emergence of the 'public' is consistently noted by Habermas, but the 'middle class' is seen less as the architect of the public sphere than as constituted by it. This insight is given strength by Geoffrey Crossick's observation that as late as the 1840s the term 'middle class', while representing a 'term of pride in oppositional politics . . . , referred less to a social group than to the right-thinking, morally upright core of British society'.[23] The significance of Habermas's argument here lies in its potential for the reconceptualisation of the 'middle class' between 1780 and 1850. In this view, what the term 'middle class' denoted in the period was not so much a clear sociological entity as a moral, cultural and political force whose identity was registered in and through the workings of the liberal public sphere, and the associated concepts of the 'public' and 'public opinion'.[24]

II

During the second half of the nineteenth century, according to Habermas, the liberal public sphere began to dissolve. From the 1880s state and civil society became subject to a process of mutual interpenetration, as large limited companies took on a 'semi-public' character and the state increasingly intervened in domains, such as welfare and industrial relations, formerly confined to the 'private sphere'. Simultaneously, the liberal public sphere was undermined by its own universalist logic as widening groups of women and workers demanded inclusion within the ranks of the 'public'.[25] I shall return to some of the consequences of this analysis later. Rather than from Habermas, however, the most significant recent theoretical perspective on bourgeois culture in the period between 1850 and 1914 has derived from the literature of 'urban modernity' associated with sociologists and cultural critics such as Georg Simmel and Walter Benjamin in the earlier twentieth century, and Marshall Berman, Elizabeth Wilson and Richard Sennett in more recent times.[26] The influence of their ideas has been registered primarily within cultural theory, but also increasingly within social and cultural history.[27]

The term 'modernity' is, of course, a vexed one, used in a variety of ways. It can denote a particular historical periodisation; a distinct 'project', usually associated with the Enlightenment; or a type of social experience, identified with the forms of public life which developed in major western cities from the mid-nineteenth century.[28] The urban modernity described in cultural theory refers to this last category, but also incorporates the substantial physical and spatial reorganisation of those cities in the period. The qualitative aspects of urban modernity highlight the flux and transience of city life; for Charles Baudelaire modernity meant 'the ephemeral, the fugitive, the contingent'.[29] Modernity also evokes the 'modern', the new, embodied in the widened streets, squares and shopping arcades which made up the changing cityscape. If this was a novel and liberating environment it was also one which is described in the literature as disorientating and anxiety-laden. The crowds of strangers and rapidity of change placed identities of class, gender and the self in question. The theoretical shift from the Habermasian public sphere to that of urban modernity thus involves the movement from a 'rational' to an 'anonymous' public.

The idea of an anonymous public sphere itself raises questions, not least for historians. If urban modernity was predicated on flux and transience, how were social identities maintained? More pertinently here, how was a 'middle-class' identity defined and upheld? Neither the theoretical nor the historical literature provides definite answers to these questions, but they do suggest a number of important ways forward.

First, following Simmel, social and cultural theorists have pointed to the preponderance of the visual over other senses in later nineteenth-century urban culture.[30] One result of this was an emphasis on visual appearance, on dress and conduct as a key indicator of class and status in a mobile society where such attributes were no longer self-evident. That appearance was a matter of increasing interest at the period is signalled by the descriptions of street life and social 'types' which featured heavily in magazines like *Punch* from the 1840s and the provincial periodical press from the 1860s.[31] The proliferation of this literature is suggestive of concern with the problems of appearance in public, but, along with manuals of etiquette, it also provided reassuring information on how to distinguish the 'true' lady or gentleman from the 'painted lady' or social 'upstart'. Codes of dress and conduct, little investigated by social historians, were clearly crucial in maintaining class and status distinctions in the highly visible world of the city.[32] Moreover, a new emphasis on visuality, on looking and seeing, did not necessarily imply a crisis of identity or the fragmentation of the self. The archetypal protagonist of urban modernity, the male *flâneur* who moved freely about the city, observing the crowds yet apart from them, appears as a liminal figure but not as a powerless or fractured one. As Judith Walkowitz has observed, the conventional notion of the *flâneur* 'presupposed a privileged male subject whose identity was stable, coherent, autonomous'.[33]

If urban spectatorship involved an implicit set of social and power relationships, so also did the layout of the city itself. The substantial reconstruction of metropolitan and provincial cities, most marked between 1860 and 1890, created new social and physical spaces. Social differences were encoded in a specific pattern of residential zoning, characterised by suburbia, workers' districts and slums.[34] Within the city centre distinct areas were created: the warehousing and business district, shopping streets, the 'official' city of town hall, monuments and public institutions, all of which were often fringed by slums, factories and workshops.[35] Each of these areas was invested with distinct social as well as functional connotations, reinforced by complex divisions of public and private space which operated within the city as well as between workplace and home. The presence of women in all-male enclaves such as 'clubland', or of factory workers in the 'official' city, was potentially charged with transgressive or political meaning. Thus the anonymous public spaces of urban modernity were classed and gendered in profoundly normative, if shifting, ways.

New codes also regulated the domain of bourgeois culture. After 1850 key cultural institutions of the liberal public sphere – art galleries, museums, concert halls – were increasingly opened up beyond the relatively small number of subscribers to a more socially amorphous audience based on cash payment. Elsewhere I have argued that classical music and the concert hall played a leading role in creating a new public domain for culture from the mid-nineteenth century. The Hallé concerts in Manchester and the Crystal Palace concerts in London, both initiated in the 1850s, deliberately broke with the subscription system of concerts, establishing a scale of differentially priced tickets and providing access for wider social groups beyond the wealthiest and most powerful sections of urban society.[36] At the same time, they established a new regime of concert behaviour. Conversation and walking about during the performance were proscribed; instead the audience was expected to sit in silent attention, to focus on the music as a work of art rather than as a background to socialising.[37] The aesthetic categories and behavioural norms centred on concerts were given wider circulation through reports in the press, where they were contrasted with the 'vulgarity' of popular forms associated with the music hall, as well as with the commercialism of events such as the promenade concerts. Classical music thus served as a principal medium by which older categories of 'high' and 'low' culture were reorganised to conflate ideas of cultural and social hierarchy and to impose them on an expanded public sphere. In the early twentieth century, as John Lowerson shows, music became defined by terms such as 'highbrow', 'middlebrow' and 'lowbrow', each with their particular social connotations.[38]

Events such as the concert series, of course, were not simply occasions for studied immersion in art, but also part of a social calendar for the rich and fashionable. They formed part of a repertoire of highly visual public rituals which marked city life between 1850 and 1914, in which the wealthier sections of urban society engaged in conspicuous display. These included fashionable promenades, civic processions and openings, and the 'centipedic funerals' of local employers and politicians. The meaning of these events was contextually specific, but in different ways they served to make power visible by the act of stylised public appearance. As a mode of symbolic address, they variously asserted the rights of 'respectability' and the identity of the city with its 'leading men' and institutions. In Habermasian terms they embodied authority 'not for, but "before" the people', indicating that the category of 'representative publicness' was not eradicated by the advent of the liberal public sphere, but continued, and even flowered, in the conditions of urban modernity.[39] Above all, as I suggest in a later essay in this volume, the function of such events was to stabilise the play of appearances in the city, and to establish, if only provisionally, a space of authority.

Thus the amorphousness of urban modernity did not preclude social practices and cultural codes which regulated its flow and enabled identities of class and gender to be sustained and elaborated in new ways. This did not apply equally to all social groups, however. In a seminal article Janet Wolff argued that by focusing on the public life of the city the concept of modernity rendered women invisible: 'the literature of modernity describes the experience of men'.[40] In accounting for this invisibility, Wolff points to the confinement of middle-class women to the private sphere and to the obsession of the emergent, masculine discipline of sociology with the world of work, politics and city life. While certain of these points carry force, there exists a mounting literature which demonstrates the extensiveness of women's engagement in the public sphere of the city and emphasises its liberating aspects. The key developments identified with this entry into the public domain were the new world of shops and consumption, the department stores in particular successfully seeking to attract a specifically female custom; the flourishing sphere of philanthropy, in which an estimated 500,000 women were engaged as voluntary workers by 1893; and the domain of politics, encompassing local government and the campaigns for women's suffrage, the mass demonstrations between 1907 and 1914 confirming in vivid terms women's arrival as political subjects on the public stage.[41] While this foothold in urban modernity was achieved in the face of considerable physical and ideological opposition, it appears to have been firm nonetheless. By the 1880s, according to Walkowitz, 'expanded opportunities for shopping, philanthropy, civic participation, and an 'independent' life ... generated a new urban female style of "being at home" in the city'.[42]

If middle-class women have been written back into the history of urban modernity, where does this leave the larger concept of the 'middle class' within this history? Clearly, both 'class' and 'modernity' were experienced differently by men and women, as well as by the expanding groups who made a claim to 'middle-class' status between 1870 and 1914, notably salaried officials, office and other white-collar workers.[43] Clearly, also, there was a strengthening identification between occupation and class in the language of social description during this period.[44] This section has further suggested the close association between the 'middle class' and the city. The city centre, in particular, was a principal site in which class identity was tested, whether in matters of appearance, ritual demonstrations of taste and public order, or in larger claims to urban leadership embodied in the monumental architecture and ceremonial of civic pride. More fundamentally still, the literature of urban modernity implies that the identity of the 'middle class' was tied up not simply with self-presentation or collective expression, but with the act of looking itself. Roland Barthes long ago suggested that bourgeois culture involved an 'ex-nominating operation': 'The bourgeoisie is defined as the social class which does not want to be named.'[45] Historians are well aware that the neutral eye which lay behind a newspaper report, official document or photograph was positioned and positioning: it was the eye of power. In the context of the later nineteenth and early twentieth centuries it was often specifically a middle-class eye, and one which though differentially gendered, was common to the female charity worker as much as to the male *flâneur*. As Mica Nava has commented:

> charity work established for [middle-class] women the right to look. It authorised the observation and classification of the homes, lives and even marital relationships of the poor. Middle-class women involved in the philanthropic enterprise were not obliged to conduct their affairs with a lowered gaze. They could indulge the pleasures of urban spectatorship – of the voyeur – with a sense of entitlement which is not so easily distinguishable from that of the male *flâneur*.[46]

If modernity privileged the visual over other senses, it did so in ways that were specifically classed as well as gendered. The privileged gaze defined the 'middle class' not only as spectators but as agents, actively intervening in and shaping urban reality, even as, following Barthes, that agency was dissolved into the anonymous, universal categories of Nation, Humanity and Nature.

III

The periodisation of urban modernity is vague, but there is a clear sense that the particular version I have described, associated with the heyday of 'bourgeois society', ended with the First World War.[47] Indeed, from a theoretical and historical perspective the early twentieth century is full of endings. For Habermas the period witnessed the collapse of the liberal public sphere, partly as a result of the tendencies to democratisation and the interpenetration of state and civil society noted earlier, but also as a consequence of other forces: the decline of the patriarchal bourgeois family, the segmentation of the public with the creation of a new stratum of 'intellectuals', and the advent of mass consumption. The result, according to Habermas, was a shift from a 'culture-debating' to a 'culture-consuming' society.[48] For historians of Britain, the First World War marked the end of Victorian Liberalism, and of the Liberal Party as a political force.[49] Meanwhile, surveying the history of the European middle class, Jürgen Kocka has argued that since 1914 the middle class has all but dissolved as a distinct social entity, along with the civil society (*bürgerliche Gesellschaft*) with which it was closely identified after 1789.[50]

There has, in fact, been little research on the middle class in twentieth-century Britain.[51] Those recent studies which have been carried out have been organised around the concepts of consumption rather than industry, social structure or politics.[52] As a concept, consumption does not refer to a single, coherent body of social or cultural theory. Interest in the subject developed in sociology in the 1980s as part of a wider debate about postmodernity.[53] Historians, of course, had already pointed to the origins of a 'consumer society' in the eighteenth century, but the twentieth century, so it has been argued, saw the development of consumption on a truly mass scale and, more contentiously, a shift from production to consumption as the organising principle of society and of social identity.[54] In constructing a theoretical frame for the study of consumption, sociologists have looked back to Veblen's *The Theory of the Leisure Class* (1899), which saw modes of consumption as the basis of social status, and the Frankfurt School's critique of mass consumption and the 'culture industry' developed between the 1930s and the 1950s.[55] The new approaches depart from these earlier analyses in two important ways, however. Whereas Veblen saw social emulation as the motive-force behind consumerism, the new generation of studies rejects any simple 'trickle down' theory of consumption. Similarly, the negative emphasis of the Frankfurt School on mass consumption as ideology, a form of political and economic manipulation, is replaced by a positive endorse-ment of its factitious character; consumption appears as emancipating in the possibilities it offers for the creation of new identities.[56]

The institution most closely identified with the development of modern consumerism is the department store, established in London and the large provincial cities from the 1860s.[57] The department store offered a previously undreamed-of variety of goods under one roof, open to all and without obliga-tion to purchase. The stores thus represented a new experience of shopping: they 'transformed merchandise into a permanent spectacle, into a show-like theatre of commodities', and in so doing turned customers into consumers.[58] In London and Paris they became tourist attractions, especially during the winter sales, and in their design evoked other sites of spectacle such as museums and industrial exhibitions, which Tony Bennett has seen as collectively forming a distinct 'exhibitionary complex' during the late nineteenth and early twentieth centuries.[59] Moreover, the department stores set out specifically to attract middle-class women as consumers; staffed by women shopworkers, and incor-porating restaurants and fashion displays, shopping at stores became an index of middle-class status and an important focus for feminine sociability in the city.[60] If the origins of the department stores lay in the context of urban moder-nity described in the previous section, they also led out to other later forms of consumption. As Mica Nava has observed, cinema-going was often associated with shopping before and after the First World War; both were identified pre-eminently with women as consumers, and were seen as evoking a 'dream' or 'fantasy' world.[61] Equally, the 'new consumerism' of the interwar years, based heavily on durable goods which doubled as a percentage of consumer expenditure in Britain between 1911–14 and 1935–38, was aimed primarily at women, through advertising techniques pioneered by the department stores.[62]

Consumption was therefore associated with women in the early twentieth century, contributing to a wider series of anxieties about the loss of patriarchal control within and beyond the family.[63] While this anxiety encompassed the unemployed working-class man by the 1930s, in the earlier decades of the century it focused heavily on a new 'lower middle class'. Consumption was identified not just with women, but with a specific social group, the 'Suburbans' as Charles Masterman termed them, composed principally of the families of office employees, minor professionals and elementary teachers.[64] Conspicuous consumption was viewed as essential to this class, though scarcely affordable, since its aspirations, in Veblenesque style, were to ape 'High Society' and to differentiate itself from its dreaded social 'other', the manual working class.[65] This type of psychological caricature persisted into the interwar years, but as recent studies have emphasised, it increasingly had to vie with depictions of the consumer-oriented, lower-middle-class suburban family as the model of a new kind of modernity. Indeed, it is possible to read both sets of representations into J. B. Priestley's well-known description of the interwar suburbs of London with their 'miles of detached bungalows, all with their little garages, their wireless sets, their periodicals about film stars, their swimming costumes and tennis rackets and dancing shoes'.[66]

The identification of the 'new consumerism' with a 'new' middle class during the interwar years can be linked to larger changes in social formation during the early twentieth century. The gradual merger of elites based on land, industry and finance between 1880 and 1939 was hastened in the interwar period both by the relative decline in aristocratic wealth and by the growing proximity of large industry to the state.[67] One result was that while during the nineteenth century large industrial, merchant and banking families were considered as part of a 'middle class', by the early twentieth century they were more likely to be seen as part of a plutocracy or 'upper class'. The 'middle class' of the interwar years was viewed as an amorphous group squeezed between Capital and Labour, akin to the 'lower middle class' of the pre-war period but more extensive than it. Speaking about the Middle Class Defence Organisation in 1911, its leader, L. P. Sydney, was unable to decide whether to define those he represented as 'lower middle' or 'middle class'.[68] Yet the very indeterminacy of this group, encompassing stockbrokers and school teachers, meant that culture and consumption became increasingly integral to conceptions of it. In an influential study written just after the Second World War, Lewis and Maude rested their definition of the 'middle class' crucially on these categories. Alongside income and occupation, they listed 'accent, spending habits, residence, culture, leisure pursuits, clothes, education' as essential ingredients for determining 'middle-class' status.[69]

During the interwar years this definition was given a specific political inflexion by the Conservative governments of the period. In an important essay Ross McKibbin has argued that the Conservative predominance between 1923 and 1939 was based on a construction of the 'public' closely aligned with a 'new' middle class: 'a huge assembly of "middle" classes, numbering 9–10 million adults, who stood between the middle classes proper and the manual working class, but who felt themselves both in their style of life and in their hostility to the unionised working class to be middle-class'.[70] This group, according to McKibbin, defined itself negatively, hostile to war profiteers and the 'idle rich', but especially to the organised working class, perceived to be endlessly engaged in grievances with their employers and scrounging off the state. Constituted as 'public opinion' by newspapers such as the *Daily Express* and the *Daily Mail*, this 'middle class' was regarded by the Conservative leadership under Baldwin as representing its core constituency. As such, it was appealed to by the Conservatives' deflationary policies, low levels of taxation, and the defence of the 'public interest' against a politicised working class. More generally, Conservative strategy was 'closely related to [the] perceived styles of life' of those who defined themselves as 'not-working class', but equally not the 'idle rich'.[71] Interwar Conservatism thus sought to mobilise politically the cultural aspirations and prejudices of a new, amorphous 'middle class', and to consolidate the identification of this class with the 'public'. Part of this strategy depended on constructing the public itself as consumers, in opposition to a class of 'producers' in the form of an organised working class, capable of holding the country to ransom. Conservatives sought to appeal to voters as consumers, as in Baldwin's analogies of the national to the household economy ('Every housewife knows what inflation means in prices'; 'Borrowing is like drink. You cannot go on for ever, and the headache is inevitable sooner or later'). A consumerist rhetoric was instinctively drawn upon, even before the introduction of 'scientific' methods of testing public opinion.[72] By the 1930s, therefore, consumption had entered public discourse as a political as well as a social marker, closely linked with the emergence of a reordered, inchoate 'middle class' as the basis of a reconstituted 'public'.

IV

I have argued that these new perspectives based on concepts of the public sphere, urban modernity and consumption, have come to exert an increasing influence in histories of the English middle class over the last decade or so. Sometimes the influence is explicit; more often, perhaps, it is implicit, hinted at in allusions to theoretical sources or buried in footnotes. They are, of course, not the only perspectives. The influence of Foucault, among others, has also been conspicuous in the formation of the new cultural history, though how far Foucauldian ideas of power and governmentality are compatible with notions of the 'middle class', or indeed with any kind of class analysis, is questionable.[73]

In so far as the perspectives described have taken hold, they differ from the older economic and political narratives in two fundamental ways. First, they do not posit a progressive, linear development expressed in the idea of the inexorable 'rise' of the middle class associated with the spread of capitalism and political domination of the state. There is no moment of the 'making' of the middle class which serves as a basis for a continuous, long-term development. Rather, the middle class is seen as subject to a constant process of formation and re-formation between the eighteenth and twentieth centuries. Secondly, and by extension, within the new perspectives the middle class is not viewed as formed primarily by economic or political factors. Neither economic development nor political interests 'give' any particular social identity, including class. Rather, identities and meanings are formed on the terrain of culture as a result of complex negotiations and conflicts, which may (or may not) take economic and political form. Historically, the term 'middle class' did not carry the same political connotations or even denote, sociologically, the same groups of people across different periods of time. Changes in economy and social structure were important in providing a context for such shifts, but the precise identity and meaning of the term 'middle class' at any time was always a matter of cultural construction.

This is not to argue that the perspectives outlined here constitute a new narrative of the middle class to replace the old. The concepts of the public sphere, of urban modernity and of consumption contain their own narratives within them, but they do not offer the basis for a continuous history of the middle class across the last three centuries. However, by describing these categories in chronological order this account has constructed its own narrative. If there is a single thread through the account it is provided by the identification of the middle class with the 'public' in different guises: the 'rational' public of the liberal public sphere, the 'anonymous' public of urban modernity, and the 'consumerist' public of the early twentieth century. These varying identities, and their inter-relationship with the shifting category of the 'private', provide one means of rethinking the history of the middle class which analyses of gender have already done much to advance.[74] Yet the very different, and even contradictory, theoretical orientations which underpin the perspectives I have described warn against any simple attempt to reconstitute that history as a single, continuous narrative. It may well be that the history of the English middle class is best understood as a narrative of disjuncture and discontinuity, which the terms 'history' and 'middle class', with their air of seamlessness and fixity, have served only to conceal.

NOTES

1 See for example S. G. Checkland, *The Rise of Industrial Society in England, 1815–85* (Harlow, Longman, 1971); A. Briggs, 'Middle-class consciousness in English politics, 1780–1846', *Past and Present*, 9 (1956); Briggs, *The Age of Improvement 1783–1867* (Harlow, Longman, 1959).

2 W. D. Rubinstein, *Men of Property* (London, Croom Helm, 1981); M. J. Wiener, *English Culture and the Decline of the Industrial Spirit, 1850–1980* (Cambridge, Cambridge University Press, 1981); L. Davidoff and C. Hall, *Family Fortunes: Men and Women of the English Middle Class, 1780–1850* (London, Hutchinson, 1987).

3 Elements of this debate can be traced through the following: J. Wolff and J. Seed, (eds), *The Culture of Capital: Art, Power and the Nineteenth-Century Middle Class* (Manchester, Manchester University Press, 1988); M. J. Daunton, '"Gentlemanly capi-

talism" and British industry, 1820–1914', *Past and Present*, 122 (1989); R. J. Morris, *Class, Sect and Party. The Making of the British Middle Class: Leeds, 1820–50*, (Manchester, Manchester University Press, 1990); D. Wahrman, *Imagining the Middle Class: The Political Representation of Class in Britain, c. 1780–1840* (Cambridge, Cambridge University Press, 1995).

  4 See for example M. Poovey, *Making a Social Body: British Cultural Formation, 1830–1864* (Chicago, University of Chicago Press, 1995); P. Joyce, *Democratic Subjects: The Self and the Social in Nineteenth-Century England* (Cambridge, Cambridge University Press, 1994); T. Bennett, *The Birth of the Museum: History, Theory, Politics* (London, Routledge, 1995).

  5 K. Marx, *The Eighteenth Brumaire of Louis Bonaparte* (New York, International Publications, 1963).

  6 J. Habermas, *The Structural Transformation of the Public Sphere: An Inquiry into a Category of Bourgeois Society*, trans. T. Burger (Cambridge, Polity Press, 1992). All subsequent references are to this edition.

  7 *Ibid.*, pp. 27 ff.

  8 *Ibid.*, p. 8.

  9 *Ibid.*, pp. 55–6.

 10 *Ibid.*, pp. 43–51.

 11 *Ibid.*, pp. 31–43.

 12 *Ibid.*, pp. 62–6.

 13 *Ibid.*, pp. 78–9.

 14 The following represent a selection of critical responses by historians and others: C. Calhoun (ed.), *Habermas and the Public Sphere* (Cambridge, Mass., MIT Press, 1992), esp. essays by Calhoun, Fraser, Ryan and Eley; A. Bermingham, 'Introduction' in A. Bermingham and J. Brewer (eds), *The Consumption of Culture 1600–1800: Image, Object, Text* (London, Routledge, 1992), pp. 9–11; S. Pincus, '"Coffee politicians does create": coffeehouses and restoration political culture', *Journal of Modern History*, 67 (1995); H. Wach, 'Civil society, moral identity and the liberal public sphere: Manchester and Boston, 1810–1840', *Social History*, 21: 3 (1996); J. Breuilly, 'Civil society and the public sphere in Hamburg, Lyon and Manchester, 1815–1880', in H. Koopman and M. Lauster (eds), *Vörmazliteratur in Europäischer Perspektive 1: Öffentlichkeit und Nationale Identität* (Bielefeld, 1996).

 15 For an elaboration of these comments see N. Fraser, 'Rethinking the public sphere: a contribution to the critique of actually existing democracy', and G. Eley, 'Nations, publics, and political cultures: placing Habermas in the nineteenth century', in Calhoun (ed.), *Habermas and the Public Sphere*; J. Landes, *Women and the Public Sphere in the Age of the French Revolution* (Ithaca, Cornell University Press, 1988).

 16 Eley, 'Nations, publics, and political cultures', p. 306.

 17 *Ibid.*, p. 294.

 18 See for example P. Borsay, *The English Urban Renaissance: Culture and Society in the Provincial Town, 1660–1770* (Oxford, Clarendon, 1991); J. Barrell, *English Literature in History, 1730–80: An Equal, Wide Survey* (London, Hutchinson, 1983); Bermingham and Brewer (eds), *The Consumption of Culture*; J. Brewer, *The Pleasures of the Imagination: English Culture in the Eighteenth Century*, (London, Routledge, 1997); P. Langford, *Public Life and the Propertied Englishman, 1689–1798* (Oxford, Clarendon, 1989); J. Brewer, *Party Ideology and Popular Politics at the Accession of George III* (Cambridge, Cambridge University Press, 1976).

 19 J. Seed, 'Gentlemen dissenters: the social and political meanings of rational dissent in the 1770s and 1780s', *Historical Journal*, 28: 2 (1985) 299–325.

 20 A. Thackray, 'Natural science in cultural context: the Manchester model', *American Historical Review*, 79 (1974); I. Inkster and J. Morell (eds), *Metropolis and Province: Science in British Culture, 1780–1850* (London, Hutchinson, 1983).

 21 *Leeds Mercury*, 2 January 1836, p. 5.

 22 Morris, *Class, Sect and Party*, p. 167.

 23 G. Crossick, 'From gentlemen to the residuum: languages of social description in Victorian Britain', in P. Corfield, (ed.), *Language, Class and History* (Cambridge, Cambridge University Press, 1991), p. 158.

24 The arguments here have some affinity with those of Dror Wahrman in his book *Imagining the Middle Class*, although I would take issue with his stress on the political dimension as against the moral, cultural and even social aspects. See also Joyce, *Democratic Subjects*, pp. 161–6 for an interesting discussion of the uses of the term 'middle class' at the period, and its relation to culture.

25 *Structural Transformation*, pp. 141–51.

26 Key works include G. Simmel, 'The metropolis and mental life' (1903) in K. Wolff (ed.), *The Sociology of Georg Simmel* (New York, Free Press, 1964); W. Benjamin, *Charles Baudelaire: A Lyric Poet in the Era of High Capitalism* (London, Verso, 1993); S. Buck-Morss, *The Dialectics of Seeing: Walter Benjamin and the Arcades Project* (Cambridge, Mass., MIT Press, 1989); D. Frisby, *Fragments of Modernity* (Cambridge, Polity Press, 1985); M. Berman, *All That is Solid Melts into Air* (London, Verso, 1983); E. Wilson, *The Sphinx in the City* (London, Verso, 1991); R. Sennett, *The Fall of Public Man* ([1977,] London, Faber and Faber, 1993).

27 It has, however, been drawn on in very different ways. See for example, W. Schivelbusch, *The Railway Journey* (Leamington Spa, Berg, 1986); J. R. Walkowitz, *City of Dreadful Delight* (London, Virago, 1992); Poovey, *Making a Social Body*.

28 P. Osborne, 'Modernity is a qualitative, not a chronological category', *New Left Review*, 192 (1992) 65–84, provides a helpful conspectus. See also P. Joyce, 'The return of history: post-modernism and the politics of academic history in Britain', *Past and Present*, 158 (1998), 213–18, for a consideration of how historians have used the term.

29 Cited in J. Mayne (ed.), *The Painter of Modern Life and Other Essays* (Oxford, Phaidon Press, 1964), p. 13.

30 Simmel, 'Metropolis and mental life'. See also T. J. Clark, *The Painting of Modern Life* (London, Thames and Hudson, 1985), for a discussion of visuality and bourgeois culture in nineteenth-century Paris.

31 The provincial periodical press remains a rich source of this type of commentary, though the papers were often short-lived. For Birmingham see *The Dart*, 1876–, and *The Lion*, 1877–; for Manchester, *The Freelance*, 1867–; Liverpool is best approached through the work of the journalist Hugh Shimmin, selections from which have been usefully reprinted in J. K. Walton and A. Wilcox (eds), *Low Life and Moral Improvement in Mid-Victorian England* (Leicester, Leicester University Press, 1991).

32 Useful insights on these questions can be found in E. Wilson, *Adorned in Dreams: Fashion and Modernity* (London, Virago, 1985), esp. ch. 7; Sennett, *Fall of Public Man*, pp. 161–87; A. St George, *The Descent of Manners: Etiquette, Rules and the Victorians* (London, Chatto and Windus, 1993).

33 Walkowitz, *City of Dreadful Delight*, p. 16. For the classic description of the *flâneur* see Benjamin, *Charles Baudelaire*, pp. 35–66.

34 R. Fishman, *Bourgeois Utopias: The Rise and Fall of Suburbia* (New York, Basic Books, 1987); R. Dennis, *English Industrial Cities of the Nineteenth Century* (Cambridge, Cambridge University Press, 1984), ch. 7.

35 For insights into this process of reconstruction and zoning see M. Girouard, *The English Town*, (New Haven and London, Yale University Press, 1990); D. G. Olsen, *The City as a Work of Art: London, Paris, Vienna* (New Haven and London, Yale University Press, 1986).

36 S. Gunn, 'The sublime and the vulgar: the Hallé concerts and the constitution of "high culture" in Manchester, c. 1850–1880', *Journal of Victorian Culture*, 2: 2 (1997) 208–28; M. Musgrave, *The Musical Life of the Crystal Palace* (Cambridge, Cambridge University Press, 1995).

37 Gunn, 'Sublime and vulgar', pp. 213–21. On the reception of classical music and audience behaviour more generally see W. Weber, *Music and the Middle Class: The Social Structures of Concert Life in London, Paris and Vienna*, (London, Croom Helm, 1975); J. Johnson, *Listening in Paris: A Cultural History* (Berkeley, University of California Press, 1995). P. Gay, *Pleasure Wars. The Bourgeois Experience: Victoria to Freud* (London, Harper Collins, 1998), pp. 75–89, also includes a consideration of the Hallé concerts.

38 This analysis draws heavily on the work of Pierre Bourdieu, especially on his ideas of the 'homology' between social and cultural hierarchies. See P. Bourdieu, *The Field of Cultural Production* (Cambridge, Polity Press, 1993), and *Distinction: A Social Critique of*

the Judgement of Taste (London, Routledge and Kegan Paul, 1984). See also John Lowerson's essay (ch. 13) in this volume.

39 A point which Habermas specifically refutes. See his critique of Sennett's, *Fall of Public Man* in Calhoun, *Habermas and the Public Sphere*, p. 426.

40 J. Wolff, 'The invisible *flâneuse*: women and the literature of modernity', in *Feminine Sentences: Essays on Women and Culture* (Berkeley, University of California Press, 1990), p. 34.

41 E. Abelson, *When Ladies Go A-Thieving: Middle-Class Shoplifters in the Victorian Department Store* (Oxford, Oxford University Press, 1989); P. Hollis, *Women in Public: The Women's Movement 1850–1900* (London, Allen and Unwin, 1979); P. Hollis, *Ladies Elect: Women in English Local Government, 1865–1914* (Oxford, Clarendon Press, 1987); M. Nava, 'Modernity's disavowal: women, the city and the department store', in M. Nava and A. O'Shea (eds), *Modern Times: Reflections on a Century of English Modernity* (London, Routledge, 1996); F. K. Prochaska, *Women and Philanthropy in Nineteenth-Century England* (Oxford, Clarendon Press, 1980); J. Rendall (ed.), *Equal or Different?: Women's Politics, 1800–1914* (Oxford, Basil Blackwell, 1987); L. Tickner, *The Spectacle of Women: Imagery of the Suffrage Campaign, 1907–1914* (London, Chatto and Windus, 1987); G. Pollock, *Vision and Difference* (London, Routledge, 1988) ; Walkowitz, *City of Dreadful Delight*, esp. ch. 2. See also the essay by Christopher Hosgood (ch. 10) in this volume.

42 *City of Dreadful Delight*, p. 46.

43 E. Hobsbawm, 'The example of the English middle class', in J. Kocka and A. Mitchell (eds), *Bourgeois Society in Nineteenth-Century Europe* (Oxford, Oxford University Press, 1993), pp. 138–41, provides an overview of the growth of these groups between 1870 and 1914.

44 B. Waites, *A Class Society at War: England 1914–18* (Leamington Spa, Berg, 1987), ch. 2; Crossick, 'From gentlemen to the residuum', pp. 166–7.

45 R. Barthes, 'The bourgeoisie as a joint-stock company' in *Mythologies* ([1957,] London, Granada, 1973), p. 150, italics as in the original.

46 Nava, 'Modernity's disavowal', p. 44.

47 Many of the classical accounts of urban modernity, such as those by Simmel and Benjamin, were either written before the First World War, or looked back to the period before it. Associated works of urban and social history, such as those of Olsen, Walkowitz and Nava previously cited, similarly take 1914 as marking an end point.

48 *Structural Transformation*, pp. 151–80.

49 The classic work remains G. Dangerfield, *The Strange Death of Liberal England* (London, Constable, 1936). See also P. F. Clarke, *Lancashire and the New Liberalism* (Cambridge, Cambridge University Press, 1971); D. Tanner, *Political Change and the Labour Party, 1900–18* (Cambridge, Cambridge University Press, 1990); T. Wilson, *The Myriad Faces of War* (Cambridge, Polity Press, 1988).

50 J. Kocka, 'The middle classes in Europe', *Journal of Modern History*, 67 (1995), 803–6; see also his chapter, 'The European pattern and the German case', in Kocka and Mitchell, *Bourgeois Society in Nineteenth-Century Europe*.

51 Though see A. A. Jackson, *The Middle Classes 1900–1950* (Nairn, David St John Thomas, 1991); M. Barlow, P. Dickens, A. J. Fielding and M. Savage, *Property, Bureaucracy and Culture: Middle-Class Formation in Contemporary Britain* (London, Routledge, 1992).

52 See for example the essays by Christopher Hosgood (ch. 10), Jill Greenfield, Sean O'Connell and Chris Reid (ch. 12), and John Lowerson (ch. 15) in this volume. Also J. Lowerson, *Sport and the English Middle Classes, 1870–1914* (Manchester, Manchester University Press, 1993); J. Benson, *The Rise of Consumer Society in Britain* (Harlow, Longman, 1994); F. Mort, *Cultures of Consumption: Masculinities and Social Space in Late Twentieth-Century Britain* (London, Routledge, 1995); M. Nava, 'Modernity's disavowal'; A. Light, *Forever England: Femininity, Literature and Conservatism Between the Wars* (London, Routledge, 1991). A new volume, A. J. Kidd and D. Nicholls (eds), *The Making of the British Middle Class? Studies of Regional and Cultural Diversity Since the Eighteenth Century* (Stroud, Sutton, 1998), esp. essays by Dintenfass, Rubinstein, Thompson and Trainor, will go some way to compensating for this neglect of the politics and social structure of the British middle class in the twentieth century.

53 R. Bocock, *Consumption* (London, 1993), pp. 1–5.
54 Among the burgeoning historical literature on eighteenth-century consumption see Bermingham and Brewer, *Consumption of Culture*; N. McKendrick, J. Brewer and J. H. Plumb, *The Birth of a Consumer Society: The Commercialisation of Eighteenth-Century England* (Cambridge, Cambridge University Press, 1982); J. Brewer and R. Porter (eds), *Consumption and the World of Goods* (London, Routledge, 1993). For arguments about twentieth-century consumption and the shift to mass consumerism see D. Miller, *Material Culture and Mass Consumption* (Oxford, Basil Blackwell, 1987); J. Baudrillard, 'Consumer society', in *Selected Writings* (Cambridge, Polity Press, 1988); M. Featherstone, *Consumer Culture and Post-modernism* (London, Sage, 1991); P. Corrigan, *The Sociology of Consumption* (London, Sage, 1997).
55 T. Veblen, *The Theory of the Leisure Class* (New York, New American Library, 1953). For the work of the Frankfurt School, notably Adorno, Horkheimer and Marcuse, see A. Arato and E. Gebhardt (eds), *The Essential Frankfurt School Reader* (Oxford, Basil Blackwell, 1978); T. Adorno, *The Culture Industry: Selected Essays on Mass Culture* (London, Routledge, 1991), has a useful introduction by J. M. Bernstein.
56 Corrigan, *The Sociology of Consumption*, ch. 2; Baudrillard, 'Consumer society'; Mort, *Cultures of Consumption*.
57 On the development of the department store in England see A. Adburgham, *Shops and Shopping, 1800–1914* (London, Barrie and Jenkins, 1989); W. Lancaster, *The Department Store: A Social History* (Leicester, Leicester University Press, 1995).
58 R. Laermans, 'Learning to consume: early department stores and the shaping of modern consumer culture, 1860–1914', *Theory, Culture and Society*, 10: 4 (1993), p. 92.
59 M. B. Miller, *The Bon Marché: Bourgeois Culture and the Department Store, 1869–1920* (London, Allen and Harris, 1981); A. Forty, *Objects of Desire: Design and Society since 1750* (London, Thames and Hudson, 1986); T. Bennett, 'The exhibitionary complex', in N. B. Dirks, G. Eley and S. B. Ortner (eds), *Culture/Power/History* (Princeton, Princeton University Press, 1994).
60 Corrigan, *Sociology of Consumption*, p. 60.
61 Nava, 'Modernity's disavowal', pp. 60–1.
62 S. Bowden, 'The new consumerism', in P. Johnson (ed.), *Twentieth-Century Britain: Economic, Social and Cultural Change* (London, Longman, 1994).
63 S. Alexander, 'Becoming a woman in London in the 1920s and 30s', in *Becoming a Woman and Other Essays in Nineteenth and Twentieth-Century Feminist History* (London, Virago, 1994), pp. 203–7.
64 C. F. G. Masterman, *The Condition of England* (London, Methuen, 1911).
65 See *ibid.*, pp. 65–77; also the essays by Hammerton (ch. 11) and Hosgood (ch. 10) in this volume.
66 Light, *Forever England*, ch. 1; Forty, *Objects of Desire*; J. B. Priestley, *English Journey* (London, Heinemann, 1934), p. 401.
67 W. D. Rubinstein, 'Wealth, elites and the class structure of modern Britain', *Past and Present*, 76 (1977) 99–126; Hobsbawm, 'The example of the English middle class', pp. 134–8.
68 Waites, *A Class Society at War*, pp. 47–54; Crossick, 'From gentlemen to the residuum', p. 174.
69 R. Lewis and A. Maude, *The English Middle Classes*, ([1949,] London, Phoenix House, 1953), p. 14.
70 R. McKibbin, 'Class and conventional wisdom: the Conservative party and the 'public' in inter-war Britain', in *Ideologies of Class* (Oxford, Clarendon Press, 1991), p. 284.
71 *Ibid.*, p. 293.
72 S. Baldwin, *Liberal Unemployment Plans Exposed* (London, 1929), cited in McKibbin, 'Class and conventional wisdom', p. 269. For comments on the development of public opinion surveys in the late 1930s see R. Graves and A. Hodge, *The Long Weekend* (London, Faber and Faber, 1940), pp. 396–7.
73 The influence of Foucault is apparent in a number of the works previously cited, notably Bennett, *The Birth of the Museum* and Joyce, *Democratic Subjects*, as also in Joyce (ed.), *Class: A Reader* (Oxford, Oxford University Press, 1995). Examples of

Foucault's scepticism towards class analysis and the concept of the bourgeoisie can be found in his 'Two lectures', reprinted in Dirks, Eley and Ortner, *Culture/Power/History*, esp. pp. 215–17.

74 See for example, Davidoff and Hall, *Family Fortunes*; M. Roper and J. Tosh (eds), *Manful Assertions: Masculinities in Britain Since 1800* (London, Routledge, 1991); C. Hall, *White, Male and Middle Class: Explorations in Feminism and History* (Cambridge, Polity Press, 1992).

PART ONE

GENDER, IDENTITY AND CIVIC CULTURE

PRELUDE

The purpose of this Prelude is to provide a brief introduction to the chapters in Part One of the book. Readers wishing to pursue the issues raised by the contributors can follow sources and arguments through the note references to each chapter and also via the selection of 'Further reading' at the end of the book, and based upon recommendations for further study made by the authors.

As already suggested in the editors' introduction, a major focus of the chapters in Part One is the extent to which, within the provincial middle-class elites of the first half of the nineteenth century, cultural identities revolved round notions of the urban and the civic. Thus, Arline Wilson in her chapter '"The Florence of the North"? The civic culture of Liverpool in the early nineteenth century', examines an early attempt to construct a cultural identity for Liverpool that was both aesthetic and bourgeois and designed to obscure the town's association with the slave trade. The Literary and Philosophical Society and other institutions central to male middle-class (elite) culture were the site for this endeavour. The Liverpool experience can be linked to that of other northern cities in the same era. Existing work on Manchester and Leeds, like Wilson's case study of William Roscoe's cultural campaigns in Liverpool, demonstrates the way in which urban leadership was regarded as a matter of creating cultural consciousness.

The role of the learned societies and notions of urban civilisation in northern towns (this time Sheffield) feature also in the contribution from Alison Twells. In the chapter entitled '"A Christian and civilised land": the British middle class and the civilising mission, 1820–42', she explores the relationship between the Christianisation of indigenous cultures abroad and the construction of a middle-class identity at home. Representation of the 'civilisation' of native peoples was a relatively unproblematic cultural icon for the recipients of missionary tales at home, reinforcing as it did a sense of superiority (difference) yet also a feeling of shared humanity (sameness). The cultural impact of the missions extended to the development of the modern human and social sciences. The ethnographic and other collections of the evangelical missionaries supported the commitment to science and to 'useful knowledge' as epitomised in the Literary and Philosophical societies. Twells explores the extent to which the latter were a site for the construction of a male middle-class identity. She examines the early development of the relationship between cultural difference and sameness of Christianised and un-Christianised peoples and the extent to which a civilised middle-class identity was being constructed in terms of difference to uncultivated races overseas (as, indeed, it was to the urban masses at home, also regarded as similar yet different).

Dianne Macleod's chapter, 'Homosociality and middle-class identity in early Victorian patronage of the arts', is one of two contributions in this volume from an art historian (the other is Louise Purbrick's). Employing the concept of 'homosociality' (social bonds between persons of the same sex in relation to class and power), she explores the construction of masculine identities appropriate for middle-class art connoisseurs and collectors during the second quarter of the nineteenth century, a time when the transition from aristocratic to bourgeois taste and patronage was incomplete. Middle-class art patrons were caught between class and gender imperatives which pivoted on notions of gentlemanly behaviour and the potential inference of effeminacy if bourgeois codes of masculine behaviour were infringed. At this moment of transition, concepts of masculinity were uncertain and unstable. Macleod examines the contrasting responses of three art patrons of modest social origins as they struggled to situate themselves in class and gender terms.

Similarly, Louise Purbrick's chapter reveals an overlap of approaches in the study of images between the concern of the art historian to 'read' an image, to explore its possible meanings, in part by a deconstruction of its symbolism/iconography, and the desire of the social historian to contextualise the image as a cultural artefact. Purbrick's study, 'The bourgeois body: civic portraiture, public men and the appearance of class power in Manchester, 1838–50', suggests the value to the social historian of understanding how to interpret the internal workings of an image and its genre, to read it as a 'text'. In her chapter, she argues that a collection of official portraits of civic leaders in early Victorian Manchester were constitutive, rather than reflexive, of middle-class power. Purbrick describes the sameness, the uniform conventions and ritual symbolism of these celebrations of bourgeois status. In doing so she explores some of the possible meanings of the relationship between political and artistic cultures and sees in these portraits a symbolic rendering of individual persons so as to position them as icons both of class and of gender. Thus cultural aesthetic and institutional ideology combine in a visual rhetoric of civic proprietorship at a crucial moment when class power seemed newly won.

In her chapter, '"Thoroughly embued with the spirit of ancient Greece": symbolism and space in Victorian civic culture', Kate Hill takes concern with civic culture and social identity forward into the mid-Victorian period. Her geographical loci are Preston, Liverpool and Birmingham. Hill argues that civic improvements (public buildings and urban spaces) represented a vision of the city and its middle-class citizens designed to enhance the status of both. First, the rhetoric of civic culture (expressed in a series of interconnecting narratives) is explored as a discourse on the meaning of the city, its history and purpose. Secondly, the use of space within the city is explored as a means of cultural control both of public behaviour and of a particular ideal of citizenship. Such issues focus on the extent to which the architecture and open spaces of the nineteenth-century town themselves represented the 'ownership' of the 'public' places by a 'private' group, the middle-class male elite. The appropriation of the 'public' by the middle class found cultural expression in a number of ways. The statues and portraits, civic ceremonial and ritual and the meetings of the various learned societies which took place in these public buildings and which were profusely reported in the local press (combined with the restriction of access to other groups and activities) are indicative of the extent to which a middle-class male elite was able to use public buildings as arenas for mutual self-endorsement and for the consolidation of an identity of rank, authority and power. Despite a rhetoric of universal access, public space was middle-class and generally male. Increasingly, however, as the century wore on other groups competed for access to this cultural arena.

This is clearly demonstrated in Simon Gunn's chapter, which explores the concept of 'modernity' as expressed in the spatial and architectural patterns of the reconstructed industrial city: Manchester in the middle and later nineteenth century. 'The middle class, modernity and the provincial city: Manchester, c. 1840–80' examines how, as the middle-class elite and the 'wider middle class' of the suburbs experienced the city, they constructed its spatial relations in terms appropriate to their proprietorial relationship with urban modernity. Gunn sums up the process as follows: 'As property-owners, investors, speculators, architects and councillors the city's male bourgeoisie were to a very large extent the agents of the new cityscape. In turn, the identity of the bourgeois elite was affirmed by the re-creation of the city itself, reinforcing the status of the elite as "our representatives", "our leading merchants, capitalists and public men".' The problem of urban space and the attempt to retain control of that urban space by an increasingly suburban middle class is Gunn's major theme. He emphasises that the new urban spaces were often conceptualised in moral terms, as places of danger and of transgression, and he explores the ways in which these spaces and places were reclaimed as sites of consumption and of respectable ritual, especially important for the 'wider suburban middle class'. This spatial renegotiation was not unproblematic as the respectable bourgeois were jostled in the streets by drunks, beggars and prostitutes. Thus, Gunn, like Hill, points to the extent to which the 'moral city' was an unstable construct. The obverse of civic pride was civic fear. Public spaces could be places of contest and confrontation especially for middle-class ladies. Thus the wider suburban middle class set out to reappropriate certain quarters of the city as arenas of high-class consumption and fashionable parade. In this, the usually private world of regularity and ritual characteristic of suburban living was intended to perform a normative function as public cultural display. This assertion of suburban rights expressed one way in which the wider middle class negotiated the conditions of urban modernity.

3

'THE FLORENCE OF THE NORTH'? THE CIVIC CULTURE OF LIVERPOOL IN THE EARLY NINETEENTH CENTURY
Arline Wilson

Cultural forms and practices are increasingly being identified as crucial elements in the making of the middle class (or classes). However, the difficulty of locating Liverpool within current historiographical paradigms has seen its cultural infrastructure receive little attention. As a great commercial entrepot, Liverpool, although in the industrial North, was not of it, thus rendering it atypical in accounts challenging the image of a philistine northern bourgeoisie.[1]

Liverpool, however, has been equally ill-served by the revisionist approaches which assert the primacy of commercial enterprise over spinning and smelting in Britain's rise to pre-eminence and accord priority to 'gentlemanly capitalism' in explanations of British economic decline. Contrary to the idea of Britain as the workshop of the world, W. D. Rubinstein asserts that it was never fundamentally an industrial and manufacturing economy but always essentially a commercial-, finance- and service-based one, focused in and around the metropolis.[2] Similarly, for Cain and Hopkins, 'gentlemanly capitalism' seems not to have extended beyond the City of London and the home counties[3] – Liverpool again is rendered exceptional, not by its source of wealth but by its geographical position. Yet, as this chapter will show, the early nineteenth century witnessed the development of an ambitious cultural infrastructure in Liverpool which was instrumental in redefining the identity of the town and its merchant elite. Moreover, the success of its cultural organisations in spanning Liverpool's deep religious and political divisions confirms Robert Morris's emphasis on the centrality of voluntary societies in uniting the dignified and independent classes of society and making them into a recognisable, self-aware and active 'middle class'.[4]

The eighteenth century had seen Liverpool's rise from an insignificant seaport at its opening, to a position at its close where the town was vaunting its position as Britain's second city. For most of this period the first line of self-definition for its newly rich merchants was through material possessions, conspicuous consumption and spatial separation from their fellow townsmen. However, from increased wealth grew increased civic pride. Identifying their wealth firmly with commerce rather than manufacturing, Liverpool's merchant classes began to define themselves against industrial Manchester whilst turning envious eyes towards the metropolis.

Although the foresight and enterprise of the merchants have generally been recognised and lauded as a dynamic element in Liverpool's economic success story, both contemporary and more recent accounts have depicted an elite characterised by the philistinism of self-made men. In his description of the town in 1795 James Wallace declared: 'Arts and sciences are inimical to the spot, absorbed in the nautical vortex, the only pursuit of the inhabitants is commerce.'[5] Yet, by the mid-nineteenth century, J. W. Hudson was drawing remarkably different conclusions:

> There is not town in the Kingdom in which there are so many temples dedi-cated to the improvement of mankind as in Liverpool, nor can any city provide equal evidence of the zeal of its Merchant Princes in raising mansions for the advancement of civilisation.[6]

Although hyperbole undoubtedly played its part in both these assessments, they are nevertheless indicative of a dramatic 'sea-change' in outside perceptions of Liverpool's civic and cultural identity.

The motivation for this redefinition can, in part, be identified with the broader national movement which, in the later eighteenth and early nineteenth centuries, saw the burgeoning provincial towns become increasingly confident and articulate in asserting their claims and status, rivalry with the metropolis being reflected on the cultural as well as the economic front.[7] William Carey, a tireless advocate of English art, queried why the arts should 'be confined to a *glutted* metropolis . . . they should be planted in every apt soil'.[8] However, it can be argued that Liverpool's place at the forefront of this movement, and its embracing of the grand conception of a 'Florence of the North', was further motivated by the changing national ideology in relation to the slave trade.[9]

For much of the century, Liverpool's share of the slave trade had been 'a thing to be envied, the legitimate reward of enterprise which everyone would have been delighted to share'.[10] However, the inauguration of the national aboli-tionist movement in 1787 saw public opinion change and Liverpool now found itself becoming increasingly isolated and facing not just a threat to its economic base but also a challenge to its cultural identity.[11] As early as 1788, Matthew Gregson (a prominent local supporter of the slave trade) was categorised as 'a proper Liverpool man' by a London correspondent, who dubbed himself 'humanity man' – the inference being that to the outside world the two terms were considered incompatible.[12] The town found itself subjected to public opprobrium in Parliament, branded as the 'metropolis of slavery', with visitors expressing a similar moral distaste. The artist Fuseli, visiting the sights of Liverpool in 1804, declared 'I viewed them with interest, but methinks I smell everywhere the blood of slaves.'[13] As Seymour Drescher concedes, the twenty years before abolition witnessed Liverpool's merchants unceasingly petitioning Parliament against abolition and their involvement in the slave trade far from diminishing actually increased. However, he draws on contemporary descrip-tions and local guides to suggest a growing disquiet at this alleged 'stain' on Liverpool's reputation, with the *Liverpool Guide* in 1789, stressing the impor-tance of the town's other commercial ties and insisting that the trade was conducted mainly by outsiders – a patent manipulation of the truth.[14] The vocif-erous criticism from neighbouring Manchester proved particularly galling and added to the resolve of the merchants to legitimise their status as Liverpool 'gentlemen'. The adoption of William Roscoe as their cultural icon and architect underlines the strength of this commitment.

In defining the spirit of Liverpool during the first third of the nineteenth century the term 'Roscoe's Liverpool' has, with justification, been considered the most appropriate.[15] William Roscoe was, for nearly half a century, a consistent factor in the evolution of Liverpool's intellectual life and his achievements were remarkable. The son of an innkeeper and market gardener, he rose to become an historian of international repute – 'within a generation Roscoe's name was as internationally famous as Gibbon's'.[16] A renowned botanist, minor poet, artist and art lover, radical politician and opponent of the slave trade, he was also a lawyer, banker and businessman, and as such involved in, and concerned for, the commercial success of the port. But William Roscoe was also a Radical and a Dissenter in a town whose leading merchants were firmly attached to High Toryism and the principles of the established Church; an ardent abolitionist in a town which considered its prosperity dependent on the slave trade, setting him firmly outside the established elite of the town.

During the last third of the eighteenth century, Roscoe, together with like-minded men such as Dr James Currie, the biographer of Burns, John Rutter, physician and mineralogist, and William Rathbone the fourth, philanthropist and social reformer, had established a number of art and literary societies in the town (including a Philosophical and Literary Society in 1779), all of which had elicited little response from the merchant community at large, and had faded away in the repressive atmosphere of the early 1790s.

However, 1796 came the publication of Roscoe's biography of Lorenzo de' Medici, a pioneering study of its subject in English, highlighting the Anglo-Florentine entente in commerce and culture, an event which has been described as 'a turning point, it not the starting point of Liverpool's intellectual life'.[17]

Roscoe's long interest in Italian writings and poetry had drawn him to the conclusions that 'everything great and excellent in science and in art, revolved round Lorenzo de' Medici, during the short but splendid era of his life'.[18] Roscoe saw in Florence and its ruler the apotheosis of the union between culture and commerce. He proclaimed his interest as literary and cultural rather than political and disclaimed the book had any relevance for contemporary problems: 'the truth is, it is a tale of other times, bearing but little on the momentous occurrences of the present day'.[19] The book tapped into a willing and ready readership and became an immediate success. It stimulated English interest in the Italian Renaissance and earned Roscoe a national and international reputation as a writer and historian. The fact that Roscoe was a self-made man who now owned 'the very estate where his father was gardener and his mother housekeeper', made him a particularly attractive role model for aspiring American merchants and professionals seeking to establish their civic and social position. For many Bostonians, he symbolised 'the intellectual breadth and elegance which might lift a Boston businessman to a loftier social and cultural level'. Numerous Americans visited or corresponded with Roscoe and at least two Bostonians named their sons after him.[20] Roscoe was now established as the model of the cultured merchant, a living symbol that humble origins, a remote northern birthplace and the pursuit of a business career were not incompatible with the highest intellectual achievement. His book also brought reappraisal of Liverpool's image and kindled interest in the cultural identity of the town. One critic marvelled that this 'model of literary endeavour' had been written and printed 'in the remote commercial town of Liverpool, where nothing is heard of but Guinea ships, slaves, blacks and merchandise'.[21]

This widespread acclaim accorded Roscoe impressed his fellow townsmen. He had rewritten history in a way that allowed Liverpool's merchants to celebrate themselves and for this they were now prepared to adopt Roscoe, the man of letters, as their cultural mentor, whilst simultaneously rejecting Roscoe, the Radical politician and abolitionist. The analogy of Liverpool and Renaissance Florence was particularly appealing. For, despite Roscoe's assertions that the book had no contemporary relevance, it was surely here that Roscoe looked for a role model for his native town. His belief in the efficacy of Lorenzo's academies, schools, libraries, associations, provided him with the blueprint for the future construction of a similar infrastructure in Liverpool. Roscoe's Italian vision made a deep impression on his native town and it continued to be evoked by his fellow townsmen of all shades of political and religious opinion long after his death, in public speeches, lectures and in papers read before the local literary and scientific societies.

In 1797, when Roscoe and his circle regrouped to establish the first of the institutions which were to provide the mainframe of Liverpool's nineteenth-century cultural infrastructure, they were greeted with a markedly different response to that which had accompanied their earlier cultural forays. The changing attitudes of Liverpool's merchants manifested themselves in widespread enthusiasm and support.

The Athenaeum, one of the largest and most imposing of the urban 'gentlemen's' libraries founded in Britain at this time, confirmed from the outset that the redefinition of the cultural identity of Liverpool was to be the creation of the town's wealthier citizens. It also presaged the role that cultural endeavour was to play in transcending traditional religious and political boundaries within this group. Despite the presence among the founders of men associated with reform and dissent, the proposals met with an immediate response. A catalogue of the Athenaeum stressed that:

> Although the proposal for founding the Athenaeum was brought forward at a time of great political excitement ... this state of public feeling was not allowed to prejudice the design. On the contrary, men of all shades of opinion, political and religious, concurred with equal zeal in promoting the success of an institution designed to facilitate the acquisition of knowledge.[22]

The oligarchic and staunchly Tory Common Council proceeded to look on the Athenaeum with favour, seeing it as a decided ornament to the town and granting it the reversionary interest in its premises. The first president, George Case, was himself a member of the Council and the Mayor was elected an honorary member. William Roscoe was vice-president of the Athenaeum from 1799 to 1801 and president, 1803–4, and remained an active committee member, devoting much time and attention to the Athenaeum library.[23] Inside two years the value of the shares had tripled with membership of the Athenaeum being seen as an essential emblem of status for Liverpool's commercial aristocracy.

The Athenaeum also proved important in establishing Liverpool's cultural identity in the international arena and the town now found itself becoming a role model for its western trading partner. The Boston Athenaeum, founded in 1807, based its laws on the Liverpool institution, with one of its founders claiming the intention to 'make ours as much like that as the different circumstances of the countries will admit'.[24] The Bostonian, Joseph Buckminster, reported to his Anthology Society in 1806:

> The City of Liverpool has now reached that point of wealth, at which societies, which have been hitherto merely mercenary and commercial, begin to turn their attention to learning and the fine arts, that is they perceive that something more than great riches is necessary to make a place worthy of being visited, and interesting enough to be admired.[25]

Although there were also institutional analogies with London, for many Bostonians 'London and the Londoners were, in a sense, merely Liverpool and William Roscoe writ large'.[26]

Encouraged by this success, the same intellectual coterie were instrumental in founding the Botanic Garden (1802), the Lyceum (1803) and the Academy of Art (1810). In 1812 Liverpool followed Manchester and Newcastle in founding a Literary and Philosophical Society.[27] The programme of the Liverpool society, however, was markedly different from those of Manchester and Newcastle where science was the dominant ethic. The Unitarian minister William Turner, progenitor of the Newcastle society, unequivocally saw its prime purpose as bringing science to bear on the primary economic needs of the district and placed papers on coal and lead firmly at the head of his agenda.[28] In the case of Manchester, it has been suggested that the main impetus for the town's Literary and Philosophical Society stemmed from the demands of the new industrial middle classes for a cultural forum where they could forge their own distinct identity, and it was science that they chose as their cultural mode of self-expression.[29] The presence of Percival and Dalton in the Society further ensured the primacy of scientific topics. By contrast, the Liverpool society reflected the influence of Roscoe (president from 1817 to 1831) who in his broad intellectual interests belonged more to the eighteenth-century classical humanitarian school than the mercantilist and industrial nineteenth century. While this lack of specialisation ensured that it never achieved the same eminence accorded to the Manchester and Newcastle societies, it nonetheless played an important role in Liverpool's intellectual life, attracting an elite and prestigious membership and orchestrating a number of public cultural activities which helped Liverpool earn recognition in the wider intellectual arena.

As with the Athenaeum, membership of the Liverpool Literary and Philosophical Society was confined to the town's middle classes with the largest occupational group coming from the business community – 31 of the first 56 names on the Society's roll being merchants or brokers. Theoretically the Society was open to anyone who resided within 5 miles of Liverpool and who could afford the entrance free of 1 guinea and the annual subscription of half a guinea, which in comparison with other literary and philosophical societies (Newcastle for example) was fairly cheap. These were not, however, the sole criteria for membership. All prospective members were balloted for, and three-quarters of the votes had to be in a man's favour before he could join. From 1814, the required proportion was increased to four-fifths and the minutes record that at least one prospective member fell foul of this regulation in the early years of the Society.[30] Membership was an all male affair and continued to be so for most of the nineteenth century. It was not until October 1883 that the first women were elected to full membership. Even then, women customarily attended only the less academic lectures and no woman was appointed to the Society's Council until about 1927.

Although the initial impetus for the Society stemmed mainly from socially marginal men (of the sixteen founder members, half can be identified as non-Anglican, while five had been 'Jacobins' or members of the Anti-Slavery Society),[31] it attracted and elected to membership West Indian merchants, Anglican priests and a wide variety of men from established sections of the middle classes. By establishing a forum, where literary and scientific topics could be discussed in a relatively informal, congenial and non-controversial atmosphere, it served to integrate the town's middle classes (whether Dissenting or established Church, anti- or pro-slavery, radical or conservative) at a time when feelings were running high in town.[32]

A number of papers presented before the Society in its early years reinforced this fellowship with panegyrics on the character and worth of the Liverpool merchant community with the Florentine analogy frequently being evoked. Liverpool's merchants, through the platform of the Literary and Philosophical Society, had no wish to distance themselves from the source of their wealth but sought to glorify the spirit of commerce as the nurse of liberty and the arts.

The importance of visual representation to Liverpool's image was a major theme of the Society in its early years, with seventeen papers being delivered on art and architecture. The architect Thomas Rickman delivered thirteen of these to an audience that included members of building and memorial committees who had begun offering commissions to local architects and sculptors to adorn the city with new buildings and commemorative statues befitting its new economic status. Rickman (like many others at that time) was at work on the principles of the Gothic style. He presented his findings to the members of the Literary and Philosophical Society and in 1817 disseminated them more widely in his book, *An Attempt to Discriminate the Styles of English Architecture, from the Conquest to the Reformation*, which became the cornerstone of the Gothic Revival.[33] It has been argued that although the town did not repudiate the neo-classic form, Rickman's influence ensured that it was Liverpool which witnessed the birth of the Gothic Revival.[34].

Two years after its inauguration, members of the Literary and Philosophical Society were instrumental in helping to establish the Liverpool Royal Institution. Here was the culmination of William Roscoe's dream of establishing a prestigious cultural centre which would exemplify the Liverpool conjunction of commerce and culture:

An attempt to institute in the midst of a great trading city a place which should be a perpetual focus for every intellectual interest, a perpetual radiator of sane and lofty views of life, a perpetual reminder of the higher needs and aspirations of men in the midst of the fierce roar of commercial competition and the clangorous appeal of these surroundings to the vulgar lust of money.[35]

Although, as the choice of name suggests, the Liverpool Royal Institution was partly inspired by its London namesake, it was never planned as purely a scientific establishment. From the outset, its stated aims were uncompromisingly cultural in character, reflecting Roscoe's cosmopolitan interests in art, science and literature. During the first half of the nineteenth century, it became one of the major provincial institutions devoted to the diffusion of learning.

The committee appointed in 1814 to direct and oversee the future development of the project demonstrated once more the success of cultural schemes in Liverpool in rallying support from and unifying the town's middle classes. It included West India merchants, American merchants, clergymen from the established church, Unitarian ministers and members of the Town Council. William Roscoe and John Gladstone were appointed chairman and vice-chairman respectively – men of widely differing political and religious views but united in their desire to see Liverpool achieve a cultural profile consonant with its economic status. The £20,000 deemed necessary to fund the Institution was raised by the issuing of share of £100 and £50. Proprietors holding £100 shares were to be entitled to a silver ticket which granted free admission to the Institution to the shareholders and members of his family, with holders of £50 shares paying half price. The term 'family', the resolution stipulated, was to include wives, children, brothers and sisters of the proprietors, but definitely 'not Housekeepers' – an indication from the outset that the Institution did not intend to draw its patrons from the lower classes.[36]

The Institution's role was to be multi-functional, the founders setting themselves a magnificent educational task, inaugurating comprehensive lecture programmes, establishing day schools and providing support and accommodation for local cultural societies and the Academy of Art. The Royal Institution, it was believed, would not only firmly establish Liverpool's cultural profile as a new Florence but would possibly even bring current and future commercial benefits to the town. The proposed schools, for example, would not only relieve local parents from the 'expence [sic] and anxiety of sending their Children to a distance', but might also attract trade to Liverpool from outlying areas by encouraging: 'Strangers to bring their families here for that purpose ... especially such as may intend any of their Sons for Trade, as they could then unite here, in some measure, Scientific with Commercial Education.' The Institution's educational programme, however, was not aimed solely at the younger generation. Through its lecture courses, the Institution hoped to become 'a rational source of Information and Recreation for Persons farther advanced in life', keeping them abreast of the 'rapid progress of Literature and Science which characterizes the present age'. Liverpool, had already achieved a measure of recognition as a literary centre and the wide-ranging lecture courses would not only further enhance this reputation but would also gain Liverpool a correspondingly high scientific profile, and thus 'in time render this great Commercial Town no less distinguished as a Seminary of Science, than as an Emporium of Commerce'.[37]

At the opening of the Royal Institution in November 1817, William Roscoe (the Institution's first president) delivered an inaugural address before a large audience (including the 8-year-old William Gladstone), in which he justified his thesis that literature and art could not, and should not be, disassociated from commerce. He traced a historical link between intellectual improvement and commerce, concluding that 'in every place where commerce has been cultivated upon great and enlightened principles, a considerable proficiency has always been made in liberal studies and pursuits'. He challenged the idea of 'art for art's sake', claiming that to suppose that the arts 'are to be encouraged upon some abstract and disinterested plan, from which all idea of utility shall be excluded, it to suppose that a building can be erected without a foundation . . . Utility and pleasure are . . . found together in an indissoluble chain.' He compared the effect that commerce had on broadening the mind to that of industry: 'it is much to be feared that the unavoidable tendency of these employments is to contract or deaden the exertions of the intellect, and to reduce the powers both of body and mind to a machine'.[38] This offered heart-warming legitimisation for Liverpool's gentlemen, and was a welcome contrast with the image of the 'Manchester Man'.

By 1820 the major part of the Institution's programme had been achieved. Lecture courses had commenced and been well received. The Classical and Mathematical schools had been opened and the Literary and Philosophical Society was housed in the Institution.[39] The Royal Institution also developed significant collections in its Museum of Natural History and Art Gallery, which fulfilled a valuable function at a time when public galleries and museums were practically non-existent and allowed the Liverpool elite an opportunity to display their talents as discerning collectors.

Roscoe was associated with every attempt made in Liverpool to establish an Academy and annual exhibitions and was the most important single influence guiding art patronage in the town for the first thirty years of the nineteenth century. The nucleus of the Institution's art collection was formed in 1819, when a group of members presented it with thirty-seven of Roscoe's pictures, which he had been forced to sell to stave off his impending bankruptcy. Roscoe's purpose in collecting his pictures had been primarily didactic and a similar intent appears to have guided the intentions of the donors. This communal action by a group of Liverpool men immersed in the world of commerce was significant and innovative, for it meant that 'for the first time in Britain a group of important old master paintings had been bought and placed on permanent exhibition with the avowed intention of improving public taste'.[40]

Roscoe's influence ensured that the Royal Institution paid particular attention to the Exhibition Room for the Liverpool Academy of Art. In a speech to the reformed Academy in 1811, Roscoe had looked forward with confidence 'to a period when the Liverpool Academy might produce artists of the highest talent, and perhaps might eventually rival the great Institution in the capital', and he envisioned a future when the name and the artists of Liverpool Academy would be known throughout the world. Liverpool's gentlemen were reluctant to see their Academy link art with the industrial developments of the day, and the principles of high art were the dominant ethic of the exhibitions held in the Royal Institution throughout the 1820s, with the majority of patrons supporting an educational programme for painters that emphasised these principles. The artists, too, had no great desire to jeopardise their economic or social positions by admitting craftsmen and the problems of applied art.[41]

By the early 1820s the president, Benjamin A. Heywood, felt able to assure his audience that the Institution was already proving influential, both in stimulating intellectual development amongst the citizens of Liverpool, and in helping to redefine Liverpool's cultural identity. 'At this moment', he claimed. 'it has a higher literary character than most provincial towns, and there is undoubtedly more general desire of mental improvement.'[42] The year 1822–23 saw the Institution attract visitors not only from Britain, but from America, Belgium, Portugal, Denmark, Jamaica, Russia, Italy, Peru, France, Germany and Canada.[43] In 1824 Heywood took particular pleasure in asserting the Institution's status (and by association that of the proprietors and of the town) as a role model for the 'the numerous institutions . . . which have been founded upon similar plans in various parts of the kingdom'.[44] Furthermore, he contended, this 'had not been confined within the limits of this country', quoting in justification of his claim an Address of a committee in New York which was planning to establish a similar institution in its own city:

> The example of Liverpool has been frequently held out to our citizens as worthy of imitation, and none can be adduced more apposite. The two cities have risen into importance almost *pari passu* – have been mutually conducive to each other's progress, and are most intimately connected in the bonds of a constant and ever active intercourse.[46]

However, for many of the founders the primary purpose for which the Institution had been created was the provision of systematic lecture courses on literature and science and for more than twenty years a determined but ultimately unsuccessful effort was made to realise this. The lectures were 'to be open to the public on such terms as may be from time to time be approved by the Committee'. The average price of the tickets was 5 shillings for a single lecture and 2 guineas for the course. The cost, coupled with the fact that many of the lectures were scheduled in the middle of the working day (the botanical lectures of Sir J. E. Smith, for example, were given at 11 a.m.), ensured that the audiences patronising the lecture programme would be drawn almost entirely from Liverpool's middle classes. The arts lecture programme covered a wide range of subjects including English poetry, Italian, French and German literature, ancient and modern history, philosophy, political economy and music. In addition, the Institution's association with the Liverpool Academy and its School of Design resulted in attempts to arrange lectures on the fine arts and on architecture. The Royal Institution followed the Literary and Philosophical Society in promoting architecture at what it believed to be a particularly important time in the town's development: 'it is highly important in this growing town, to adhere to what is correct in architecture, and cultivate the taste to appreciate and adopt what is excellent'.[46] Lectures in scientific subjects were also given fairly frequently during the early years of the Institution, although it was only in medical subjects that anything like systematic coverage was provided – a development that was largely responsible for the establishment (within the Institution) of the Liverpool Medical School in 1834, the forerunner of Liverpool University's Faculty of Medicine. Other science courses included geology, astronomy, zoology, botany, electricity and courses on miscellaneous science subjects.

This wide-ranging programme led to recognition by contemporary observers of the potential of the Royal Institution to function as the north of England's first university college. In 1818, *Blackwood's Edinburgh Magazine* pointed out the difficulties that beset parents in northern England who sought higher education for their offspring and believed that the Liverpool Royal Institution was admirably fitted to remedy this situation. It claimed that of all the cultural projects supported by the town's merchant community the Royal Institution was 'infinitely more worthy of all their exertions and all their liberality than any which has ever before become candidate for their approbation'.[47] Unfortunately, the Institution itself seemed unable to decide whether the prime function of the lecture programme was to provide professional education of a university type for young people or supplementary education in liberal studies for adults. The Institution endeavoured to realise both objectives, and possibly would have succeeded if it had possessed adequate financial resources to carry them out properly. Sadly, this was not the case, for apart from a grant of £150 from the Town Council and a few hundred pounds from investments, the Institution was entirely reliant on fees paid by students other than proprietors.[48]

The aim of the founders of the Liverpool Royal Institution to provide secondary education for sons of the local middle classes proved to be longer-lasting and pioneering in its influence. The 'Establishment of Academical Schools' had been the first objective listed in the detailed plan of 1814, aiming to give the proprietors and their social compeers the opportunity of educating their sons 'in the highest departments of science and literature, without the necessity of sending them to distant and expensive establishments'. The plan of 1814 favoured a school which would be innovative in its curriculum, moulding young Liverpool gentlemen who would exemplify the tenet that the union of commerce and culture was both possible and desirable. The school was to have no religious or political affiliations – 'the object of the Liverpool Royal Institution being altogether unconnected with Political or other Party'.[49] Although Roscoe, in particular, remained convinced of the importance of a classical education, the pupils were also to be given the opportunity to study scientific and commercial subjects. This commitment to combining classical and commercial education led to the plan of the Liverpool Royal Institution School becoming a role model for the new proprietary day schools founded in other large provincial cities.[50]

The leaders of the Royal Institution were also instrumental in a number of other important educational and cultural initiatives in Liverpool, notably the founding of a Mechanics' Institution in 1825. However, the attitude of the Town Council towards this working-class project was markedly different to that displayed towards the Royal Institution. The association of Liverpool's cultural reputation with commerce rather than manufacturing was now adroitly adopted by the opponents of the Mechanics' Institution, who insisted that 'Liverpool not being a manufacturing town, such an institution is not here requisite'.[51] Despite the presence among the founders of Alderman Thomas Case (Mayor in 1817), a request to the Corporation for a grant of £500 in 1825 was 'negatived by a large majority'.[52] The Mayor refused permission for the general meeting of June 1825 to be held in the Town Hall, 'though he was requested to do so by a requisition signed ... by a great number of parties', and, in the same year, the Earl of Derby declined to contribute.[53] Support from the town at large was also less than had been expected, many of the established elite proving far less willing to help the School of Arts than they had been to aid the Royal Institution. For the majority of Liverpool's wealthy, investment in cultural enterprise appeared to be firmly allied with self-interest. Altruism had little part to play – for these men, polite culture was a means of defining themselves as the elite of the town, a valuable accoutrement to their status as gentlemen.

By the mid-1840s, the heyday of the voluntary cultural societies was passing, as they fought a losing battle against the rising tide of public enterprise. Writing in 1851, J. W. Hudson declared that: 'Institutions like all great works, flourish or decay in proportion to their value and utility to the age in which they exist.'[54] This proved prophetic in the case of Liverpool. By the second half of the nineteenth century, its merchant elite were legitimated and secure and their concern lay more in reinforcing their individual status rather than in asserting their group identity through joint cultural enterprise.[55] With the realisation that the Roscoe ideal of the Liverpool businessman–scholar had not been, nor seemed likely to be, accomplished by the existing societies and institutions, many of Liverpool's leading citizens now turned their energies towards coordinating municipal cultural provision and the establishment of a university – designated by one Liverpool historian as the 'spiritual and material heir of the Royal Institution'.[56] Evidence, however, that Liverpool's commercial elite continued to celebrate the compatibility of 'high culture' and business values, can be seen in the building of the Walker Art Gallery (1877). Surrounding the gallery's porch are three statues – Raphael on one side, Michelangelo on the other, with Commerce on the top!

Modern Liverpool's distinctive cultural identity, is generally regarded as the creation of its working classes. However, it is interesting to note that in recent years, with Liverpool again seeking to improve its economic fortunes and redefine its image, it is celebrating the city's rich architectural heritage, promoting art festivals and seeking city-of-learning status. Liverpool is, perhaps, looking back to the cultural values and the value placed on culture of its founding merchant elite.

Notes

1 See for example J. Wolff and J. Seed (eds), *The Culture of Capital: Art, Power and the Nineteenth-Century Middle Class* (Manchester, Manchester University Press, 1988).

2 W. D. Rubinstein, *Capitalism, Culture and Decline in Britain, 1750–1990* (London, Routledge, 1993).

3 P. J. Cain and A. J. Hopkins, 'Gentlemanly capitalism and British expansion overseas: 1:

the old colonial system 1688–1850', *Economic History Review*, 39 (1986), 501–25.

4 R. J. Morris, *Class, Sect and Party. The Making of the British Middle Class: Leeds 1820–1850* (Manchester, Manchester University Press, 1990), p. 96.

5 James Wallace, *A General and Descriptive History of the Ancient and Present State of the Town in Liverpool* (Liverpool, Crane & Jones, 1797), p. 283.

6 J. W. Hudson, *The History of Adult Education* (London, Longmans, 1851), p. 96.

7 P. J. Corfield, *The Impact of English Towns* (Oxford, Oxford University Press, 1982), p. 10

8 Quoted in T. Fawcett, *The Rise of Provincial Art: Artists, Patrons and Institutions outside London, 1800–1865* (Oxford, Clarendon, 1974), p. 9.

9 Seymour Drescher, 'The slaving capital of the world: Liverpool and national opinion in the age of abolition', *Slavery and Abolition*, 9 (1988), 128–43.

10 J. Ramsey Muir, *A History of Liverpool* (London, Williams & Norgate, 1907), p. 193.

11 Drescher, 'The slaving capital of the world', 129.

12 David Samwell to Matthew Gregson, n.d. [c. 1788], *Gregson Correspondence*, Liverpool Record Office, 920 GRE/17/41.

13 Quoted in Emily A. Rathbone (ed.), *Records of the Rathbone Family* (Edinburgh, R. & R. Clark, 1913), p. 36.

14 Drescher, 'The slaving capital of the world', 128–43.

15 F. E. Hyde, *Liverpool and the Mersey: An Economic History of a Port 1700–1970* (Newton Abbott, David & Charles, 1971), p. 43.

16 J. R. Hale, *England and the Italian Renaissance* (London, Faber, 1954), p. 85

17 C. Northcote Parkinson, *The Rise of the Port of Liverpool* (Liverpool, Liverpool University Press, 1952), p. 3.

18 William Roscoe, *Life of Lorenzo de' Medici, called the Magnificent*, 7th edn (London, 1846), p. xiii.

19 William Roscoe to Lord Lansdowne, n.d. [c. 1795], Roscoe Papers, 2327.

20 Ronald Story, 'Class and culture in Boston: the Athenaeum, 1807–1860', *American Quarterly*, 27 (1975), 185.

21 Quoted in Henry Roscoe, *The Life of William Roscoe*, 2 vols (London, T. Cadell, 1833), 1, p. 169.

22 *Catalogue of the Athenaeum Library, Liverpool* (London, 1864), p. xiii.

23 In 1817, as a consequence of Roscoe's financial troubles, a number of his personal books were purchased by his friends and donated to the Athenaeum to form a 'Roscoe Collection'. Roscoe Papers, 454.

24 Quoted in Story, 'Class and culture in Boston', 186.

25 *Ibid.*, 184.

26 *Ibid.*, 187.

27 Local chroniclers invariably point to the connecting links with the short-lived Philosophical and Literary Society which existed in the town from 1779 to 1783. Of the first names enrolled in the 1812 Society, two members belonged to the earlier society, and six other other members were the son of members.

28 R. S. Watson, *The History of the Literary and Philosophical Society of Newcastle Upon Tyne (1793–1896)* (London, Walter Scott, 1897), p. 36.

29 Arnold Thackray, 'Natural knowledge in a cultural context: the Manchester model', *American Historical Review*, 79 (1974), 672–709. In 1922, John James Taylor, a member of the Manchester Literary and Philosophical Society, observed, 'Mechanics and chemistry are all the vogue in this district . . . literature is quite beaten off the field by science – even though we have a Literary and Philosophical Society.' Quoted in Revd H. McLachlan, *Essays and Addresses* (Manchester, Manchester University Press, 1950), p. 68.

30 *Laws and Regulations of the Literary and Philosophical Society of Liverpool (1812)*, recorded in *Liverpool Literary and Philosophical Society Minute Book*, 1, (13 April 1812); *Laws and Regulations of the Literary and Philosophical Society of Liverpool (1815)* (Liverpool, 1815).

31 *The Liverpool Literary and Philosophical Society Centenary Roll, 1812–1912*, complied by J. Hampden Jackson. Liverpool Record Office, 060 LIT 3/1/2.

32 Divisions between Liverpool's American merchants and West Indian merchants had been intensified in the years leading up to 1812, by the effects of the Orders in Council. America's Embargo Act had left the American merchants fearing for their livelihood,

while the West India merchants were delighted that America had cut off its own trade with Europe and the colonies. Many of the American merchants were Dissenters seeking to avoid the taint of slavery. Of 14 presidents of the American Chamber of Commerce between 1801 and 1821, 6 were Unitarian, 2 Quakers, 3 of unknown religion but prominent reformers. C. D. Watkinson, 'The Liberal Party on Merseyside in the nineteenth century', unpublished Ph.D. thesis, University of Liverpool, 1967, pp. 48–9.

33 C. P. Darcy, *The Encouragement of the Fine Arts in Lancashire 1760–1860* (Manchester, Chetham Society, 1976), pp. 99–100.

34 Quentin Hughes, *Seaport: Architecture and Townscape in Liverpool* (London, Lund Humphries, 1964), p. 116. Hughes claims that Liverpool also saw the death of the Gothic Revival, the town's Anglican cathedral being – 'a final blaze of Gothic, in scale unprecedented – a fitting consumation of a great period'.

35 Ramsay Muir, *A History of Liverpool*, p. 293.

36 This is confirmed by an analysis of the list of 202 subscribers in 1822. Out of the 170 subscribers whose occupation can be traced, 111 were engaged in business as merchants, brokers or bankers. Others included 6 physician/surgeons, 9 lawyers, 8 clergymen (4 Anglican, 4 Dissenting), and 12 who classified themselves as gentlemen. There are 4 lady proprietors.

37 *Address at a General Meeting of the Subscribers to the Liverpool Institution, held on the 18th April* (Liverpool, 1817), Sydney Jones Library, University of Liverpool, R. I. Arch.50.9.

38 William Roscoe, *On the Origin and Vicissitudes of Literature, Science and Art and Their Influence on the Present State of Society: a Discourse, delivered on the Opening of the Liverpool Royal Institution, 25 November 1817* (Liverpool, Harris, 1817).

39 *Resolutions, Reports and Byelaws of the Liverpool Royal Institutions, 14 March 1820*, Sydney Jones Library, University of Liverpool, G34.32 (5).

40 Edward Morris, 'The formation of the Gallery of Art in the Liverpool Royal Institution, 1816–1819', *Transactions of the Historic Society of Lancashire and Cheshire*, 142 (1992), 88.

41 Darcy, *The Encouragement of the Fine Arts*, p. 39.

42 *Resolutions, Reports . . .* , 27 February 1822.

43 *Book for inserting the Names and Places of Abode of Strangers, April 1822–1834*, R.I.Arch.19.

44 *Addresses delivered at the Meetings of the Liverpool Royal Institution on the 27th February, 1822 & 13th February, 1824, by B. A. Heywood, Esq. President* (Liverpool, 1824).

45 *Address delivered . . . on the 11th February 1825 by B. A. Heywood, Esq. President* (Liverpool, 1824).

46 *Resolutions, Reports . . .* , 14 March 1820, p. 14.

47 *Blackwood's Edinburgh Magazine*, 2 February 1818, 535–6.

48 T. Kelly, *Adult Education in Liverpool: A Narrative of Two Hundred Years* (Department of Extra-Mural Studies of the University of Liverpool, 1960), pp. 17–18.

49 *Royal Institution Minutes*, 29 March 1820.

50 H. Perkin, *The Origins of Modern English Society 1780–1880* (London, Routledge & Kegan Paul, 1969), pp. 296–7.

51 *The Kaleidoscope*, 5 (21 June 1825), 430.

52 *Liverpool Institute Schools' Records*, Directors' Minute Book, 4 August 1825. Liverpool Record Office. 373 1/1/1.

53 *The Kaleidoscope*, 5 (7 June 1825), 413. *Directors' Minute Book*, 7 September 1825.

54 Hudson, *The History of Adult Education*, p. 168.

55 B. G. Orchard criticised what he considered gifts inspired by desire for personal aggrandisement rather than by concern for the intellectual life of the town. He informed his readers that Sir William Brown's gift of the Brown Library, was motivated by the prospect of a baronetcy rather than any native generosity. He was similarly critical of Sir Andrew Barclay Walker, the brewer and distiller who gave Liverpool the Walker Art Gallery. Orchard, *Liverpool's Legion of Honour* (Birkenhead, privately printed, 1893), pp. 213, 689.

56 H. Ormerod, *The Liverpool Royal Institution: A Record and a Retrospect* (Liverpool, C. Tinling, 1953), p. 4.

4

'A CHRISTIAN AND CIVILISED LAND': THE BRITISH MIDDLE CLASS AND THE CIVILISING MISSION, 1820–42
Alison Twells

In Sheffield General Cemetery there stands a weathered and disintegrating memorial to George Bennet (1775–1841), local evangelical, philanthropist and missionary, who travelled as a representative of the London Missionary Society (LMS) to the South Pacific, New Zealand, Australia, South-East Asia, India, East Africa and Cape Town between 1821 and 1829. Broad-based and standing square, the memorial celebrates Bennet's missionary success. The north face carries his claim that he had 'made an honest comparison of multitudes of persons of nearly all climes, colours and characters' and was therefore able to testify to the superiority of Christian cultures: 'that having traced the world around,/And search'd from Britain to Japan,/I still have no religion found,/So just to God, so true to Man'. It is the carving on the south side of the monument, however, that is most striking. Here Bennet is depicted in a scene of missionary triumph, standing against a background of palm trees and cacti, his right arm resting on a globe, with a Bible in his hand and a broken idol at his feet.

This chapter focuses on George Bennet's visit to the South Pacific, the main destination of his missionary voyage, to explore the significance of the 'civilising mission' for the construction of middle-class identity and cultural authority in Britain in the early to mid-nineteenth century. It draws upon and contributes to the now well-established critique which suggests that 'British' history does not occupy a sphere which is separate and distinct from that of 'the empire', but that 'domestic' and 'colonial' histories need to be discussed as part of the same area of study.[1] This critique has been developed in a number of different contexts over recent years, most notably: in the debate within schools' history, sparked by the proposals in the late 1980s for a new National Curriculum, concerning the place of empire in Britain's social, cultural, economic and political formation;[2] in women's history, in response to the political critiques by black women of the failure of white feminisms to address issues of racism and difference stemming from the colonial legacy;[3] and in the influence of a more explicitly theoretical body of knowledge, developing in part from the discussions and debates surrounding the publication in 1978 of Edward Said's *Orientalism* which, focusing on the various cultural forms – philology, lexicography, history, political and economic theory and fiction – through which the West constructed the Orient as 'other', raised crucial questions concerning the relationship between power and knowledge.[4]

In focusing on the 'civilising mission' in the late eighteenth and early nineteenth centuries, this chapter is shaped by these developments. Its concern is not with missionary activity in terms of its impact 'out there' – its success or otherwise in the 'mission field', its relationship with other cultures or to other agencies of colonial power – but with the significance of the 'civilising mission' within the domestic cultural context. My particular interest is in the missionary project within the context of changing relationships of class and gender in Britain; and especially the relationship between the self-representation of many Britons as agents of civilisation and their identities as middle-class men and women at home.

Recent writing on class formation in Britain has tended to downplay the extent to which a 'middle-class' culture can be said to have existed in the late eighteenth and early nineteenth centuries.[5] My research, however, supports the view that the many intersecting and overlapping local and regional networks, within which the men and women of the 'middling sorts' navigated their lives, enabled the development in this period of a culture and identity which, while by no means homogenous, can be broadly termed 'middle class'.[6] The theory and practice of 'mission' provided a central site in this process. While many early overseas missionaries, like the scorned 'consecrated cobblers' of Serampore, were men of the artisanate, those who formed and led the missionary societies, who sat on committees, raised funds and wrote pamphlets, encouraged and selected men (and later women) for overseas work and attempted to reform the poor at home, were members of newly developing and diverse urban elites. Through their commitment to shared discourses of enlightenment, progress and civilisation, they contributed to the emergence of a new 'social' and global sphere of cultural intervention, and to a new articulation of the relationship between the 'savage' and the 'civilised', between 'Christian' Britain and the 'heathen' world, which placed the British middle class at the apex of civilisation.

This chapter explores these themes through a focus on the LMS mission to the South Pacific in the late eighteenth and early nineteenth centuries. The first part of the chapter places evangelical interest in the South Pacific in the context of the wider missionary impulse of the late eighteenth and early nineteenth centuries which, shaped by the tension within both evangelicalism and enlightenment thought, stressed a belief in a hierarchy of cultures alongside a commitment to the essential capacity for improvement of all of humankind. The second part focuses on the public representations in Sheffield of Bennet's voyage, which included: the promotion of his trip and publication of extracts of his letters in the pages of the *Sheffield Iris*; the inclusion of some of the 'spoils of gospel' – artefacts such as weapons, dress, utensils and idols sent home by Bennet – in the new ethnographic collection of the Literary and Philosophical Society Museum; the publication in 1831 of his *Voyages and Travels*, edited by James Montgomery, the Sheffield poet, journalist and philanthropist, and Bennet's close friend;[7] and culminating in the memorial, constructed in 1842 by a public subscription organised by the Sheffield Literary and Philosophical Society, of which Bennet was an honorary member.

I

Prior to the arrival in Tahiti of the first missionaries of the London Missionary Society in 1797, the South Pacific already occupied a special place in the public imagination in Britain. Knowledge of the islands had come from the publicity surrounding the voyages of James Cook and other navigational explorers and scientists of the 1760s and 1770s. The popular representation constructed from their accounts was that of the 'noble savage': of peoples characterised by a harmonious relationship to their environment, by a beautiful and dignified physical form, and a culture uncorrupted by the greed and commercialism and restrictive sexual morality of western civilisation.[8] The publication in 1773 of the journals of Cook, Banks and Forster had inspired a 'Polynesian vogue' in late eighteenth-century Britain as 'Tahitian' toys, jewellery, tattoos, verandas for country houses, 'polynesian' wallpaper and artificial South Sea lakes became fashionable among the well-to-do. The South Pacific was further celebrated in paintings of the scene of Cook's death at Kealakekua Bay, Hawaii, in Coleridge's *Rime of the Ancient Mariner* (1798), in a pantomime performed in 1785 at the Theatre Royal in Covent Garden entitled 'Omai, or a Trip around the World', and in sex shows organised by a London prostitute named Charlotte Hayes, based on voyeuristic descriptions of public sexual activity drawn from the journals of explorers and sailors.[9]

For evangelical Christians, however, the Pacific islands were far from paradise. For them, while the Fall had resulted in sin and degradation on a global scale, the people of the South Seas represented the most morally depraved of humankind. In his first sermon to the newly formed London Missionary Society in September 1795, Dr Thomas Haweis had contested the notion of the 'noble savage' through contrasting the natural beauty of the islands with the moral and spiritual degradation of the people. The 'new world' which 'hath lately opened up before our eyes', he wrote, contained lands

> which seem to realise the fabled Gardens of Hespirides, – where the fragrant groves which cover them from the sultry beams of the day, afford them food and clothing; whilst the sea offers continual plenty in its inexhaustible stores; and the day passes in ease and affluence, and the night in music and dancing. But amidst these enchanting scenes, savage nature still feasts on the flesh of its prisoners, appeases its Gods with human sacrifices – whole societies of men and women live promiscuously, and murder every infant born among them.[10]

This focus on the practices of idolatry, human sacrifice, cannibalism and infanticide, placed against the backdrop of an idyllic Tahitian landscape, became a convention of missionary writing in the pages of the *Evangelical Magazine* and in the increasing numbers of missionary memoirs published from the early nineteenth century. Perhaps most famously, William Ellis, author of *A Tour through Hawaii* (1827) and *Polynesian Researches* (1831), challenged the inaccuracies of the popular belief, generated by Cook's *Voyages*, that the Pacific islands

> were a sort of elysium, where the highly favoured inhabitants, free from the toil and care, the want and disappointment, which was the happiness of

civilised communities, dwelt in what they called a state of nature, and spent their lives in unrestrained gratification and enjoyment.

Missionaries who had lived among the people, learned their language and observed their customs, could in Ellis's view, form 'more just and accurate conclusions' about their state of civilisation.[11]

Missionary interest in the South Pacific had emerged in Britain in the context of the evangelical revival of the late eighteenth century. Beginning with the Great Methodist Revival which swept through the country in the 1780s and 1790s, these years had seen growing congregations, an expansion in church and chapel building and general enthusiasm for evangelical practice within both the Anglican Church and Old Dissent, most notably the Congregationalist and Baptist denominations. While fractured by denominational antagonism and fears of 'irregularity', evangelical culture was also characterised by a shared concern with the *social* functions of religious belief and practice. In Britain, in the context of the radical political activity which followed the French Revolution and the general upheaval caused by the dislocations of war and industrialisation, the men and women who formed the leadership of the new domestic missionary societies drew on both evangelicalism and new understandings of poverty and the poor shaped by political economy in their aim to inculcate self-discipline, morality, industry, and a belief in the divine necessity of inequality and social hierarchy among the lower classes. By the end of the decade, these concerns were resonant in a range of texts and social practices, from the Sunday-school movement, the early monitorial system of education and visiting societies such as the Society for Bettering the Condition of the Poor (1796) to the writings of Hannah More and Thomas Malthus.[12]

Many of the same men and women who flocked to the domestic missionary societies also gave their support to the new overseas missionary bodies – the Baptist, London and Church missionary societies, formed between 1792 and 1799, and which focused their activities on India, the South Pacific and West Africa respectively.[13] Moreover, the processes of cultural reform at home and overseas shared many themes and practices. Both were shaped not only by the theology of mission but by a secular model of cultural change which, originating in the 'histories of civilisation' developed by philosophers of the Scottish Enlightenment, saw all cultures progressing through various stages of social and economic development, from savagery, through barbarism to civilised society. Writers such as John Millar, Adam Ferguson and William Robertson had drawn upon travellers' accounts, including the journals of Cook, Banks and Forster in the Pacific, to identify various factors in this process, including: a transition in the mode of production from hunting and gathering, to settled agriculture and finally to commerce; changes in the law, in social and political institutions, and in custom, culture and manners; and a greater degree of respect for women, expressed in terms of their location in the 'domestic sphere'.[14] In the words of William Robertson, author of the influential *History of America* (1777):

> In every part of the Earth, the progress of man hath been nearly the same; and we can trace him in his career from the rude simplicity of savage life, until he attains industry, the arts, and the elegance of polished society.[15]

In seeking to explain cultural difference – and in particular Scottish development in the eighteenth century – these writers had developed a framework in
which the 'savage' and the 'civilised' were placed on the same developmental
continuum. By the 1790s this body of theory had become common currency,
providing the basis of more specialised disciplines, including ethnography and
the incipient anthropology which focused on cultures overseas, and investigations into the domestic poor inspired by political economy at home.

The significance of stadial theory lay both in its insistence on the capacity for improvement of all peoples throughout the world and its location of the
culture of the British middle class, with its commitment to commerce and public
life and to 'separate spheres' and an orderly family and home life, at the apex of
civilisation. This had a particular resonance for evangelical Christians.[16] For
them, the language of the 'civilised' and the 'savage' easily mapped onto that of
the 'Christian' and the 'heathen'. The inculcation of Christianity was, they
believed, a prerequisite for the civilising process; Christian religious belief and
practice necessarily led to the abandonment of cultures of barbarism and
savagery. The mission became, in Mary Louise Pratt's words, a 'contact zone',
a site for cultural intervention and reform of other peoples on a global scale,
and from which middle-class self-representation as the agents of civilisation was
produced.[17]

In towns throughout Britain, interest in overseas and domestic missions
developed concurrently. In Sheffield, George Bennet's home town, the first
two decades of the nineteenth century saw the emergence of a dense network
of societies which combined a focus on religious conversion with a concern
with moral and domestic reform. Including the Society for Bettering the
Condition of the Poor (1804), the Aged Female Society and Bible Society
(both 1810), the Sheffield Sunday School Union (1812), the Lancasterian and
National schools (1809–15) and the Methodist, London and Church missionary societies (1813–16), these societies drew their overlapping memberships
from Sheffield's growing manufacturing and professional classes.[18] A significant minority of these were either already members of, or were becoming
affiliated to, Sheffield's Unitarian community, while a great many more were
evangelical, members of either the Methodist or Congregational denominations, or supporters of the evangelical interest within the established Church.
In their ability to accommodate both denominational loyalty and a wider
commitment to 'progress' and 'improvement', such societies were of great
significance in the construction of a new sphere of 'social' activity, generating
shared values which centred on an understanding of their members as agents
of progress and civilisation.[19]

Both men and women participated in this new social world. While
excluded from committees and seats of power, middle-class women assumed the
role of lady visitors to the homes of the poor, and in deploying publicly their
'private' and 'domestic' skills, played a crucial role in the construction of a class
culture in which the domestic was seen as a crucial site of social reform.[20] For
middle-class men, their positions of authority on the committees of the new
societies made important connections with other sites of power and authority
within the new civic order – in Sheffield as Overseers of the Poor, Town Trustees

and members of the Highway Board, gas and water companies and committees of the General Infirmary and Dispensary, all of which were important to the administration of the town's affairs prior to incorporation.[21]

George Bennet was an important figure in this network. A member of Queen Street Congregational Chapel since his conversion to evangelicalism at the turn of the nineteenth century, Bennet had run the Sunday school in his home, was involved with the Society for Bettering the Condition of the Poor from 1804 and, along with an interdenominational group of friends and acquaintances,[22] had been a founder and committee member of the Aged Female Society, Bible Society, Sunday School Union and Boys' Lancasterian School. He was also a prominent member of both Rotherham College, an institution for the training of young men for the Independent ministry, and the (Congregationalist) West Riding Auxiliary Missionary Society. Bennet was seen by the directors of the LMS, therefore, as an ideal candidate for their deputation of the early 1820s.

The purpose of Bennet's and Tyerman's visit to the South Pacific was supervisory. LMS directors were anxious to resolve the conflicts that had broken out both between missionaries and between the missionaries and the parent body, as the former expressed their anger at the meagre salary and supplies and what some understood as the general patronising attitude of the directors.[23] During the early nineteenth century, due to the extension of LMS mission stations from Tahiti to the islands of Eimeo, Huahine and Raiatea (the island group known by the British as the Society Islands) and general Christian progress, symbolically represented by the conversion of King Pomare in 1814, the area had become a central focus of the missionary gaze. Celebrated in the pages of the *Evangelical Magazine*, it had inspired LMS expansion to India, Ceylon, Africa, the West Indies and New Brunswick, as well as the formation of supportive auxiliary missionary societies in towns throughout Britain. Indeed, despite conflicts and disappointments, such intense interest continued into the Victorian period, as the mission spawned two of the most popular early Victorian missionary heroes, William Ellis and John Williams, both of whom had arrived with a new group of men in 1817.

Between September 1821, when Bennet and Tyerman arrived in Tahiti, and May 1824, when they set sail for New Zealand, the two men spent their time evaluating the successes of the established mission stations and assessing the possibility for extension to the smaller islands. They made their acquaintance with kings, queens and chiefs, spending many hours discussing with them the nature of Christian progress and improvement. They visited *maraes* (the sites of idolatrous worship and human sacrifice), conversed with women about the practice of infanticide, quizzed the newly converted as to the specifics of the Scriptures and attended Christian baptisms, weddings and funerals, and sermons in newly built chapels. In regular letters and reports to the directors of the LMS, they detailed the growth in Christian religious practice and its concomitant cultural change. They also corresponded with their friends and acquaintances at home, contributing to the production of a new knowledge about the world and Britain's place at the helm of the 'civilising mission'.

II

George Bennet's missionary voyage to the South Pacific had from the outset generated considerable interest within evangelical circles in Sheffield. In his capacity as newspaper editor, James Montgomery had publicised his friend's impending trip in the *Sheffield Iris*, and solicited donations – of Sheffield hardware (edge tools, cutlery, Britannia metal and saws), scissors, razors, fish-hooks, earthenware, cooking utensils, paper for tracts and children's books, and looking-glasses, linen and bed furniture – which, the public were informed, were in particular demand in the South Seas and would serve as appropriate gifts for Bennet to bestow on potential converts and friends.[24] Joseph and Elizabeth Read, Bennet's long-standing friends, held a farewell party for him at their home at Wincobank Hall, north of Sheffield, presenting him with a portfolio of scarlet leather for his use on his travels, and a selection of missionary maps, drawn by their fifteen-year-old daughter, Catharine.[25] Whilst in the South Pacific, Bennet continued to receive gifts for Pomare and his wife from Elizabeth Read who, with the rest of her family, wrote him regular letters. Even little Edmund, who was just six years old at the time of Bennet's departure, picked flowers and feathers from the garden at Wincobank – which the missionary passed on to a young Tahitian boy at the mission school named John Williams, who was encouraged to send Edmund shells in return.[26]

Bennet's letters home to his friends served to affirm their sense of themselves as participants in a global missionary enterprise. Usually written to the Reads, Montgomery, Rowland Hodgson or Bennet's nephew Edward MCoy, his letters home were infrequent, reliant on a passing whaler or returning missionary for their passage. In accordance with the author's wishes they were copied and circulated within a larger missionary circle, thus ensuring that his news reached friends and acquaintances in other parts of the country. Bennet's letters discussed his domestic arrangements and the state of his health, and provided lengthy descriptions of the landscape and scenery, of the 'delightful fatigues of climbing mountains, tracking streams and viewing the Ruins of Idolatrous temples', and of his adventures at sea.[27] He delighted in sending snippets of enjoyable experiences concerning the progress of Christianity. To Elizabeth Read, for example, he wrote of the joys of taking his Scripture class, telling her that she too, as a Sunday-school teacher, would enjoy 'sitting cross-legged upon a little native stool in the native houses and conversing with them and questioning them from their Catechism or from the sacred Scriptures'.[28] Writing to Catharine Read he confessed his decision to present the scarlet portfolio as a gift to the newly crowned four-year-old king, Pomare III, with the intention that it be used to carry the Bible and a copy of the new laws of the land at all future processions,[29] while to Edmund he wrote of the Christian coronation of the child-king, comparing him to Edward VI, with his pretty crown with crimson silk and satin, and gold lace coronet decorated with pearls and a cross.[30]

Knowing that such information was in safe hands, Bennet was able to write relaxed and amused accounts of what he perceived to be 'cultural confusion' of the Pacific people as they received commodities from other, 'advanced', cultures. Discussing the superior, more respectable dress of Tahitian women in comparison with the scantily clad inhabitants of the Sandwich Islands, Bennet told Elizabeth Read of the attitude to English clothing of some of the men: 'Some dress [sic] very oddly at first we could not help smiling', he wrote, proceeding to tell a tale of a chief who had attended a feast held for the deputees wearing a mat around his loins, an English Black-coat buttoned up with the collar halfway up his back, a frilled shirt open on top and reaching down to his thighs, and nothing on his legs and feet. On another occasion, enquiring of a gown he had given to a woman, he was informed that her husband was wearing it – the arms and body tied round his waist, skirt hanging down his legs.[31] Such cultural 'hybridity', the missionary assumed, represented the first steps towards 'civilisation' for 'these recent heathens' and affirmed the rightful role of British men and women as leaders in the global mission.

Extracts from Bennet's letters also found their way, under Montgomery's guidance, into the pages of the *Sheffield Iris*. Here they served a different function, assisting in Montgomery's concern to educate the general public as to the value of overseas missions. Montgomery had long reported missionary miscellany, promoting the belief in the general capacity for improvement of 'other' peoples. Thus, whether applauding the work of the Serampore Baptists in India and giving support to missionary petitions against their exclusion from the East India Company's protection in 1813; celebrating the conversion of Pomare in 1814 and the role of Moravian missionaries in the transformation of Native Americans from 'barbarism' to Christianity; or reporting the guest appearance of returned missionaries – such as the CMS secretary Edward Bickersteth, present at both the CMS and BMS anniversaries in Sheffield on his return from Sierra Leone in 1818 – Montgomery adopted a framework which was both historical and progressive, assuming a gradual movement of 'primitive' peoples towards 'civilisation'.[32] In July 1824, he gave over two columns of the *Iris* to mourn the deaths of the Queen and King of the Sandwich Islands during a visit to London. Reflecting his involvement with the newly formed Anti-slavery Society, Montgomery represented them as model Christian converts: 'Let those who talk of Blacks not being fit to be intrusted with freedom', he wrote, 'study the character and conduct of the King of the Sandwich Islands.'[33]

In November 1824, the *Iris* printed extracts from two letters recently received from Bennet, written from Eimeo and Huahine in January and May of that year, and which celebrated the general missionary success, evident in the increasing numbers of converts and in the Christian coronation of the young King Pomare.[34] In May of the following year, Montgomery printed a poem written by Bennet and sent to Elizabeth Read, expressing his sorrow on leaving Tahiti and his joy at 'what God has done' for the islanders who were now under the 'universal sway' of the gospel:

> Then, dear delightful scenes, farewell!
> Tahiti's shores adieu!
> Through life 'twere happiness to tell
> What God has done for you.
>
> Once *hell* and *sin* were here combin'd
> And Satan reign'd alone

But Jesu's Gospel, now we find,
Hath hurl'd him from his throne.[35]

Placed alongside this was Bennet's sensational account of his 'perils' among the 'cannibals' of New Zealand, a story of near-death at the hands of the Maori, who were reputed to have murdered and eaten the captain and a crew of an earlier vessel unlucky to have sailed into the same harbour. Descriptions of 'savages' with 'faces, already hideous from their *tatauings*, [and] rendered even more so by their anger', brandishing axes and spears and 'raising warsongs, accompanied by the most horrid gesticulations', contrasted with the gentle, subdued, Christian island of Tahiti to startling effect.[36]

Bennet's letters also became a resource for Montgomery's speeches at the anniversaries of the Sheffield Sunday School Union. In 1826 he drew on Bennet's account of the prevalence of infanticide in the Pacific to inform a few thousand local children of the 'oppression' of children in heathen cultures.[37] Such material formed part of a regular evangelical diet, undoubtedly aiming to instil a sense of gratitude at being born into a civilised, Christian land. Indeed, this points to the uses in the domestic missionary context of a language of heathenism, both to legitimate the attempt to reform the lower orders and affirm Britain's position at a higher level on the scale of civilisation.

Montgomery's desire both to affirm the missionary project and to educate the unconverted were combined in his decision to edit Bennet and Tyerman's *Voyages and Travels*, first published in 1831. These two volumes, which condensed extracts from journals and letters written by Bennet and Tyerman during their travels and narratives produced by Bennet on his return to Britain, engaged with popular non- and anti-missionary discourses on race, civilisation and cultural progress which were in circulation in the 1820s and 1830s. Writing in a now well-established missionary tradition, Montgomery claimed in his introduction to reveal their 'real condition': the despotism, infanticide, murder and cannibalism which amounted, in his view, not to noble savagery but to '*a state of nature fallen FROM innocence*'.[38] At the same time, however, he was anxious to refute the increasingly popular argument that peoples of the Pacific and 'primitive' peoples generally were biologically different, inferior to white people and essentially unreceptive to methods designed for their improvement.[39] Focusing on the progress of the civilising mission on the islands, Bennet, Tyerman and Montgomery present evidence that this 'surprisingly teachable' people, who were quick to express both their piety and their sorrow at their earlier sins, demonstrated a capacity for civilisation.

The central narrative of *Voyages and Travels* emphasises the 'moral miracle' of Tahiti and the islands of the South Pacific and the central role of the missionary in the process of civilisation. Bennet's writing details religious progress: the swelling congregations at newly constructed chapels and schools; the increasing numbers of people opting for Christian baptisms, marriages and burials; the formation of missionary prayer meetings and charitable societies; the aptitude of the people in answering questions on points of the Scriptures and their willingness to discuss the positive changes in their lives brought by their conversions to Christianity. Combining an evangelical celebration of social change with the common focus of ethnographic and travel writing on the declining 'savage' cultural practices of the islanders, *Voyages and Travels* documents women's expressions of regret at their past practice of infanticide, seen to signify the positive impact of Christianity in the promotion of the ideals of a civilised society. The decline of heathen religious practices was also discussed in Bennet's and Tyerman's descriptions of their visits to *maraes*, sites of idol worship believed to have been abandoned after the abolition of idolatry by Pomare II in 1816, where they participated in ceremonies at which idols were broken and burned. Indeed, the volume abounds with accounts of the two men pushing huge and grotesque structures over cliff tops and into the sea, in scenes symbolising Christian triumph.[40]

A central focus of *Voyages and Travels* concerns the missionaries' perceptions of the domestic reform – the adoption of new patterns of marriage and monogamy and the reconstruction of gender roles – which was so crucial to advancement from savagery and barbarism. Men were apparently becoming more sober, frugal and hard-working, willing to learn 'useful arts' such as carpentry, with which they could make sofas, beds and other comfortable furniture for their homes, while their wives were being taught needlework and domestic management and were adopting western styles of dress. Families moved to newly constructed settled villages of plastered and windowed dwellings with separate living and sleeping accommodation. They were encouraged to sleep at night rather than during the day, and to eat in moderation and at regular intervals.[41] Women's dress, and comfortable houses with western commodities, were central to a new sense of progress. In the words of Mahamene, native of Raiatea: 'Look at the chandeliers over our heads; look at our wives; how becomingly they appear in their gowns and bonnets.'[42]

Such domestic order was seen to be having a positive impact on society generally. At Huahine, a previously itinerant people had abandoned their former homes to their pigs and since their occupation of 'humble, but neat dwellings' near to the bay had become changed in their characters and manners:

> While these village erections are thus coming forward, a new form of society is growing up with them ... The gospel may be said to have first taught them the calm, enduring, and endearing sweets of home, which their vagabond forefathers, and many of themselves, hardly knew to exist, till the religion of Him who had nowhere to lay his head, taught them how good and how pleasant a thing it is for brethren to dwell together in unity, instead of roving like fishes, or littering like swine.[43]

Voyages and Travels documents the decline of 'savage' forms of entertainment, such as 'licentious' dancing, cock-fighting and other cruel sports. Feast times, previously characterised by 'surfeiting, drunkenness, debauchery, quarrelling and murder', had become pleasant occasions, partly due to the civilising presence of women who were newly participant at such events.[44] A public festival at Raiatea in December 1823 was quite a spectacle, with 241 sofas and over a hundred tables, an awning of cloth, much food, and people dressed in their best clothes, including women wearing bonnets. Dinner was followed by addresses, during which aspects of the new life, the 'feasting, their improved dress, their purer enjoyments, their more courteous behaviour, the cleanliness of their persons, and the delicacy of their language in conversation', were compared with 'their former gluttony, nakedness, riot, brutality, filthy customs and obscene talk'.[45]

Such representations of cultural change inevitably reveal more about missionary concerns than the beliefs of the people under study. As has been argued by anthropologists, the agency of the people on the receiving end of the missionary enterprise meant that the missionary relationship was by no means unproblematic; while successful in infusing cultures with new signs and commodities, missionaries had little control over the interpretation of their message and the ways in which it was shaped by the indigenous cultural experience.[46] Indeed, in his private correspondence with the LMS board, George Bennet was more willing to acknowledge the anxieties of conversion, such as the persistence of idolatry and sexual misconduct, and of King Pomare's continued taste for alcohol.[47] While later nineteenth-century accounts, written in the light of shifting understandings of racial difference, emphasised the disappointments of the mission,[48] in the climate of the 1820s the keenness to establish missionary authority and to contest arguments asserting the futility of Christian interventions in 'primitive' cultures ensured that such anxieties were not placed on public display.

Voyages and Travels drew upon a hierarchical, familial model to represent the relationship between the missionary and the missionised. Bennet and Tyerman were insistent that all peoples, whatever their degree of savagery, were part of the same human family. 'Primitive' peoples, however, were represented as younger members of that family, as children awaiting instruction by their parents and elder siblings. The missionaries articulated different degrees of infantilisation among the cultures they experienced. The Tahitians were, they believed, a 'surprisingly teachable people'. Indeed, in a statement which raises important questions concerning the categories of race and class in this period, the missionaries likened them to the poor at home: 'As to original capacity', they wrote, 'we cannot doubt that the reclaimed Savages . . . need not to be ashamed to measure their standard with that of the bulk of mankind in civilised countries.'[49]

In contrast, however, Bennet and Tyerman were appalled by the Hawaiians, who they believed practised infanticide and other abominations, advertised dram shops, were scantily dressed, slept for much of the day, played cards and scrapped over their food – a situation explained in terms of their lesser contact with Christianity. They were especially disgusted by the Hawaiian royal family who, far from being dignified rulers, they saw as more idle, irreverent and uncouth than even ordinary Christian Tahitians. *Voyages and Travels* contains rich descriptions of this particular cultural encounter. On their first meeting the two men were shocked to discover the queens, two of whom were over 6 feet tall, covered in flowers and ferns, with two or three of their front teeth, in Bennet and Tyerman's words, 'barbarously dismantled'. The women showed no shame, eating their food without using a knife, fork or spoon, and even feeding their male attendants from ladles; on one occasion they were caught enjoying being pushed around in a wheelbarrow by 'two stout men'. The King and his chiefs were similarly idle, spending their days 'loitering and looking about with vacant eyes, or humming a low, dull, monotonous air without melody, as if they know not what to do with themselves'. Such irreverence extended to their behaviour at chapel: at one service the king 'had lain full length on a bench, resting his head on one attendant whilst being fanned by another', while the ladies 'sat and lolled in a group . . . from time to time handing a pipe about themselves'. On the occasion of one of William Ellis's sermons, the chiefs had again 'flung themselves upon their backs, on the floor, lolling or dozing with utter indifference'; at the end of the service, the king had marched out, 'swinging his stick about with an air of barbarian dignity'.[50]

It seemed to the missionaries that the further they travelled, the more savage and infantile their hosts became. At their next port of call – a Methodist mission station at Whaarongoa Bay, New Zealand – they endured the most harrowing experience of their journey as they found themselves in a confrontational situation with a group of Maori and believed they were to be killed and eaten at a cannibal feast. The conflict had begun when, amidst a peaceable discussion, the cook of their ship had discovered that clothing and kitchen equipment had been stolen, and had confronted the leaders of the group. The description in *Voyages and Travels* evokes the horror of the situation:

> Tremendous were the howlings and screechings of the barbarians, while they stamped and brandished their weapons, consisting principally of clubs and spears . . . [A Chief] brought his huge tatooed [sic] visage near to Mr Bennet's, screaming, in tones the most odious and horrifying, 'tangata New Zealandi, tangata Kakino? (man of New Zealand a bad man?). Happily Mr Bennet understood the question.[51]

Yet while the Maori were represented as 'savage and filthy', their appearance, manners and violence evidence that they occupied a considerably lower level of civilisation than did the South Sea Islanders, they became 'magnificent barbarians' as Bennet and Tyerman reached Sydney and encountered the 'abject natives' of New Holland.[52] Australia's blacks were, in the missionaries' estimation, dirty, idle, slovenly, practitioners of infanticide and superstition, and given to drink, violence and cruelty to their wives; 'the lowest class of human beings', they were less civilised than even the 'Hottentot'.[53]

Such a reference to the South African Khoi evokes a sense both of the degradation of native Australians and of their capacity for improvement, for while the humanity of the 'Hottentot' had been questioned by white Europeans they were, the missionaries believed, now in the process of conversion to Christianity:

> The Hottentot and the Negro have proved themselves men, not only by exemplifying all the vices of our common nature, but by becoming partakers of all its virtues; and, that the day of visitation will come to the black outcasts of New Holland also, we dare not doubt.[54]

Bennet and Tyerman were appalled at the attitudes of the white settler population who, refusing to believe in the humanity of blacks, supported their murder.[55] Indeed, the missionary model of cultural difference received further confirmation in Australia, where the presence of the 'worst class of white men' – those English and Irish convicts, described by Bennet and Tyerman as 'repulsive' and 'miserable', with the 'looks of fallen beings' – who added to the degradation of native Australians. 'Those are the most degraded who are brought into contact with their civilised invaders!', Bennet and Tyerman wrote to Governor Brisbane in 1824.[56] It was Christianity which was to be the catalyst of improvement, and hope was present in the children attending the Paramatta Sunday school, who wept for their parents' sins.[57]

Voyages and Travels is an important intervention in the debate concerning cultural difference, and one firmly located in a new genre of missionary writing. In it, James Montgomery marshalled the evidence from the pens of Bennet and Tyerman to present an argument for the cultural basis of human difference and the role of the missionary and Christian instruction in propelling people closer to civilisation. While asserting the capacity for improvement of all peoples, however, Bennet and Tyerman emphasised hierarchy, both in terms of the differing degrees of savagery and, of course, in the location of white middle-class Europeans at the top of the scale of civilisation. It was they who had the ability to teach and to nurture, the supervisory authority necessary to enable others to reach adulthood.

Such self-representation is evident in the uses in Sheffield of a second body of material sent home by George Bennet. As many missionaries and travellers, Bennet collected ethnographic, geological and natural-history specimens, including artefacts such as cloth, shells, fishing hooks, spears and vessels. Although they were acquired as gifts or bartered for knives, forks, scissors and other imported goods, these artefacts were for the missionaries much more than items of exchange. Writing to ask his friends Montgomery and Hodgson to select pieces for themselves and their mutual friends as gifts and tokens of remembrance, Bennet emphasised that his intention was for the cases to be bestowed not only for friendship and 'the good cause', but 'for the interests of Science'.[58] His expectation was that the cases to arrive in Sheffield in 1824 would be deposited at the museum of the Rotherham Academy, the nearby Congregationalist college. During 1823, however, the interests of science in Sheffield had become best represented by another institution: the newly formed Literary and Philosophical Society. James Montgomery, elected president of the Society in 1824, decided to commit some of Bennet's material to the collections of its newly opened museum.[59]

Sharing the enlightenment language of progress, middle-class evangelical men formed a central constituent of the new wave of scientific societies to sweep the nation in the early 1820s, joining those manufacturers, merchants and medical men, many of them Unitarian, whose commitments to science and 'useful knowledge' stretched back into the late eighteenth century. The Sheffield Literary and Philosophical Society, as stated by Montgomery in his opening address, claimed to promote 'the diffusion of liberal knowledge amongst all classes', enabling 'every man of the least taste or refinement, or elevation of mind' to become acquainted with 'the progress of society'.[60] The Society's membership, however, was solidly middle class; comprising surgeons, school masters, solicitors, journalists and a handful of manufacturers, it reflected less the participation of 'progressive' men of all classes than, as has been argued by Ian Inkster and Roger Cooter, a site for the construction of a shared culture within the urban elite.[61]

Alongside the Experimental Science and Natural History collections, Bennet's 'spoils of gospel' formed the beginnings of the Ethnographic collection in the museum. In 1824, his first 'two boxes of Curiosities from Otaheite, consisting of War Instruments, Dresses, Musical Instruments', were received by the Society. A further donation of geological specimens, collections of shells, birds and ethnographic material – including cloth, jewellery, domestic utensils, weapons of war and idols – was made to the museum in 1831, after his return to Britain.[62] At around the same time the museum acquired other natural-history and ethnographic donations, including a poem 'written in the ancient language of Ceylon on the leaf of the Talipot tree', two casts of the heads of New Zealand chiefs, a lioness, two leopards and a tiger, mother of pearl from Botany Bay and the skeleton head of a hippopotamus from South America.[63] Writing in 1885, local historian J. D. Leader remembered visiting as a child the 'sombre apartment beneath the Music Hall' and seeing a stuffed fawn and tiger, a long case of minerals and fossils and the head of a New Zealander, with long black hair, behind the president's chair.[64]

While in the 1820s and 1830s such displays were designed for a limited audience, the museum not yet a public institution, the emphasis on the historical development from primitive to civilised society anticipated the taxonomic organisation of later museums. As described in the *Annual Report* of 1841, Bennet's donations were

> memorials of a state of society gone by in the South Sea Islands, where society had previously not changed a feature of its aspects for ages beyond the memory of man, having been apparently incapable either of improvement or degradation.[65]

As Ludmilla Jordanova has argued, the very practice of display – the taxonomies involved, the process of comparing, contrasting and labelling specimens – is central to the construction of the categories through which narratives of human progress are made. It also serves as a reminder of the means of acquisition, in this case eliciting admiration for missionary enterprises and the progressive civilised culture which had produced them.[66] In the words of the 1842 *Report*, the value of Bennet's 'spoils' lay not in any intrinsic worth of their own but in 'the associations awakened by their presence, in a Christian and civilised land'.[67]

George Bennet's writing and the 'spoils of gospel' sent home to Sheffield from the South Pacific in the 1820s and 1830s contributed to the construction of a new relationship between Britain and the 'heathen' world in the first half of the nineteenth century. Shaped by evangelical and enlightenment notions of human 'likeness', of all peoples as members of one family, this relationship was also based upon an assertion of cultural inequality and difference, expressed in terms of a model of social change whereby all peoples were positioned on a developmental continuum from savagery to civilisation. This relationship had a particular significance for the British middle class, and especially its male members who, as symbolised by Bennet's civic memorial of 1842, received public acclaim for their participation in the process of global improvement. George Bennet's obituary, published in the Sheffield Literary and Philosophical Society *Annual Report* of 1842, ends with an adaptation of a quotation from the Bible: '"Let there be light", and even upon them shall "be light".'[68] It is this representation of 'them', in the process of being civilised by Christian belief and practice, which enabled the articulation of the 'us' of the already enlightened, already civilised British middle class.

NOTES

1 For an overview of this argument, see Antoinette Burton, 'Rules of thumb: British history and 'imperial culture' in nineteenth- and twentieth-century Britain', *Women's History Review*, 3:4 (1994), 483–500.

2 For reflections on this debate, see Shula Marks, 'History, the nation and empire: sniping from the periphery', *History Workshop Journal*, 29 (Spring 1990), 111–19; Alison Twells, *The Empire in South Yorkshire* (Sheffield Development Education Centre, 1992); Julia Bush, 'Moving on – and looking back: teaching colonial history', *History Workshop Journal*, 36 (Autumn 1993), 183–94.

3 See bell hooks, *Ain't I a Woman? Black Women and Feminism* (London, Pluto Press, 1982); Hazel V. Carby, 'White women listen! Black feminism and the boundaries of sisterhood', in Centre for Contemporary Cultural Studies (eds), *The Empire Strikes Back: Race and Racism in 70s Britain* (London, Hutchinson, 1982), pp. 212–35; Valerie Amos and Pratibha Parmar, 'Challenging imperial feminism', *Feminist Review*, 17 (Autumn 1984), 3–19; Clare Midgley, *Women against Slavery: the British Campaigns, 1780–1870* (London, Routledge, 1992); Vron Ware, *Beyond the Pale: White Women, Racism and History* (London, Verso, 1992); Catherine Hall, *White, Male and Middle Class: Explorations in Feminism and History* (Oxford, Polity Press, 1992); Antoinette Burton, *Burdens of History: British Feminists, Indian Women and Imperial Culture, 1865–1915* (Chapel Hill, University of North Carolina Press, 1994).

4 Edward Said, *Orientalism* (London, Penguin, 1978) and *Culture and Imperialism* (New York, Vintage, 1993). For various contributions sparked by this and subsequent scholarship, see Mary Louise Pratt, *Imperial Eyes: Travel Writing and Transculturation* (London, Routledge, 1992); Billie Melman, *Women's Orients: English Women and the Middle East, 1718–1918* (London, Macmillan, 1992); Nicholas Thomas, *Colonialism's Culture: Anthropology, Travel and Government* (Oxford, Polity Press, 1994). For a useful overview of the 'orientalism debate', see John M. MacKenzie, *Orientalism: Theory and the Arts* (Manchester, Manchester University Press, 1995).

5 See Dror Wahrman, *Imagining the Middle Class: The Political Representation of Class in Britain, c. 1780–1840* (Cambridge, Cambridge University Press, 1995).

6 Following John Smail, it is my argument that developments at the local level in the late eighteenth century, which included the emergence of the missionary society, provided important points for convergence for middle-class men and women, enabling the construction of regional and national networks and a shared and coherent culture. See John Smail, *The Origins of Middle-Class Culture: Halifax, Yorkshire 1660–1780* (London, Cornell University Press, 1994), pp. 3–18 and 191–236. For a sympathetic argument for the study of the 'local' in terms of colonial discourse, see Thomas, *Colonialism's Culture*.

7 James Montgomery (ed.), *Voyages and Travels by the Reverend Daniel Tyerman and George Bennet, Esquire, deputed from the London Missionary Society to visit Their Various Stations in the South Seas, China, India, etc, between the years 1821 and 1829*, 2 vols (London, Frederick Westley and A. H. Davies, 1831).

8 The popular representation at home was often quite different from the detail of 'ignoble savagery' contained in their journals. See Nicholas Thomas, 'Liberty and licence: the Forsters' account of New Zealand sociality', in Chloe Chard and Helen Langdon (eds),

Transports: Travel, Pleasure and Imaginative Geography, 1600–1830 (New Haven, Conn., Yale University Press, 1996).

9　See Bernard Smith, *European Vision and the South Pacific, 1768–1850* (London, Oxford University Press, 1960); Alan Morehead, *The Fatal Impact: An Account of the Invasion of the South Pacific, 1767–1840* (London, Hamish Hamilton, 1966); Gavan Daws, *A Dream of Islands: Voyages of Self-Discovery in the South Seas* (Honolulu, Hawaii Mutual Publishing Company, 1980); Nigel Rigby, 'A sea of islands: tropes of travel and adventure in the Pacific' (unpublished Ph.D. thesis, University of Kent, 1995).

10　Quoted in Smith, *European Vision*, p. 107.

11　William Ellis, *Narrative of a Tour through Hawaii, or Owhyee* (London, H. Fisher, Son and P. Jackson, 1827), pp. 2–4.

12　See Robert Hole, *Pulpits, Politics and Public Order in England, 1760–1832* (Cambridge, Cambridge University Press, 1989); Eileen Janes Yeo, *The Contest for Social Science: Relations and Representations of Gender and Class,* (London, Rivers Oram Press, 1996), pp. 3–31.

13　See Richard Lovett, *A History of the London Missionary Society, 1795–1895,* vol. 1 (London, Henry Froude, 1899); C. S. Stock, *The History of the Church Missionary Society: Its Environment, Its Men and Its Work,* vol. 1 (London, Church Missionary Society, 1899). The Wesleyan Methodist Missionary Society, although not formally established until 1813, originated in Thomas Coke's visits to the West Indies in 1786–87. See N. Allen Birtwhistle, 'Methodist missions', in Rupert Davies, A. Raymond George and Gordon Rupp (eds), *A History of the Methodist Church in Great Britain,* vol. 3 (London, Epworth Press, 1983), pp. 1–19.

14　See P. J. Marshall and Glyndwr Williams, *The Great Map of Mankind: British Perceptions of the World in the Age of Enlightenment* (London, J. M. Dent, 1982); Ronald L. Meeks, *Social Science and the Ignoble Savage* (Cambridge, Cambridge University Press, 1976); Jane Rendall (ed.), *William Alexander's History of Women from the Earliest Antiquity to the Present Time* [1777] (Bristol, Thoemmes Press, 1994), Introduction.

15　William Robertson, *History of America,* quoted in David Spadafora, *The Idea of Progress in Eighteenth Century Britain* (London, Yale University Press, 1990), p. 273.

16　See Leonore Davidoff and Catherine Hall, *Family Fortunes: Men and Women of the English Middle Class, 1780–1850* (London, Hutchinson, 1987).

17　Pratt, *Imperial Eyes,* pp. 6–7. Many of the missionaries sent to overseas fields, however, were drawn from the lower classes, and often had a complex relationship to this culture. For both its promoters and its subjects, guided by their middle-class patrons, their own moral worthiness was to be confirmed through their missionary practices. For the conflictual relationship between missionaries in the South Pacific and the LMS directors in London, see Neil Gunson, *Messengers of Grace: Evangelical Missionaries in the South Seas, 1797–1860* (Oxford, Oxford University Press, 1978).

18　Unlike the development of bourgeois voluntary culture in Bradford as described by Theodore Koditschek, the emergence of Sheffield's middle-class network was less dependent upon the town's emergent capitalist bourgeoisie. While the involvement of the big industrialists developed with the coming of the 'steel giants' from mid-century onwards, public life in early nineteenth-century Sheffield was dominated by smaller manufacturers and professional men. See Theodore Koditschek, *Class Formation and Urban-Industrial Society, Bradford, 1750–1850* (Cambridge, Cambridge University Press, 1990), pp. 252–319.

19　For voluntary religious societies and the formation of the public sphere, see R. J. Morris, 'Voluntary societies and British urban elites, 1780–1850: an analysis', *Historical Journal,* 26:1 (1983), 95–118; John Seed, 'Theologies of power: Unitarianism and the social relations of religious discourse, 1800–1850', in R. J. Morris, *Class, Power and Social Structure in British Nineteenth Century Towns* (Leicester, Leicester University Press, 1986); Davidoff and Hall, *Family Fortunes,* pp. 416–49.

20　See Davidoff and Hall, *Family Fortunes.*

21　The Municipal Corporations Act 1835 was resisted in Sheffield until 1843. See Derek Fraser, *Power and Authority in the Victorian City* (Oxford, Basil Blackwell, 1979), pp. 139–48; Richard J. Childs, 'Sheffield before 1843', in Clyde Binfield et al. (eds), *The*

History of Sheffield, 1843–1993, vol. 1 (Sheffield, Sheffield Academic Press, 1993), pp. 7–24.

22 Most notable among these were James Montgomery, the journalist, who was born a Moravian but developed Methodist evangelical sympathies; Rowland Hodgson, a gentleman, and Samuel Roberts, a manufacturer, both of whom were Anglican; the Congregationalist silver-plate manufacturer Joseph Read, and Thomas Asline Ward, a cutlery manufacturer and a Unitarian. See M. Walton, *Sheffield: Its Story and Its Achievements* (Otley, Amethyst Press, 1948), p. 158; R. E. Leader, *Reminiscences of Old Sheffield: Its Streets and Its People* (Sheffield, Leader and Sons, 1876), pp. 300–10.

23 See Gunson, *Messengers of Grace*, especially pp. 119–20.

24 *Sheffield Iris*, 14 November 1820 and 6 March 1821.

25 George Bennet to Catharine Read, 21 April 1820 (Mary Anne Rawson Papers, H. J. Wilson Collection, Sheffield City Archives, hereafter MAR/SA). Bennet had played an important role in their evangelical family life, donating a Bible when Joseph Read opened his own chapel in their grounds for the neighbouring poor and supporting his daughters' philanthropic and missionary commitments. For the Read family and missionary childhoods, see my 'Happy English children: class, ethnicity and the making of missionary women in the early nineteenth century', *Women's Studies International Forum*, 21:3 (June 1998), special edition on gender and colonialism.

26 George Bennet to Elizabeth Read, November 1822 [n.d.]. Daniel Tyerman complained that the abundance of gifts from Sheffield put Bennet and himself in an unequal relationship, particularly as it seems that Bennet refused to let him participate in their distribution; as a result, Tyerman felt obliged to give away his clothes. Daniel Tyerman to Rowland Hill, 3 October 1823 (G. Bennett, Letters and Reports (LMS Archive, School of Oriental and African Studies Library, London)).

27 George Bennet to Elizabeth Read, n.d.; to Edmund Read, 14 November 1822; and to Catharine and Eliza Read, 30 September 1823 (MAR/SA); Edward MCoy to James Montgomery, n.d., 22 January 1822, 20 March 1823, 17 April 1823, 22 May 1825 15 August 1825 (James Montgomery Collection, Sheffield City Archives, hereafter JM/SA) George Bennet to Rowland Hodgson, 14 January 1822 (LMS Archive, SOAS Library). Unfortunately none of the letters written to Bennet appears to be extant.

28 George Bennet to Elizabeth Read, 29 September 1823 (MAR/SA).

29 George Bennet to Catharine Read, 30 September 1823 (MAR/SA).

30 George Bennet to Elizabeth Read, 13 April 1824 (MAR/SA).

31 George Bennet to Elizabeth Read, n.d. (MAR/SA).

32 See *Sheffield Iris*, 13 April 1813, 20 April 1813, 21 June 1814, 24 January 1815, 2 June 1818, 13 July 1819.

33 *Sheffield Iris*, 13 and 20 July 1824.

34 *Sheffield Iris*, 30 November 1824.

35 'Farewell to Tahiti', George Bennet to Elizabeth Read, 13 April 1824 (MAR/SA).

36 *Sheffield Iris*, 24 May 1825.

37 *Sheffield Iris*, 10 May 1826.

38 *Montgomery (ed.), Voyages and Travels*, vol. 1, Introduction, p. viii.

39 See Catherine Hall, 'Missionary stories: gender and ethnicity in England in the 1830s and 1840s', in C. Hall, *White, Male and Middle Class* (Oxford, Polity Press, 1992), pp. 205–54.

40 Montgomery (ed.), *Voyages and Travels*, vol. 1, pp. 71–2, 74, 91, 113, 163–4, 181, 196, 201, 265, 277, 285, 449, 458.

41 *Ibid.*, vol. 1, pp. 132, 218.

42 *Ibid.*, vol. 1, p. 512. Jean and John Comaroff have talked about missionary reconstructions of the 'black body' through dress, grooming and deportment. They see such 'bodywork' as part of a more general attempt to construct 'free individuals' and introduce European commodities. See Jean and John Comaroff, *Ethnography and the Historical Imagination* (Oxford, Westview Press, 1992), p. 41.

43 *Ibid.*, vol. 1, pp. 201–3. For an account of Bunaauia, where 'provident and well-regulated modes of living' had apparently replaced the 'grossness, confusion and filthiness' of earlier domestic arrangements, see p. 164.

44 *Ibid.*, vol. 1, pp. 94, 348.

45 *Ibid.*, vol. 1, p. 533.

46 See Jean and John Comaroff, *Of Revelation and Revolution: Christianity, Colonialism and Consciousness in South Africa* (Chicago, University of Chicago Press, 1991) and *Ethnography and the Historical Imagination*; Thomas, *Colonialism's Culture*.

47 George Bennet, Letters and Reports (LMS, Archive, SOAS Library).

48 See Lovett, *A History of the London Missionary Society*, pp. 290–4.

49 Montgomery (ed.), *Voyages and Travels*, vol. 1, p. 335.

50 *Ibid.*, vol. 1, pp. 380–3, 411–13, 451–3, 469–71.

51 *Ibid.*, vol. 2, pp. 133–6.

52 *Ibid.*, vol. 2, pp. 130 and 174.

53 *Ibid.*, vol. 2, pp. 141–82.

54 *Ibid.*, vol. 2, p. 148.

55 'The white settlers have generally speaking not the least feeling of humanity towards the blacks', Bennet wrote to James Montgomery, 'but would rejoice and have them killed off a thousand times sooner than have them instructed and civilised.' George Bennet to James Montgomery, 25 December 1824 (JM/SA). 'Degraded as they are', wrote Tyerman in a letter to LMS director George Burder, 'they still have souls . . . as vigorous as our own.' Daniel Tyerman to George Burder, 8 February 1825 (LMS/SOAS). As an expression of their faith in the potential for change, the deputation supported the proposal of Lancelot Threlkeld to establish a mission to the Aborigines near Sydney.

56 George Bennet and Daniel Tyerman to Governor Brisbane, 11 October 1824 (LMS/SOAS).

57 Montgomery (ed.), *Voyages and Travels*, vol. 2, p. 167.

58 Letters from George Bennet to James Montgomery, 10 August 1823, 26 January 1824, 17 May 1824 (JM/SA).

59 Bennet was pleased with this arrangement. He also requested that material be sent to his friends John Clapham at Leeds, who was active in the Sunday School Union and later an intermediary with the Literary and Philosophical Society; the Reverend M Alliott at Nottingham, a conchologist; and Joseph Gilbert at Hull. Letter to James Montgomery, 15 May 1826 (JM/SA).

60 *Sheffield Iris*, 17 December 1822, 24 December 1822.

61 For the role of such societies in forging a common middle-class identity in the early nineteenth century, see Ian Inkster and Jack Morrell (eds), *Metropolis and Province: Science in British Culture, 1780–1850* (London, Hutchinson, 1983); Roger Cooter, *The Cultural Meaning of Popular Science* (Cambridge, Cambridge University Press, 1984).

62 Letter from Edward MCoy to James Montgomery, 10 May 1824. Bennet also sent material to Literary and Philosophical Society museums at Leeds and Whitby and to the museum at Saffron Waldon. Sheffield material became part of Sheffield City Museum, and some was sent to the British Museum in the late nineteenth century.

63 Sheffield Literary and Philosophical Society, *Annual Reports* (Sheffield, James Montgomery, 1823 and 1824; William Todd, 1825; John Blackwell, 1828; and George Ridge, 1832).

64 Sheffield Literary and Philosophical Society, *Annual Report* (Sheffield, Leader and Sons, 1885), p. 25.

65 Sheffield Literary and Philosophical Society, *Annual Report* (Sheffield, Leader and Sons, 1841).

66 Ludmilla Jordanova, 'Objects of knowledge: a historical perspective on museums', in Peter Vergo, *The New Museology* (London, Reaktion Books, 1989), p. 32.

67 Sheffield Literary and Philosophical Society, *Annual Report* (Sheffield, Leader and Sons, 1841).

68 Sheffield Literary and Philosophical Society, *Annual Report* (Sheffield, George Ridge, 1842).

5

HOMOSOCIALITY AND MIDDLE-CLASS IDENTITY IN EARLY VICTORIAN PATRONAGE OF THE ARTS
Dianne Sachko Macleod

Robert Vernon, John Sheepshanks and Jacob Bell have long been recognised for their pioneering patronage of British art. The first members of the emerging Victorian middle class to give their art collections to the public, they rode the crest of a new wave that coursed over the aristocracy's protean patronage of living artists in early Victorian England. The tendency, however, to treat these early benefactors homogeneously overlooks the differences in gender and class identity which characterise their individual subjectivities, interactions with artists and aesthetic expectations. In this chapter I will argue that, while these men were responsive to the incipient Victorian definition of manliness which emphasised moral circumspection and 'earnestness, selflessness and integrity', each, nonetheless, engaged in a form of homosocial behaviour that subverted that norm.[1] Bachelors three, Vernon, Sheepshanks and Bell depended on social networks of male companions, clubs and fraternal organisations to fashion more imaginative identities for themselves which pointedly deviated from the middle-class myth of masculinity that was rapidly gaining credence in these years of economic and political transformation. Their personal preferences, in turn, affected the constitution of their art collections. Yet, when Jacob Bell followed Vernon and Sheepshanks in donating his art treasures to the nation, in 1859, it was readily apparent that, despite their dissimilarities, these early Victorian patrons fostered art forms that reinforced the social and cultural imperatives of the patriarchy.

'Homosocial', according to Eve Sedgwick, 'is a word occasionally used in history and the social sciences, where it describes social bonds between persons of the same sex' and is distinguished by its 'intimate and shifting relation to class'.[2] She adds the observation that 'in any male-dominated society', there is a special relationship between male homosociality' and 'the structures for maintaining and transmitting patriarchal power'.[3] Male homosociality was a long-standing feature of the elitist British art world whose institutions found justification for their 'gentlemen only' prescription in the eighteenth-century philosophy of taste which excluded women in all but a peripheral way. Given theoretical foundation by the philosophers of the Scottish Enlightenment, the concept of taste was extrapolated from the Lockean principle that anyone could learn to master a subject, with the significant caveat that sufficient leisure and access to fine works were necessary to complete this process of education in the arts. While David Hume, in *Of the Standard of Taste* lamented the fact that the fine arts 'are always relished by a few only, whose leisure, fortune and genius, fit them for such amusements', Archibald Alison, in his *Essays on the Nature and Principles of Taste,* argued that the lower orders were incapable of acquiring taste because their 'vulgar and degrading occupations disfigure their minds'.[4] In contrast, the intelligentsia and wealthy urban bourgeoisie were deemed capable of accessing the intangible virtues which had previously been enjoyed only by the landed classes, providing that they earnestly dedicated themselves to the pursuit of culture. Nonetheless a tension remained between the civic humanist model of learning with its assumption of hereditary authority 'derived from the warrior ethic of aristocratic societies', and the more egalitarian model of apprehension advocated by the moneyed members of the middling ranks and the intelligentsia.[5]

The debate over whether the aristocrat and the arriviste were equally suited to adjudicate over aesthetics plagued the nascent Royal Academy under the leadership of Sir Joshua Reynolds. Reynolds initially defended the natural superiority of the landed elite, even though he was an outsider himself. The son of a schoolmaster who was granted a knighthood in reward for his role in establishing the British school of art, Sir Joshua quickly identified with the ruling class. In his public lectures, Reynolds recreated the language of civic humanism with its concomitant exclusivity.[6] To the founding president of Great Britain's first official school of art, the ideal Georgian gentleman was a man of rank and substance who trained for his leadership role in the republic of taste by indulging in the unhurried contemplation of beauty. Reynolds captured one such connoisseur on canvas in his portrait of Viscount Keppel (1754, Greenwich Maritime Museum) with whom he spent three years as paid cicerone on a Grand Tour of the continent. Reynolds elevates his subject to the ranks of the cognoscenti by positioning him in the pose of the *Apollo Belvedere* which invests him with the power of a cultural symbol and, in the process, verifies Keppel's claim to social and cultural superiority. The *Apollo Belvedere* was also a trope favoured by Allan Ramsay who, in his portrait, *Norman, Twenty-Second Chief of MacLeod* (1752, Dunvegan Castle), likewise reinforces his subject's right to a privileged position in society. Reynolds later tempered his canonisation of the ideal British gentleman after he realised that the untitled members of the middling ranks were a lucrative source of patronage; however, in the *Discourses* he delivered at the Royal Academy, he continued to insist on the importance of the timeless over the temporal. This legacy was categorically rejected by Victorian patrons, as was his ideal of manhood.

The effeminacy apparent in these portraits inspired by the *Apollo Belvedere* was incompatible with the dawning Victorian middle-class concept of masculinity which was based on a more stalwart and practical value system. Historians of fashion credit the emerging middle class with the subsequent shift to more sober and manly appearances. Termed the 'Great Masculine Renunciation' by J. C. Flugel, this change occurred gradually as hierarchical distinctions in dress were replaced by attire that was classless and more efficiently businesslike.[7] Similarly, Quentin Bell, in *On Human Finery*, notes that 'idleness was no longer the usual sign of wealth. The man who worked was not infrequently in receipt of a larger income than the men who drew rents off him; an industrious life no longer implied a poor or laborious existence and therefore ceased to be dishonourable'. Bell goes on to comment on the new 'uniform' promoted by the man of business: 'black coat, cylindrical hat, spotless linen, [and] carefully rolled umbrella'.[8] Although this transformation was a fait accompli by the middle of the nineteenth century, it was more problematic for middle-class males who desired to 'pass' as gentlemen in the elitist world of art connoisseurship in the years prior to the passage of the Reform Bill in 1832. The result, in some cases, was a construction of male subjectivity that formed an unusual collage of disparate entities.

Robert Vernon (1774–1849), for instance, paradoxically modelled himself after the pre-emptory aristocratic connoisseur and the hard-driving businessman, the military officer and the effete dilettante, and the self-made man and the country squire. As the eldest of the three early Victorian patrons whose collections provided the basis for the nation's holdings of British art, Vernon had few middle-class role models to follow in the art world. Moreover, the concept of masculinity itself was particularly unstable in the anxious years of social change following the Napoleonic Wars, when an economic boom shifted attention from the warrior model to the businessman. Commenting on such societal transformations, Mangan and Walvin insightfully observe: 'it would be wrong to imagine that manliness was a simple, single, coherent concept . . . it was, in effect, a portmanteau term which embraced a variety of overlapping ideologies . . . which changed over time and which, at specific moments, appear to be discrete, even conflicting, in emphasis'.[9] Uncertain about which path to follow, Vernon fashioned himself into a medley of contradictory types.

Henry Pickersgill's portrait of Robert Vernon (figure 1), painted in 1847, the year that he announced his gift to the nation, reveals some of these incongruities. There is little to indicate that the subject is the owner of a carriage-for-hire business.[10] Elegantly attired in an embossed satin dressing-gown with velvet trim and cuddling a King Charles spaniel on his lap, he appears somewhat foppish. Moreover, Vernon's feathered hairstyle, combined with his erect bearing, suggests a military role model based on his hero the Duke of Wellington, which further removes him from the middle-class realm of commerce and, by association, places him in counterpoint to the goals of his native social group, since Wellington had bitterly opposed the passage of the Reform Bill.[11]

Nonetheless his esteem for the Iron Duke led him to commission several works of art which featured the intrepid soldier.[12] Because Vernon's portrait formed part of his gift to the nation, it is tempting to speculate that he wished to announce himself as a patriot who shared the values of the aristocratic warrior class, as well as one of the company of connoisseurs who sat on the board of trustees of the National Gallery, men such as Baron Monteagle and the Marquess of Lansdowne, with whom he corresponded about the terms of his donation.[13] The exposure that he enjoyed to these lords of the land was a definite cut above the circles into which he had been born. The son of a hackneyman and stable owner, Vernon expanded his inheritance into a highly profitable enterprise that catered to clients who included the Prince and Princess of Wales, the Earl of Bristol and the Duke of Bedford.[14] Just as he parlayed his patrimony into

Fig. 1 **Henry Pickersgill,** *Robert Vernon***, 1847, oil on canvas.**

a business empire that extended to rental property throughout the West End and a palatial country house and estate in Berkshire, he also augmented the small collection of Old Master paintings he inherited from his father into a landmark assemblage of modern British art. While the refined image Vernon conveys in his portrait may have been a public proclamation of the height to which he had risen on the social scale, he made no secret about his modest beginnings.

On the contrary, Vernon habitually broadcast disinformation about his

social origins.[15] Like Mr Bounderby in Charles Dickens's *Hard Times*, Vernon
pretended that his childhood was less advantageous than it actually was. So
widespread was the myth of the self-made man in Victorian England, that
Harold Perkin describes this phenomenon as 'one of the most powerful instruments of propaganda ever developed by any class to justify itself and seduce
others to its own ideal'.[16] Much like the backlash against affirmative-action policies in the USA today, this propaganda was directed against the disadvantaged
who were believed to be social parasites lacking in the tenacity to persevere in
the school of self-help that was the training ground for the self-made man.
Vernon's motives for subscribing to the myth, no doubt, were bound up in his
need to attract attention to himself by making his accomplishments seem all the
more praiseworthy in comparison to his understated origins; nevertheless, he
was acutely sensitive to society's whims and must have sensed a social advantage to denigrating his origins.

The social diversity of the Athenaeum Club to which Vernon aspired to
belong was conducive to his myth-making. Founded in 1824, the humble origins
of many of the Club's early members indicate the increasing prevalence of the
homo novus legend in the 1830s: sculptor Francis Chantrey was a Sheffield
carpenter's son, painter Daniel Maclise's father was a private in a Highland
Regiment, ornithologist John Gould was the son of a gardener at Windsor
Castle, artist William Frith's father was a butler and social reformer Richard
Cobden had once been a commercial traveller.[17] In his bid for membership,
Vernon would have recognised an advantage in understating his patrimony as a
way of earning more recognition for his perspicacity. But before he could be
taken seriously as a devotee of the arts, he had to dispel the prejudice of one of
the Athenaeum's most formidable members, National Gallery trustee Lord
Landsdowne, who paradoxically insisted that men involved in the creative arts
be excluded 'as we shall otherwise be overrun with all the pretenders to literature and the arts, than whom there is not anywhere a more odious race'.[18]
Vernon's enormous art collection, elegant attire, Pall Mall mansion and country-
squire life style, which included running with the Berkshire hounds, must have
worked in his favour because he was elected a member in 1838.[19] Like the
fictional Mr Ainsley, a cotton lord who was angry at the ridicule he suffered at
the hands of the gentry, Vernon was determined to win their respect by appearing as someone to the manner born.[20] But, at the same time, he could not resist
claiming the kudos awarded to self-made men. Vernon's fractured subjectivity is
also apparent in his contradictory interactions with artists.

On the surface, Robert Vernon was a model patron, one who lavished
attention on artists and offered them a forum for homosocial camaraderie at his
London home at 50 Pall Mall and at Ardington House, his Berkshire retreat.
The list of painters he entertained reads like a *Who's Who* of the early Victorian
art world – Eastlake, Turner, Callcott, Landseer, Maclise, Pickersgill, Cook,
Stanfield and Roberts were among those he graced with invitations. Yet, Vernon
could be a difficult host, as Daniel Maclise attested, when he compared the
struggles and squabbles of the ducks in the pond at Ardington House with the
way artists felt about trying to get through the day as his house guests.[21] His
nephew, Vernon Heath, who was conscripted as his general factotum, frankly

noted that his uncle 'was a strange and singular man. One day he would be generous and liberal, considerate and sympathetic; the next the very reverse'.[22] This assessment holds true in Vernon's mercurial behaviour towards Landseer. Knowing that the artist had painted the royal family and was invited to some of the grandest houses, Vernon treated him with deference; nonetheless, when Landseer was delinquent in completing a painting of his beloved King Charles spaniels, Vernon was quick to reprimand him. Some of this ambivalence can be attributed to Vernon's indecision about whether he should imitate the domineering commands of the soldier, the lordly manners of the cognoscenti, the more egalitarian conduct of the businessman or the ingratiating obeisance of the self-made man. Because standards of patronage were in a state of flux in the early Victorian years, even artists responded to them in different ways.

Whereas Landseer felt harassed by Vernon's rebukes, Constable found him open-minded and liberal. Constable far preferred Robert Vernon to landowner William Wells of Redleaf, for instance, who insisted on his claim to the proverbially infallible eye of the connoisseur in assessing artistic technique. After Wells paid a visit to his studio in 1833, Constable vented his frustration in a letter to his friend C. R. Leslie:

> I had, on Friday, a long visit from Mr Wells alone. He saw hundreds of my things – I sincerely believe nothing amongst them made any impression upon him nor did they come into his rules, or whims, of the art. I told him ... I looked on <u>pictures</u> as things to be <u>avoided</u>. Connoisseurs looked on them as things to be <u>imitated</u>. (Constable's emphasis)[23]

What rankled with Constable was Wells's presumption that he was qualified to assess his artistic efforts. The scenario repeated itself two years later when Wells once again visited Constable's studio and criticised his work in progress on *The Valley Farm*, only this time Vernon arrived on the scene just after Wells had left and rescued the situation. As Constable reported to Leslie, 'Mr Vernon came soon after ... he saw it free from the mustiness of old pictures – he saw the daylight purely – and bought it – it is his.'[24] Constable's admiration of Vernon, however, was not universally shared by artists. John Horsley complained that the patron haggled over prices, both with him and Thomas Webster; Frederick Lee also must have been aghast when he discovered that Vernon had asked another painter to add a figure to one of his compositions.[25] While the nobility and gentry assumed it was their prerogative to dictate to artists, Victorian middle-class patrons were increasingly inclined to treat them as fellow professionals.[26] Vernon, however, chose to refer back to older and more elitist codes of behaviour.

There is no evidence that Robert Vernon managed to acquire the visual acuity of the leisured connoisseur. His correspondence with artists contains few references to aesthetics or the artistic process. Rather it was the subject matter of his paintings which most concerned him and in this regard he anticipates the mainstream businessmen-collectors of the next generation who were unwilling to invest the time required for a lengthy Grand Tour of the continent. Thus the cadence of connoisseurship was eventually overpowered by the louder rhythms of the narrative refrain.

In its emphasis on content over form, Vernon's collection conforms to an emerging middle-class aesthetic. While approximately two-thirds of his gift to the National Gallery consisted of the history paintings, poetic subjects and landscapes that characterised upper-class taste, the remaining third featured the small and unpretentious anecdotal scenes from daily life which had begun to capture the attention of middle-class patrons in the years surrounding the passage of the Reform Bill. Commenting on this trend, the *Edinburgh Review* noted, in 1834: 'The majority would rather see the likeness of something they have seen before, than stretch their faculties to understand a story told on canvas, or try to imagine whether a great event in history is adequately represented in the picture before them.'[27] In offering the nation a well-balanced survey of the British school of art, it behoved Vernon to temper his elitist inclinations with a strong sampling of popular anecdotal subjects that celebrated the daily lives of ordinary folk.

John Sheepshanks (1787–1863), on the other hand, was less equivocal about his middle-class identity. Thirteen years younger and two generations further removed from the source of his family's fortune, Sheepshanks was more accepting of his social status. He did not try to ingratiate himself with the landed gentry like Vernon, preferring middle-class Blackheath to Berkshire. A descendant of a family of Leeds cloth manufacturers and merchants who had prospered during the Napoleonic Wars by supplying scarlet and white fabric for the clothing of troops, John Sheepshanks retired from the family business before his fortieth birthday and moved south permanently.[28] His social outlook, however, had already been moulded in the crucible of Leeds's radical politics.

Concern about social unrest, both on the local and international levels, infiltrated the discourse on art. W. C. Taylor, writing in the *Art Journal* in 1849, recommended art education as a means to 'securing the foundations and strengthening the bonds of social order'.[29] Referring to recent political disturbances on the continent, Taylor reasoned:

> 'Taste', we are told, 'will not extinguish Revolutionary tendencies'; probably not, but will neglect of taste produce this desirable result? We are not very much surprised, though we are very deeply grieved, at the doubts which the insurrections of Berlin, Vienna, and Paris, have excited respecting the expediency of the intellectual training of the masses; but we have shown that while there is an element of danger, there is also a corrective, of which society can easily avail itself as a counterpoise.

Endorsing this view that art held the potential to benefit the working classes, Sheepshanks designated the public as 'shareholders' in the collection he donated to the South Kensington Museum whose administrators were more sympathetic to his altruistic intentions than the conservative trustees of the National Gallery.[30] Henry Cole and Richard Redgrave shared the benefactor's democratic views and thereby abided by his wish to make the 233 oils and almost 300 watercolours, drawings and etchings in his gift available to the working classes on Sunday afternoons and in the evenings by installing gas lighting in the galleries where Sheepshanks' collection was displayed. Welcomed by the inviting setting, viewers were delighted to discover that over half of the oil paintings were narrative subjects which they could easily understand. Attempting to

Fig. 2 **William Mulready, *John Sheepshanks*, 1858. Chalk, pencil and wash.**

explain the popularity of the collection, Richard Redgrave concluded that 'the subjects are such as we can live by and love'.[31] These scenes from daily life and popular literary texts were drawn from common experience rather than the remote past and, unlike the generalised compositions favoured by eighteenth-century connoisseurs, introduced telling and often amusing details to guide their viewer's visual comprehension. Its physical and aesthetic accessibility made the Sheepshanks collection an immediate success with the general public.

Sheepshanks' appearance was consistent with his egalitarian principles. His informality was captured in a chalk sketch by William Mulready in 1858 (figure 2). Disdaining a cravat, the patron is casually dressed in a jacket and sweater. His nonchalant attitude towards clothing sometimes led him to be mistaken for one of his gardeners when strangers came to call and even once caused him to be refused admittance to a first-class carriage on the railway.[32] By all appearances, it would seem that Sheepshanks was so comfortable with himself that he felt no need to impress the outside world. Yet that observation does not tell the whole story, nor does it account for the tense facial muscles we observe in his portrait, or the vulnerable expression in his eyes.

That a more complex private side existed to Sheepshanks' character is hinted at in his relations with artists. Like Vernon, he enjoyed the homosocial atmosphere of artists' studios. Sheepshanks, however, was more at ease with the artists and engravers whom he entertained at his boisterous Wednesday 'at homes', so much so that he sometimes enjoyed himself to the point of inebriation.[33] That a close bond was forged between artists and patron in this convivial clime is not surprising. Landseer, who described his evenings at Sheepshanks' home as consisting of 'fine works of art – agreeable conversation – eating, drinking and laughter', was particularly sensitive to his host's temperament.[34] On one occasion, anxious to clear up a misunderstanding, the artist pleaded, 'it was unlike you to treat me as a stranger in this matter. In what have I offended you? I write this in haste to say it is to me greatly mortifying to find one of my oldest friends putting his boot on me with not telling me why.'[35] Landseer's tone reveals that, despite Sheepshanks' informality, he still symbolically signified the pre-Victorian image of the patron as a charismatic father figure who evoked a desire in his wards to please and to obey, a desire which was intensified by the absence of a mother figure.[36]

Banished from this inner circle, women intervened only on canvas. Sheepshanks' attitude to the female subjects in the paintings he commissioned is telling: he stated that the death by drowning of the despondent female figure in Francis Danby's *Disappointed Love* (1821), would be no loss because she was so ugly, and justified his verdict by referring to the precedent established by a judge who sentenced a woman to death after refusing to believe in her innocence because she was so homely.[37] Taken in concert, then, one could argue that Sheepshanks' intensive homosociality and denigration of the female sex were simply manifestations of the prevailing masculinist outlook of his time were it not for the existence of a private cache of images of little boys that he withheld from the public.

Painted by another of his intimate correspondents, artist William Henry Hunt, this series of large watercolour paintings featuring beautiful pre-pubescent youths was passed down to Sheepshanks' heirs and still remains in their possession today.[38] The fact that Sheepshanks conceived of these images as a separate group suggests a parallel with a pair of pictures that were commissioned from Reynolds by the Duke of Dorset for similar purposes. *Cupid as Link Boy* and *Mercury as Cut Purse* represent suggestively posed five- or six-year-old boys who form what James Steward describes as 'a kind of before and after pair, an infantine sexual progress from the erect to the pendulous'.[39] While Hunt's little boys are not as blatantly sexual, their choir boy innocence can also be construed as erotic according to theoreticians of the male gaze who argue that 'repressed homosexual voyeurism' is an essential element in same-sex viewing.[40] I am not suggesting that Sheepshanks' homosocial relations with artists spilled over into homosexuality. Rather it is the inequality of their homosocial bond which concerns me, in as much as the artists' eagerness to satisfy the desires of their patron shaped their production. Hunt, for instance, was known to pinch his young sitters when they failed to maintain the expressions he wanted.[41] Homosociality, after all, was but another gendered kinship system defined by capital. 'A kinship system', explains Gayle Rubin, 'is an imposition of social ends upon a part of the natural world. It is therefore "production" in the most general sense of the term: a molding, a transformation of objects (in this case people) to and by a subjective purpose.'[42] Therefore, in Hunt's case, it was a question of the end justifying the means if the pleasure of the charismatic patron was to be satisfied.

That assessment throws a new light on one of the better-known images of children which Sheepshanks allowed to be released to the public domain, Landseer's *The Naughty Child* (1834, Victoria and Albert Museum). This oil painting features a petulant little boy about four years of age who defiantly looks out from a corner of a room where he has been sent to be punished for breaking the mirror which lies shattered at his feet. Unusual in Landseer's oeuvre, this representation has traditionally been viewed in conjunction with the several pictures by William Mulready dealing with instructive moments in childhood which also formed part of Sheepshanks' gift. Mulready's images, however, promote instead of defy patriarchal prerogatives as their titles suggest: *The Fight Interrupted* (1826), *The Wolf and the Lamb* (1820), and *Giving a Bite* (1834). Landseer's, by contrast, invites sympathy for the transgressive behaviour of the child by giving him a halo of tousled golden curls and by drawing attention to the putto-like plumpness of his body which is provocatively revealed by his torn frock. These features invest *The Naughty Child* with a thinly disguised eroticism which, when considered in tandem with the representations of little boys that Sheepshanks did not wish the public to see, indicates that his private fantasies did not accord with those of the Victorian paterfamilias. But for the public record, he endorsed the values of his class. Although the Landseer he donated raises the spectre of paedophilia, its impact was overshadowed by the narratives of Mulready and the messages of the other anecdotal painters represented in his gift, which reinforced the notion that the authority of the patriarchy rested on the education and control of children.

Jacob Bell (1810–59) likewise is said to have exhibited unorthodox tendencies. According to William Frith, who met him while they were both art students at Sass's Academy, Bell, who was raised a Quaker, was expelled from the Society of Friends because he dressed in women's clothes so that he could sit on the ladies' side of the chapel.[43] Amusing as this tale is, it contradicts the official records held by the Society of Friends which state that Bell was disowned by his sect many years later, in 1855, 'having for a considerable time past, habitually absented himself from our religious Meetings'.[44] Moreover, Bell's subsequent behaviour works in counterpoint to the implications of cross-dressing. After he quit art school to train with his father in the family's chemist shop, he dedicated himself to helping artists escape the taint of effeminacy that had long plagued an occupation which was synonymous with the sexed traits of emotion and imagination.

The problematic of the feminised artistic professional, according to Herbert Sussman, was a central issue in the refashioning of Victorian masculinities. The solution for the artist, he maintains, was to develop a public persona 'as entrepreneurial man, the independent producer of commodities for sale on the art market'.[45] Jacob Bell, accordingly, showed his artist friends how to manipulate the manly and mercantile standards he mastered in his own struggle to professionalise his career as a pharmaceutical chemist.

Richard Ormond has documented how indispensable Bell was to Landseer's career as a friend, adviser and informal business manager, observing that 'without Bell it is difficult to see how he could have pursued his professional career'.[46] This claim is borne out by the private correspondence between artist and patron where Landseer asked Bell to counsel him regarding Robert Vernon's 'abusive letters' and the 'tyrannical' dealer Ernest Gambart.[47] Because of the advice Bell imparted to Landseer about dealing with print publishers, even artists he did not patronise, such as the young John Everett Millais, consulted him about how much to ask for a copyright. The long list of artists he advised includes William Frith, H. H. Briggs and the Count d'Orsay; it is no wonder that Landseer complimented the collector for his 'angelic patience'.[48] The guidance which Bell willingly imparted to artists who were struggling to shirk the passively feminised persona of their occupation and learn the aggressive ways of the businessman paralleled the strategies he was practising in his own professional life.

Bell was instrumental in separating pharmacy from the practice of medicine. W. J. Reader, in his study of the rising Victorian professional classes, notes: 'The apothecaries were the third of the recognised "orders" of medical practitioners. The physicians regarded them with even greater contempt than the surgeons, and even the surgeons would not admit to their Fellowship anyone who practised pharmacy.'[49] Bell's solution was to establish a separate professional body, the Pharmaceutical Society, in 1841, for which he commissioned his former teacher at Sass's, Henry Briggs, to design its diploma (it is still in use).[50] That same year, Bell started a journal, later known as the *Pharmaceutical Journal*, directed towards chemists and druggists throughout the country, which he edited, wrote for, and financed for eighteen years. Because the professional class underwent a dramatic expansion in the first half of the Victorian period (it almost tripled in size between 1841 and 1871), it was imperative that it have Members of Parliament among its ranks.[51] When his pharmaceutical peers asked him to stand for election in 1850 to defend their interests, it must have been a sweet victory for Bell, since Quakers had originally been excluded from the House of Commons due to their refusal to subscribe to the Thirty-nine Articles of the established Church.[52]

Bell willingly represented the pharmaceutical cause in Parliament and as an ambassador at large, despite the nervousness he felt about speaking in public. At the time of the Great Exhibition in 1851, he agreed, with some trepidation, to deliver a lecture at the Society of Arts on the pharmaceutical products displayed there. Bell's appearance on that memorable evening is recorded in a drawing published in *Drug Price Current* in 1851 (figure 3). The pharmacist's frozen visage, heavily hooded eyes and aggressively protruding lower lip conceal the true range of emotions that flickered across his face during the course of his lecture. According to the description that accompanied this drawing:

> To have seen Mr. Bell at this moment was worth a great deal; he did not look stern, because sterness is akin to the iron-hearted despotism of men of war – and Mr. Bell is, as will be seen by and bye [sic], a strenuous advocate for peace; but he looked petrified, monumental – the solemn image of himself in bronze.[53]

Jacob Bell recovered from his nerve-wracking debut at the Society of Arts to continue to serve both his pharmaceutical peers and his artist friends. As disparate as his two interests seem to be, they frequently overlapped in the homosocial realm. On one level, he good-naturedly indulged the hypochondria of his friends in the art world by supplying them with prescriptive medicines.[54] But on another level, he continued his campaign to masculinise the artistic calling by involving artists in his professional arena. I have already mentioned that he employed his friend Briggs to design the pharmaceutical diploma. In addition, he commissioned Sheepshanks' favourite watercolourist William Henry Hunt to paint the interior of his chemist's shop in Oxford Street. Although the original work cannot be traced, an engraving made by J. G. Murray in 1842 is still in circulation. It is an unusual example of genre painting in the service of commerce in that it captures a characteristic moment in the daily life of laboratory assistants with the obsessive attention to detail that is the hallmark of Hunt's style. Because of its fidelity to particulars, this mezzotint is frequently reproduced in histories of pharmacy as an example of the state of that science in the early Victorian years. The image is not as well known to art historians, however, since Bell excluded it from his gift to the National Gallery, along with *The Alchemist's Study* by R. T. Lonsdale, another work in his original collection that overlapped with his professional interests.[55] Like Sheepshanks, Bell gave the nation narratives that were more instructive and less personal.

Bell's bequest to the National Gallery represented only a small portion of his collection: he selected 16 pictures from the more than 150 paintings, drawings, prints and sculptures he owned which included 5 Landseers, Frith's *Derby Day* (1856–8) and Rosa Bonheur's *Horse Fair* (1855).[56] It is apparent, however, that his choices were based on aesthetic as well as well as narrative standards. As a former art student, Bell valued the intricacies of composition, colour and mood. The catalogue he wrote when he exhibited the cream of his collection at the Marylebone Literary and Philosophical Institution in 1859, just months before his early death at the age of forty-nine, is the work of a trained observer. He comments, for instance, on Landseer's 'vigour of execution' and 'tone of colour'.[57] Bell displayed a facility that was to become increasingly rare by the

Fig. 3 *Jacob Bell delivering a Lecture at the Society of Arts, Drug Price Current* (1851), 361.

mid-Victorian period among middle-class collectors who, like Vernon and Sheepshanks, valued content over technique. Yet, despite his regard for the artistic process, Bell also firmly believed that art should communicate on an ideological plane. In writing about Frith's *Derby Day*, Bell attested: 'The picture "points a moral" . . . [and] is like a book written in many languages and addressing itself to each spectator in his own mother tongue'.[58] This image, significantly, plays on the same prominent theme of the Sheepshanks gift: the transmission of the symbolic power of the patriarchy from father to son through the vignette of the acrobat who casts a watchful and concerned eye over his young offspring. The gap between art and life was breached by the patronage of men like Bell who encouraged artists to celebrate and to promote the middle-class values of their time and, in the process, to transform the universal and timeless ideals of their eighteenth-century forebears into temporal imperatives.

The fact that each of the three earliest public benefactors of Victorian art had a private homosocial agenda does not alter the collective significance of their generosity in making a democratic form of art available to everyone, even if that generosity served to inculcate class-based values. Vernon's motives in supporting this popularising trend were perhaps as disingenuous as his fabricated background and effete appearance, just as Sheepshanks' public beneficence only hinted at his private fantasy world of child love. Jacob Bell, despite his lapsed Quakerism, more closely resembled the stalwart patriarchal paradigm of the high Victorian years, both in public and in private, due to his dedication to channelling the residue of femininity that remained in the early Victorian concept of the artist into manly enterprise.

NOTES

1 J. A. Mangan and James Walvin (eds), *Manliness and Morality: Middle-Class Masculinity in Britain and America 1800–1940* (Manchester, Manchester University Press, 1987), p. 1.

2 Eve Kosofsky Sedgwick, *Between Men: English Literature and Homosocial Desire* (New York, Columbia University Press, 1985), p. 1.

3 *Ibid.*, p. 25.

4 David Hume, *Of the Standard of Taste,* and Archibald Alison, *Essays on the Nature and Principles of Taste,* cited in Andrew Hemingway, 'The "sociology" of taste in the Scottish Enlightenment', *Oxford Art Journal*, 12:2 (1989), 16 and 26.

5 Hemingway, 'The "sociology" of taste', 12.

6 See John Barrell, *The Political Theory of Painting from Reynolds to Hazlitt* (New Haven and London, Yale University Press, 1986), pp. 2 and 69 ff.

7 J. C. Flugel, *The Psychology of Clothes* (London, Hogarth, 1930; reprinted. 1950), pp. 110–13. For an analysis of Flugel, see Kaja Silverman, 'Fragments of a fashionable discourse', in Tania Modleski (ed.), *Studies in Entertainment: Critical Approaches to Mass Culture* (Bloomington, Indiana University Press, 1986), pp. 139–52.

8 Quentin Bell, *On Human Finery* (London, Hogarth, 1976), p. 141.

9 Mangan and Walvin, *Manliness*, p. 3.

10 On Vernon's background, see Robin Hamlyn, *Robert Vernon's Gift: British Art for the Nation 1847* (London, Tate Gallery, 1993), pp. 11–14, and Dianne Sachko Macleod, *Art and the Victorian Middle Class: Money and the Making of Cultural Identity* (Cambridge, Cambridge University Press, 1996), pp. 22–6 and 484–5.

11 See Harold Perkin, *Origins of Modern English Society* (London and Toronto, Routledge and Kegan Paul, 1969; reprinted. 1985), pp. 348–9.

12 See Macleod, *Art and the Victorian Middle Class*, p. 26.

13 See Vernon Heath, *Recollections* (London, 1892), pp. 17–18.

14 Hamlyn, *Vernon*, p. 12. For Vernon's network of rental properties, see his correspondence and inventories, Jenkyns Papers II, Balliol College, Oxford.

15 See, for instance, *Dictionary of National Biography*.

16 Perkin, *Modern English Society*, p. 225.

17 F. R. Cowell, *The Athenaeum Club and Social Life in London 1824–1974* (London, Heinemann, 1975), p. 13. For the currency of the self-made-man myth in the 1830s, see François Crouzet, *The First Industrialists: The Problem of Origins* (Cambridge, Cambridge University Press, 1985), p. 39.

18 Lord Lansdowne, cited in Anthony Lejeune, *The Gentlemen's Clubs of London* (London, Macdonald and Jane's, 1979), p. 40.

19 On Vernon's election to the Athenaeum, see David Robertson, *Charles Eastlake and the Victorian Art World* (Princeton, Princeton University Press, 1978), p. 48.

20 For Ainsley, see Elizabeth Stone, *William Langshawe, the Cotton Lord*, 2 vols (1842), discussed in Ivan Melada, *The Captains of Industry in English Fiction, 1821–1871* (Albuquerque, University of New Mexico Press, 1970), p. 116.

21 On Vernon's relations with artists, see Macleod, *Art and the Victorian Middle Class*, pp. 38–9.

22 Heath, *Recollections*, p. 1.

23 Constable to C. R. Leslie, 2 March 1833, 'Constable Correspondence III', ed. R. B. Beckett, *Suffolk Records Society* 8 (1965), 94–5.

24 Constable to Leslie, March 1835, *ibid.*, 124.

25 Mrs Edmund Helps (ed.), *Recollections of a Royal Academician by John Callcott Horsley, R.A.* (London, John Murray, 1903), p. 58. For the episode of Vernon's asking George Lance to alter Lee's *The Cover Side*, see Lance to Vernon, 3 September 1844, Jenkyns Papers II, Balliol College.

26 Macleod, *Art and the Victorian Middle Class*, passim.

27 *Edinburgh Review*, 43 (1834), 63.

28 For Yorkshire and Sheepshanks, see Herbert Heaton, *The Yorkshire Woollen and Worsted Industries* (Oxford, Clarendon Press, 1965), p. 280. For Sheepshanks' biography, see Macleod, *Art and the Victorian Middle Class*, pp. 473–4.

29 W. C. Taylor, 'On the cultivation of taste in the operative classes', *Art Journal* (January 1849), 3.

30 *Art Journal* (December 1863), 241, and Henry Cole, *Fifty Years of Public Work*, 2 vols (London, George Bell and Sons, 1884), 1, pp. 188–93.

31 Richard Redgrave, *Inventory of the . . . Gift of John Sheepshanks Esq.*, with an Introduction by Richard Redgrave (London, South Kensington Museum, 1857), p. 3.

32 *Art Journal* (December 1863), 241.

33 Charles Henry Cope, *Reminiscences of Charles West Cope* (London, Richard Bentley, 1891), p. 121.

34 Landseer to Sheepshanks, 1842, Sheepshanks Family Papers, private collection.

35 Landseer to Sheepshanks, 21 November 1848, Sheepshanks Family Papers.

36 For a parallel situation involving the charismatic father figure in artist–pupil relationships, see Abigail Solomon-Godeau, *Male Trouble: A Crisis in Representation* (London, Thames and Hudson, 1997), p. 50.

37 F. M. Redgrave, *Richard Redgrave: A Memoir* (London, Cassell, 1891), pp. 170–1.

38 One of Sheepshanks' descendants agreed with the interpretation which follows, while a second did not. William Henry Hunt struck an intimate tone when he plaintively wrote to Sheepshanks: 'unknown to myself I must have given you some cause for offence' (20 October [1854–55], Sheepshanks Family Papers).

39 James Steward, *The New Child: British Art and the Origins of Modern Childhood, 1730–1830* (Berkeley, University Art Museum, 1996), p. 210.

40 Steve Neale, 'Masculinity as spectacle: reflections on men and mainstream cinema', in Steven Cohan and Ina Rae Hark (eds), *Screening the Male: Exploring Masculinities in Hollywood Cinema* (London, Routledge, 1993), p. 13. See also Joseph Kestener, *Masculinities in Victorian Painting* (Aldershot, Scolar Press, 1995), p. 31.

41 Wolverhampton Art Gallery, *William Henry Hunt 1790–1864* (Wolverhampton, 1981), p. 6.

42 Gayle Rubin, 'The traffic in women: notes on the "political economy" of sex ', in Rayna R. Reiter (ed.), *Toward an Anthropology of Women* (New York, Monthly Review Press, 1975), p. 176.

43 William Frith, *My Autobiography and Reminiscences*, 3 vols (London, 1887–88), 1, p. 43.

44 Kingston MM Minutes, 1853–65, p. 135, Society of Friends Library, London. For Bell's biography, see Macleod, *Art and the Victorian Middle Class*, pp. 391–3.

45 Herbert Sussman, *Victorian Masculinities: Manhood and Masculine Poetics in Early Victorian Literature and Art* (Cambridge, Cambridge University Press, 1995), p. 153. On the gendering of genius, see Susan Casteras, 'Excluding women: the cult of the male genius in Victorian painting', in Linda Shires (ed.), *Rewriting the Victorians: Theory, History, and the Politics of Gender* (London, Routledge, 1992), pp. 116–46.

46 Richard Ormond, *Sir Edwin Landseer* (Philadelphia and London, Philadelphia Museum of Art and Tate Gallery, 1981), p. 11.

47 Edwin Landseer to Jacob Bell, Friday [undated], and Bell to Landseer, 6 November [undated], Jacob Bell Papers, Royal Institution.

48 Landseer to Bell, 31 August 1845, Royal Institution. For Millais and Bell, see Malcolm Warner, 'The professional career of John Everett Millais to 1863, with a catalogue of works to the same date,' Ph.D. thesis, Courtauld Institute of Art, University of London, 1985, p. 104.

49 W. J. Reader, *Professional Men: The Rise of the Professional Classes in Nineteenth-Century England* (New York, Basic Books, 1966), p. 40. For Bell's apprenticeship, see G. E. Trease, 'Pioneers, Jacob Bell,' *British Journal of Pharmaceutical Practice*, 1 (November/December 1979), 26.

50 Leslie G. Matthew, 'Statesman of pharmacy Jacob Bell, 1810–59', *The Chemist and Druggist* (6 June 1958), 611.

51 Bell was a member of the Liberal Party. He advocated free trade but was opposed to the endowment of the Roman Catholic clergy. He served in Parliament from 1850 to 1852. See Michael Stenton (ed.), *Who was Who in Parliament*, 4 vols (Hassocks, Harvester Press, 1976–81), 1, p. 28.

52 M. W. Kirby, *Men of Business and Politics: The Rise and Fall of the Quaker Pease Dynasty of North-East England, 1700–1943* (London, George Allen and Unwin, 1984), p. 6.

53 'Society of Arts. Mr. Bell's Lecture', *Drug Price Current* (1851), 361.

54 Bell provided 'long-life pills' to Landseer and other artists and even found a product on his shelves for d'Orsay to use in polishing his sculptures. See letters from Landseer to Bell, 1844 and 1845, Jacob Bell Papers, Royal Institution, and Count d'Orsay to Bell, 21 August 1844, Pharmaceutical Society of Great Britain.

55 The young boy in the Hunt watercolour is John Simmons who successfully trained as a laboratory assistant. See Jacob Bell and Theophilus Redwood, *Historical Sketch of the Progress of Pharmacy of Great Britain* (London, Pharmaceutical Society, 1880), p. 190. See also 'A Business BELL [sic] founded', *The Chemist and Druggist* (6 June 1959), 615.

56 I have determined the size of Bell's collection from an undated inventory contained among his papers at the Royal Institution. Also in this archive is a receipt dated 29 June 1859 signed by Sir Charles Eastlake, director of the National Gallery, for fourteen of the pictures Bell agreed to bequeath. It does not include his replica of Rosa Bonheur's *Horse Fair* which Bell had lent to the dealer Ernest Gambart to exhibit along with the larger original. Nor is Frith's *Derby Day* on Eastlake's receipt because Gambart owned the copyright and was exercising his right to exhibit it in 1859. See Jeremy Maas, *Gambart: Prince of the Victorian Art World* (London, Barrie and Jenkins, 1975), pp. 181–2.

57 [Jacob Bell], *Descriptive Catalogue of Pictures, etc. Exhibited at Marylebone Literary and Scientific Institution* (London, 1859), p. 15.

58 *Ibid.*, p. 6.

6

THE BOURGEOIS BODY: CIVIC PORTRAITURE, PUBLIC MEN AND THE APPEARANCE OF CLASS POWER IN MANCHESTER, 1838–50
Louise Purbrick

PRESENTATION AND PORTRAITURE

On 28 October 1842, at a meeting of Manchester Borough Council, a letter from one of its members, Alderman John Brooks, was read out. The letter, dated three days earlier, was addressed to the mayor. It asked for permission to present a portrait (figure 4):

> My Dear Mr Mayor, – I beg leave to present to the Mayor and the Corporation of Manchester, the original portrait of Sir Thomas Potter, painted by William Bradley. The picture is at Mr. Agnew's, and I have given him directions to have it delivered when called for.
>
> I remain, my dear Sir,
Your obedient servant
John Brooks[1]

Thomas Potter, the portrait's subject, has featured in popular histories of the struggle for incorporation in Manchester and in academic studies of the relationship between dissenting religion, liberal politics and the formation of middle-class power. He was a cotton merchant, a Unitarian and a Liberal. He owned warehouses in the centre of Manchester, on Portland Street, and belonged to Cross Street Unitarian Chapel close by. He became the first mayor of Manchester, holding office from 1838 until 1840.

In 1842, Potter was no longer mayor but was still a member of the Borough Council. The point of the portrait was to honour him by its display in Council premises. The portrait painter, William Bradley, had been commissioned to produce an image that was appropriate as a presentation piece. Brooks's letter was only a formality. Potter's portrait was always going to be accepted; it was ready and waiting at Agnew's, to be 'delivered when called for'. As expected, the Council meeting agreed to receive the portrait and thanked Brooks, instructing the Town Clerk to 'transit a copy of this resolution inscribed on vellum'[2] to him. Writing on expensive paper is usually a sign that some kind of ceremony is coming to an end: the Council's reply concluded the formalities of portrait presentation.

Thomas Potter's portrait was the first to be presented to the Borough and

the exchange of letters, the written offer of a portrait soliciting its formal acceptance, established a procedure which was repeated as others followed. These
formalities served two purposes: to enable the Council to keep records of its
acquisitions and to ensure collective agreement about accepting a portrait of a
particular individual. Personal loyalty and political partisanship might motivate
portrait presentation but acceptance should be by the Council as a whole. The
ceremony, then, had a unifying function and its content became more elaborate
and formal, indeed more ritualistic, with time.

At a meeting on 23 October 1850, Manchester Borough Council
responded to a letter sent the day before about three portraits: of Alexander Kay
(figure 6), John Potter and W. B. Watkins (figure 7). Addressed to 'the Council
of the Borough', the letter began by announcing the 'great satisfaction' of its
signatories on the presentation of the three portraits. It continued:

> Of the services rendered to the borough by Mr Kay, as an active member of
> the Council, and especially during the two years in which he filled the office
> of Mayor; – by Mr Alderman Watkins, as both Chief Magistrate and for so
> many years one of your body; – and by our present worthy Mayor, whilst one
> of your number, and especially during the past two years, in which he has so
> worthily upheld the dignity of his office, and so efficiently discharged the
> responsible duties devolving upon him, it is quite unnecessary to speak.[3]

Despite this denial, the letter identified the reasons why portraits of Kay,
Potter and Watkins had been painted and were being presented. Each had held
office within the administration of Manchester: Kay and Potter were mayors
and Watkins a magistrate. Position was not all. Each had a quality for which
they were praised: Kay for activity, Potter for efficiency and Watkins for
longevity. They had demonstrated, in different ways, the capacity for work. The
completion of a period in office rendered them suitable portrait subjects, but
what was being valued in the painting was effective performance of public
work. Their portraits had been paid for, the letter explained, in order to show
that their 'services have been generally appreciated'.[4]

The letter was signed by ten men, who had commissioned the portraits,
together with a list of over a hundred who had subscribed to them. Six of the
ten, were, or had been, members of the Council and three of these (Elkanah
Armitage, James Kershaw, William Neild (figure 5)) were, or were about to
become, portrait subjects themselves. Thus portrait presentation appears as an
act of self-congratulation: Councillors commissioned images of themselves. Put
less cynically, individuals were acknowledged by the collective to which they
belonged and in doing so individual qualities were confirmed as collective
values. The portraits endorsed public work.

Once again, the meeting agreed to receive the portraits of Kay, Potter and
Watkins. The response, which followed procedure, was grateful acceptance. The
Council recorded its 'satisfaction' on their receipt and explained what its act of
acceptance meant:

> ... such portraits are accepted by this Council for the purpose of being placed
> within the Town Hall, and thereby testifying that the valuable services rendered
> by those gentlemen as members of the Municipal Body, and especially whilst

filling the office of Mayor, have been gratefully recognised, and also as a proof of the high estimation in which they are so deservedly held by their fellow citizens.[5]

While the formality of language seems insincere and consistent with the notion of ceremony as empty form, ceremonies should not be mistaken for mere formalities; they are ritual displays and the repetition of expected phrases is better understood as the enactment of a script. The procedural acceptance of a portrait at a Council meeting was a secular ritual which ensured that its subject was officially acknowledged. There is a simple symbolism at work here: the portrait image represents the individual.

A portrait must portray an individual otherwise it is not a portrait, just a picture. But this is too blunt. Joanna Woodall has provided a more precise definition in her introduction to a recent collection of critical essays on portraiture. She states: 'naturalistic portraiture [is] a physiognomic likeness which is seen to refer to the identity of the living or once-living person depicted'.[6] There are, then, two distinct functions of portraiture: it performs the work of resemblance and reference. A portrait offers an appearance of a body which is indicative of an identity; an external form refers to an internal entity. Reference in portraiture, Woodall explains, works on the ideological premise that an individual is constituted with a body and an identity which are attached but different from each other. Portraiture assumes a being with an outside and an inside; it articulates the idea of individualism. The operation of reference, therefore, is not a simple switch from body to identity, image to individual.

What has been also called into question is the individual as the object of reference. 'The portrait has no unproblematic referent', Marcia Pointon has argued, 'it cannot be explained as a correlative to the text of a subject's life.'[7] That an individual may not be the destination of signification unsettles the understanding of portraiture as a biographical form and sustains an argument about its wider work which, Pointon stated, is definition, 'in terms of class, rank and gender'.[8]

The issue of identity and the question of complexity of reference in imagery raised in art-historical work on portraiture are also themes of recent social histories which attend to, or have 'turned' to, language. Such histories, more specifically, use literature, examining fictional as well as documentary written forms. Visual forms are less evident in the expansion and revision of the social-history archive. A traditional aversion to art as a high, elite or dominant cultural practice may explain some absences but more important is that despite a similar concern with identity, one of its constitutive forms – biography – is positioned differently within the two disciplines. The point of departure for critical art histories of various kinds is the limitation that a biographical framework can impose on the interpretation of art. Biography, within social history, is considered more insightful and is deployed in an attempt to deal with the difficulties of analysing experience. The argument here, therefore, will be developed in relation to these current concerns of social history, although in some important respects it runs counter to them. It assumes that the historical formation of the bourgeoisie as a ruling class was being completed in the first half of the nineteenth century, and that their portrait images were constitutive of the success of their class formation. Portraiture is productive, effective and powerful. It is a form of power, a practice of confirming it, celebrating it and eliciting admiration for its holder.

THE COLLECTION AND THE COUNCIL

During the nineteenth century, the Council received, on behalf of the Borough, thirty-six portraits. All were in oil paint. By the first quarter of the twentieth century, oil painted portraits were being replaced by photographic ones. However, the subject of both media was the same: past mayors of Manchester. The entire collection is still held and housed by the city administration.

My concern here is with the formation of the collection and thus with the earliest portraits, in particular, the first twelve. Seven of the twelve were mayors of Manchester: Thomas Potter (figure 4), William Neild (figure 5), James Kershaw, Alexander Kay (figure 6), W. B. Watkins (figure 7), Elkanah Armitage (figure 8) and John Potter. The other five were their political friends and parliamentary allies: John Bright, Joseph Brotherton, Mark Philips, Charles James Stanley Walker and George Wilson. Brotherton and Philips were the first Members of Parliament (MPs) for Salford and Manchester respectively; Bright held a Manchester seat between 1847 and 1857; Walker was a Council member and Wilson was chairman of the Anti-Corn Law League. Some names are famous while others are less well-known, yet the twelve form a coherent historical group, linked by the location of their portraits.

The portraits hang in the so-called State Rooms in Manchester's Victorian-gothic Town Hall designed by Alfred Waterhouse and built in 1877 in Albert Square. Initially, the early ones hung in offices in King Street, the Council's first town hall and the only other location of its portrait collection. King Street and Albert Square are several hundred yards and a few roads apart. The portraits, then, have not moved very far and have always been housed in the same type of site: municipal buildings in Manchester's city centre.[9] Continuity of location is characteristic of a presentation collection. Since ownership is institutional, the images are unlikely to be exchanged and moved around after market transactions. The value of such collections derives, in part, from the fact that they are stationary. They define the history of the institution which they decorate and have both a material and an historical presence, depicting the people who once worked within the walls on which their portraits hang.

Manchester's Town Hall collection is treated as part of the fabric of the building. The collection is managed by a direct works department, Buildings Services, which is responsible for the security, structural maintenance and decorative order of the Town Hall as well as the arrangement of its furniture and furnishings. The portraits have not, then, been accorded any special status as art objects. Their oil paint and gilt frames indicate art, but they have not been subjected to the usual strategies of upkeep associated with the display of art in public buildings. The hanging of the collection depends upon the demands placed on municipal space and does not adhere to the deliberate organisation of art objects found inside public buildings dedicated to display, like museums.

Fig. 4 **William Bradley, *Thomas Potter*, 1842, Manchester Town Hall.**

Fig. 5 **Benjamin Rawlinson Faulkner,** *William Neild,* **1849, Manchester Town Hall.**

Fig. 6 George Patten, *Alexander Kay*, 1850, Manchester Town Hall.

Fig. 7 George Patten, *W. B. Watkins*, 1850, Manchester Town Hall.

Fig. 8 George Patten, *Elkanah Armitage*, 1852, Manchester Town Hall.

The portraits are neither classified nor labelled. They are not ordered nor are they purposefully lit or put behind glass. They have not been conspicuously displayed. They are just there in the building. The purpose of the building is not, of course, the upkeep of art but the administration of the city; the function of the Town Hall imposes conditions on how its portraits can be seen.

There are two ways to see the portraits: deliberately, as a Town Hall tourist, or almost accidentally, as one of its users. Manchester's councillors, Council workers, Council lobbyists, its political parties, trade unions and community groups use the rooms where the portraits hang. The State Rooms are regularly booked for political meetings and community purposes, when the portraits might be seen in the background or glanced at in a bored moment during a meeting, but viewing them is not the reason for entering the room. When the rooms are empty, tourists are free to wander in and focus their attention on the framed images on the walls. This is more like the intentional viewing in a museum except for the absence of information about the objects under scrutiny. There is no published catalogue, no leaflet to pick up, no floor plan to follow and no labels next to the portraits. The collection is not identified for viewing and its existence is not advertised. It is not easily accessible. Tourists are conspicuous in the corridors of the Town Hall and without signs inviting them to see the portraits, they may become lost and feel the burden of too much leisure in a place of work. Yet while the Town Hall collection is not arranged for viewing by visitors, it is public and was public from its inception. 'Public' is the condition of the collection regardless of whether it is easily accessible.

I need to define 'public' with some precision here in order to sustain it as a description of the Town Hall collection. The usual and official claim made about public institutions of all types is that they are open, enabling forms of freedom to be exercised within them. Yet, on entering a public building physical and social behaviour is actually very carefully regulated. Visitors to town halls, for example, are chiefly involved in two activities: walking and waiting. Corridors and anterooms are spaces set aside where visitors slowly move about or are supposed to be still. Barriers and signs clearly mark when access is denied. Routine business is protected from outside intrusions; town halls are public buildings which prohibit visitors from most of their interior. Providing access is not their primary purpose. Inviting visitors in is the expressed intention of other public institutions such as museums, libraries, parks and gardens. However, these places also contain parts which are closed off. Signs warn visitors away from the inner interior of museums and libraries. Even exterior public places, the outside space of parks and gardens, are no less prescriptive. Similar codes of conduct apply. Speed of movement is restricted and other forms of disorderly behaviour, making noise or spreading dirt, are either prevented by informal chastisement or official penalties. Freedom from restriction is not, therefore, a necessary feature of public places nor is openness a common characteristic. Public is more accurately identified as somewhere people arrive separately for the same purpose. The purpose is participation in an activity not primarily economically accumulative, although money might change hands in the form of taxes, fees or fines. Thus 'public' is social space where the activities which occur within it are managed and market transactions are excluded by some kind of state authority.

State-managed and market-driven activities have been cast in opposition as public and private. Within liberal theory, state and market are distinct spheres and in liberal practice there is a continuous attempt to separate the political from the profitable. But state and market do not lie either side of an interior–exterior line. The operations of both take place in public and both are spatially separate from a private domestic environment.[10] A gendered division between public and private is understood as fixed by the mid-nineteenth century while the state–market opposition is maintained only by an illusion of a pure political realm absent from personal gain, from private interest. Both separations, structural and imagined were used to legitimate bourgeois authority. Public status and political power accrued to those who could distance themselves from the private sphere and appear to act without regard for family or finance. Women, on the whole, could not qualify; their economic position was too dependent on family relationships. One of Jürgen Habermas's formulations of the public defined against the private provides a seductive summary at this point: 'The bourgeois public sphere may be conceived above all as the sphere of private people come together as a public.'[11]

I have argued that 'public' is the condition of the Manchester Town Hall collection and it can be understood as such in a number of ways. It is public because it belongs to a state authority and is located in one of its social spaces, somewhere outside the home but separate from the market. The content of the collection is also public; it contains 'private people who have come together to form a public'. In the period when the collection was formed, only men moved successfully from private to public and the portraits reflect this. The first twelve portray the fathers and capitalists who formed the first Borough Council in Manchester, private men who created a public institution and in doing so made political subjects of themselves.

Seven of the twelve were members of the first Borough Council in Manchester elected in December 1838 after Manchester's incorporation under the provisions of the 1835 Municipal Corporations Act. This Act is often understood as a codicil to the 1832 Reform Act but it was an important measure in its own right.[12] It provided for the replacement of existing corporations with councils elected on a ratepaying household suffrage qualified by three years residency and it allowed unincorporated urban centres, such as Manchester, to petition for a Charter of Incorporation. Once the Charter was granted, the reforms of the Act would apply.[13]

Until 1838 Manchester was 'subject to the jurisdiction of the county magistracy' with some degree of self-government through the 1829 Manchester and Salford Police Act.[14] Incorporation in Manchester, and the 1835 Municipal Corporations Act more generally, have been interpreted as either class or party measures: the political empowerment of the middle class in their industrial strongholds, or the consolidation of the Whig–Radical alliance in the recently created parliamentary seats; either a victory over the aristocracy or over the Tories. Gatrell's history of Manchester's incorporation argues the latter. A 'temporary resolution' of a 'feud' between the Tory High Church oligarchy and

the Liberal Dissenters, incorporation was a struggle structured by party affiliation which occurred within an urban middle class.[15] Contemporary accounts
allow new municipal government in Manchester greater historical significance.
Richard Cobden's 1837 pamphlet *Incorporate Your Borough*, depicted a struggle
between the aristocracy and the city. The former were invading pirates from
which the latter required protection in order that commercial freedoms and
political equalities, at least between wholesaler and retailer, could be
sustained.[16] Cobden exaggerated and Gatrell's carefully considered analysis is
more accurate. Yet, the heightened sense of historical struggle cannot be
explained away as melodramatic radicalism. The liberal *Manchester Guardian*
used terms similar to Cobden's. The paper described a popular victory over
feudalism. '[T]he inhabitants of this important and populous borough', it
announced, 'have made the first step towards ridding themselves of the old
feudal government under which they have laboured.'[17] Feudalism had not been
operationally in place for centuries and the aristocracy had been a capitalist class
for almost as long. The confusion of categories in contemporary accounts,
mixing Tories with aristocracy and aristocracy with feudalism, may have been
mistaken but was in fact testimony to the ideological success of the first Borough
Council. The implication was that incorporation was a class fight between the
city and an older economic system. The government of Manchester and the
representation of the middle class were seen as the same virtuous achievement.
Moreover, the sectional interests of the bourgeoisie were aligned with a larger
and more diverse middle class now unified as a municipality.

THE PORTRAITS

Thomas Potter's portrait (figure 4) is full-length and the framed canvas is large:
about 3 metres in height by 2 in width. The subject occupies its central space and
faces the viewer. His body is formally posed. His legs and feet are placed slightly
and diagonally apart, left in front of the right, with his weight on the latter. His
arms curve slightly and gently away from his body. His right arm is closest to his
body, almost hanging by his side with his hand holding a paper, perhaps a letter.
His left arm is raised to allow his forearm and hand to rest upon a stone column.
Potter's head is held straight; it is neither downcast nor upturned. His face shows
seriousness; he neither smiles nor sneers. His expression is quiet, representing
either the calmness that accompanies confidence rather than arrogance, or atten-
tiveness without subservience, and is probably intended to indicate both. Potter
looks directly out to meet his expected audience.

As the viewer considers the carefully composed figure of Manchester's first
mayor, some small signs of disorder intrude. Papers and quills are scattered on a
table covered with a red cloth and partially obscured by Potter's figure. These are
traces of interrupted activity, of work. They are part of the background but in fact
perform meaningful work, descriptive and symbolic. Things in use show a busy
man and papers are emblems of public office. Other parts of the background lend
themselves to a symbolic reading. The billowing baroque red plush curtain, the
colour of which, like that of the tablecloth, indicates high office and state power;

the column, upon which Thomas Potter appears to lean weightlessly, is also a symbol of political authority. The portrait combines signs of work with symbols of rule. Or rather, it inserts work into established conventions of state portraiture.[18]

There are a series of strategies in the portrait which attempt to establish the political legitimacy of the bourgeois subject as ruler. The portrait makes historical references which align him with older forms of authority while the expression and colour depart from the conventions of display used to portray his immediate aristocratic predecessors. The stone column is an obvious classical reference and the image as a whole has a classical gloss, the smooth finish of a statue. Most significantly, Thomas Potter's figure echoes classical form. His pose adheres to its basic principles: he is whole, erect and in proportion. As a portrait subject he is not simply still, composed so that he can be properly or fully seen, his body has been codified. His portrait painter, William Bradley, has borrowed an outline from the tradition of Roman portraiture in order to indicate an ideal ruler. His portrait is reminiscent of a Roman magistrate, although his body is more relaxed, it assumes the same shape. The arms and hands of a Roman subject are always expressive, used to show civic function or political power, and although Potter's are not forced into gesture, the significance of his hand holding a piece of paper seems to increase as the Roman reference is pursued. Classicism has been selectively used by Bradley, appropriated to enable his subject to appear as a contemporary inheritor of historical political power.

The most obvious contemporary signs are clothes. Potter is dressed almost entirely in black. His shirt, a small triangle visible on his upper chest, is white. But the rest is black: black shoes, black trousers, black waistcoat, black tail or frock coat, black cravat. A recent work by John Harvey traces the use of black clothes and the meaning of the darkly dressed male.[19] He observes that male dress gets darker after the first quarter of the nineteenth century and by mid-century black is the general fashion. With its universal use, its early meanings are altered. Black was the colour of death, loss, grief, humility, shame, sin, disease, pollution, danger. It kept its gravity in the mid-nineteenth century, it was still a serious colour, although no longer so dreadful, signifying abstinence more often than loss. Black becomes bourgeois moderation articulated against aristocratic sumptuary display and it had its own message of wealth. Harvey describes the black frock coat and black cravat as 'the dress of wealth and financial authority' which 'already carries, in its colour, associations of spirituality and spiritual power'.[20] The black clothes worn by many more of the Manchester Town Hall portrait subjects display the middle-class mix of materialism and religion.

There are two ways to interpret colour and clothing which conflict while at the same time they produce the same overall meaning for the portraits. One interpretation applies Harvey's account of black and assumes the portraits to depict clothes always worn. That black clothes are widely worn demonstrates the acceptance of middle-class values and is a sign of the persuasiveness of middle-class power. Catherine Hall and Leonore Davidoff have emphasised the political importance of clothing with a comparison particularly resonant for an interpretation of Manchester liberals. 'By the 1840s, the success of the middle-class challenge to aristocratic leadership', they write, 'was as clear in the standard of masculine dress as it was in the repeal of the Corn Laws.'[21]

The other interpretation places black within a tradition of portraiture rather than dress. Black is an element with white in a rational aesthetic of nineteenth-century male portraits. Their monotones repeat the colour scheme of seventeenth-century Dutch burgher portraiture and allude to an historical association between merchant and industrial subjects. Female portraits are, by contrast, colourful, aligning women with the aristocracy. 'This gendered difference', Joanna Woodall suggests, 'seems somewhat more exaggerated in portraiture than in surviving dress.'[22] For her, the colour of paint is more effective than that of fabric. While, there is a theoretical issue here about which practice (fashion or portraiture) and which person (sitter or artist) produced the most meaning, the power of the middle-class subject is secured either way.

ALWAYS THE SAME

The key representational strategies of Thomas Potter's portrait, clothing the body of a Roman ruler in the colour of capitalism, are repeated throughout the collection. It is, apart from two half-length portraits, made up of full-length front views. Subjects are positioned in the same way: they are placed in the middle of the 2 by 3 metre canvas. They appear, then, in a standard enlarged size. Framing considerations mean that they are the same height, but they also have the same body shape, somewhere between slim and portly. The reproduction of formal poses had a standardising effect. All subjects face front with their weight on one foot. Legs are slightly diagonally apart. Arms curve away from the body with arm actions that are asymmetrical. One hand usually holds or rests upon the documents which indicate office, the other is less expressive and allowed a more contemporary gesture. The look of calm independence recurs and heads are held straight, faces show quiet confidence, eyes meet the viewer directly. And they all wear bourgeois black. In sum, the men in Manchester Town Hall always look the same. Their portraits are 'varied clichés', to apply a term used to describe Roman state portraits whose images 'published the official appearance of the ruler'.[23] The Manchester Town Hall portraits perform the same function.

There are limited variations within the overall scheme of sameness. Some figures are more conspicuously and classically posed than others. Benjamin Rawlinson Faulkner's portrait of William Neild (figure 5), Manchester's second mayor, has stuck quite close to an ancient form and used a Greek rather than Roman source. Neild's appearance derives from the *Apollo Belvedere*. Others are more contemporary. One completely contemporary gesture is allowed in the case of John Bright. John Prescott Knight's portrait displays him with folded arms. He appears more impatient and more independent than the other subjects. That he was an MP of reputation rather than a Borough councillor may have given him more control over the making of his image; but if so, he had only a limited influence for his image conforms to the conventional format in all other respects.

Such variations, small inconsistencies within the same scheme, could be explained by referring to the portrait painter, to his training in portraiture or development of his artistic style. Four painters produced the first twelve portraits: William Bradley, Benjamin Rawlinson Faulkner, John Prescott Knight and George Patten. Bradley and Faulkner were self-taught Manchester-based portrait painters who could be termed artisans. Prescott Knight and Patten were both Royal Academicians whose reputations were based on institutional presentation portraits. Prescott Knight was a prominent London painter and Patten had practices based in London and Liverpool. But far more striking than any variations that could be associated with the individuality of the artist or sitter are the similarities in the portraits no matter who was actually responsible for them. Compare William Bradley's Thomas Potter (figure 4) and George Patten's Elkanah Armitage (figure 8). Apart from a chair which has replaced a pillar, everything is pretty much the same.

The sameness of the portraits did not go unnoticed at the time. One nineteenth-century critic singled out seven portraits by George Patten for comment. 'There is very little', he opened in the Manchester journal, *The Sphinx*, 'to be said for these portraits':

> They are of the most stereotyped kind; very fair likenesses no doubt, reasonably correct in drawing, harmless in colour, but utterly devoid of force or individuality, and amusing for the sameness of their design and accessories. In fact taking the portraits all round, it is remarkable how little invention is shown. There are so many identical table-cloths, so many tables with parchments on them, and so may editions of what, at all events, looks like the same curtain. It is the same with the attitudes. Sir John Potter has his hand on a table, with parchments; Sir E Armitage has his hand on a chair; Mr Alexander Kay has his hand on a table, so has Mr WB Watkins, so has Mr Mark Philips (but without parchment this time, for a wonder), and so, no doubt, would Messrs George Wilson and Charles Walker, but being only half-lengths, they have not the opportunity.[24]

The Sphinx called itself a journal of criticism and humour; it was a satirical magazine, a provincial *Punch*. Its review of the Town Hall portraits was not necessarily a serious assessment of their artistic merit, never mind their social purpose. The anonymous art critic's comments are callously put, but he does have a point. There is no doubt that the portraits conform to a type. The problem is not that they are unlike their subjects. In fact, our critic concedes that they are accurate images of the sitters: 'correct in drawing' and achieving 'fair likenesses'. His praise only for technical competence probably intentionally points to the absence of originality: 'little invention is shown' and the portraits were anyway 'devoid of force or individuality'. Therefore, according to him, the images resemble their subjects without showing strength and character. They represent individuals but are not expressions of their individuality. The implication of *The Sphinx* piece is that sameness is a problem of artistic practice.

Of course, the men in the portraits may look the same because they are. The twelve subjects have an historical profile which was once caricatured so often that its actual existence is now in danger of being overlooked in the search for complexity of class structure. These are the bourgeoisie; they are urban industrial capitalists operating in the textile sector. Most were cotton manufacturers or cotton merchants: the Potters, Joseph Brotherton, James Kershaw, Mark Philips and John Bright. William Neild was a calico printer and George Wilson a starch manufacturer. There were two professional men: Alexander Kay and W. B. Watkins. The religious and political affiliations of the twelve were the proper historical match for their economic interests. These were the liberal dissenters who organised the incorporation of Manchester and who initiated, or at least supported, the Anti-Corn Law League. All were members of the League and some were among its most important advocates.

The precise forms of dissenting liberal politics are not as uniform as the portraits might suggest. Unitarians and Quakers are dominant and party ranged from Radical through Liberal to Whig. Division is highlighted in the opposition of John Potter and John Bright who contested the same Manchester parliamentary seat in 1857. Political division and religious difference are smoothed out in the similar poses, but all is not the work of representation. Location has a part. The collection is constituted by its enclosure in the Town Hall. The basis for coherence is presentation to the Borough and acceptance by the Council. Its politics determined the limits of division and difference. The Council established itself in the absence of, and in opposition to, Toryism and the high established Church. It was a liberal institution which looked after the bourgeois interest. Perhaps, therefore, all that the portraits display is the actual or real relationship among political affiliation, economic position and appearance. They look the same because they share the same historical subjectivity. However, I cannot quite endorse this argument, because it takes no account of the representational power of the portraits. I want to conclude by offering two accounts of sameness which recognise relationships between social structures, political institutions and aesthetic practices and examine how such relations have given forms.

It should be noted that sameness is a characteristic of civic portraiture and is not a peculiar feature of the collection in Manchester Town Hall. Sameness detracts from the status of civic portraiture as art. All portraiture viewed as a sign of the sitter rather than of the work of the artist is problematically positioned between an historical document and an aesthetic object. The possibilities of being art rather than deploying artistic skill are reduced by sameness; a portrait within a civic collection is not exceptional enough and presents the problem of seeing significant detail in a repeating pattern. Seeing the always expected has a dulling effect. John Berger, however, has argued that civic portraits are typical of portraiture. 'If one is considering portraiture as a genre, it is no good thinking of a few extraordinary pictures', he claims, 'but rather of the endless portraits of the local nobility and dignitaries in countless provincial museums and town halls.'[25] Endless is opposed to extraordinary and only the extraordinary is art. Its conventionally essential quality is uniqueness which is understood as the effect of individual expression. Berger observed that painting a portrait rarely turned into an expression of individuality (either the artist's or the subject's) because that was not the intention. The purpose of a portrait was not to portray an individual but to position its subject. The 'satisfaction' of portraiture, which we should remember was the emotion expressed when Manchester's Town Hall portraits were offered and accepted, was 'the satisfaction of being personally recognised and confirmed in one's position'. According to Berger, social position is privileged over individual identity. 'The function of portrait painting was to underwrite and idealise a chosen social role for the sitter . . . it was not to present him as "an individual" but, rather, as an individual monarch, bishop, landowner, merchant.'[26] Thus, successful portraiture represents an individual who can be recognised as a type. It produces some differences as well as sameness within them. Broad typologies distinguish rank (a monarch set above a bishop) and class (a landowner is set against a merchant).

Charlotte Townsend-Gault also argues that absence of individuality is characteristic of portraiture which she calls 'official', but insists that this should not be interpreted as a problem of art since it is the basis of the power of portraits as representations. They are 'eminently satisfactory symbolic expressions', she claims, 'not of the nature of the individual sitter, but of the institution which endorsed it'.[27] Civic portraiture is easily recognised in the larger official category. It shares its fundamental features: the composed figure, dark hues, glossy surface, gilt frame. Official portraits are the same and sameness is an effect of institutional power. Overarching authority is assumed by Townsend-Gault: 'The portraits are controlled, at all stages of their realisation, by the institution.' Subject, artist, site and access are selected by its procedures ensuring that any particular values can be preserved.[28]

Townsend-Gault and Berger point to different causes of the same thing. For her, it is an institutional representation. For him, it is the artist who fitted an individual into a predictable social type. Both accounts are relevant to the collection in Manchester's Town Hall, where class attributes and institutional ideology are collapsed into each other. Bourgeois characteristics are presented as qualities appropriate for good government in Manchester. Commitment to public work is naturalised by and through the collection as the necessary desire of a ruling body. The work of the collection is reinforced with each portrait because all are the same. Sameness is a visual demonstration of unity within, and continuity of, both the bourgeoisie and the Borough Council.

NOTES

This work is the outcome of a cataloguing project of the nineteenth-century portraits in Manchester Town Hall funded by a Paul Mellon Research Fellowship at the University of Manchester in 1994. Professor Marcia Pointon, who initiated the project, gave the work direction in its early stages. It also benefited from discussions at the 'History of the British Middle Classes' Conference at the Manchester Metropolitan University in 1996 and with its organisers and the editors of this collection since. Any errors are mine.

1 Minutes of Manchester Borough Council Meetings, Manchester Central Library, p. 84.

2 *Ibid.*, p. 85.

3 *Ibid.*, pp. 225–6. *Kay, Watkins* and *Potter* were respectively the fifth, sixth and seventh portraits to be presented to the Manchester Borough Council. Those presented after Thomas Potter's and before these three were *William Neild* by Benjamin Rawlinson Faulkner in 1849, *Joseph Brotherton* by William Bradley in the same year and *James Kershaw* also by Bradley in 1850.

4 *Ibid.*, p. 226.

5 *Ibid.*, p. 228.

6 J. Woodall, *Portraiture: Facing the Subject* (Manchester, Manchester University Press, 1997), p. 1

7 M. Pointon, *Hanging the Head: Portraiture and Social Formation in Eighteenth Century England* (Yale, Yale University Press, 1993), p. 4

8   *Ibid.*, p. 4

9   There are a few exceptions. *George Wilson* by George Patten is unlocated as is John Prescott Knight's portrait of Joseph Heron, Manchester's first Town Clerk, presented in 1870. Three portraits are on long term loan to Manchester's City Art Gallery: *Lord Strange* by Edward Penny, presented in 1852, and Samuel William Reynolds's half-lengths of Thomas and Richard Potter, both presented in 1859.

10 C. Pateman, 'The fraternal social contract', in J. Keane (ed.), *Civil Society and the State: New European Perspectives* (London, Verso, 1988), p. 102.

11 J. Habermas, *The Structural Transformation of the Public Sphere: An Inquiry into a Category of Bourgeois Society* (Oxford, Polity Press, 1989), p. 27.

12 D. Fraser, *Power and Authority in the Victorian City* (Oxford, Basil Blackwell, 1979), pp. 9–11.

13 *Ibid.*, p. 5

14 V. A. C. Gatrell, 'Municipal reform and the pursuit of liberal hegemony in Manchester 1790–1839', in D. Fraser (ed.), *Municipal Reform and the Industrial City* (Leicester, Leicester University Press, 1982), p. 22.

15 *Ibid.*, p. 23.

16 Extracts from *Incorporate Your Borough* are quoted at length in Gatrell, 'Municipal reform', pp. 48–50, and in Fraser, *Power and Authority*, p. 17.

17 Quoted in A. Redford, *The History of Local Government in Manchester*, 3 vols (London, Longmans, 1940), 3, p. 9.

18 Woodall, *Portraiture*, p. 22. She notes the 'association of the full-length format with images of sovereigns' from the sixteenth century and the introduction from this time of a 'visual repertoire' in state portraiture which included chairs and curtains.

19 J. Harvey, *Men in Black* (London, Reaktion Books, 1995).

20 *Ibid.*, pp. 14–15.

21 L. Davidoff and C. Hall, *Family Fortunes: Men and Women of the Middle Class 1780–1850* (London, Hutchinson, 1987) p. 410.

22 Woodall, *Portraiture*, p. 5.

23 R. Brilliant, *Gesture and Rank in Roman Art* (Connecticut, Connecticut Academy of Arts and Sciences, 1963), p. 195.

24 *The Sphinx: A Journal of Criticism and Humour*, 3 (1869), p. 35.

25 J. Berger, 'No more portraits', in P. Barker (ed.), *Arts in Society* (London, Fontana, 1977), p. 47.

26 *Ibid.*, pp. 47–8

27 C. Townsend-Gault, 'Symbolic facades: official portraiture in British institutions since 1920', *Art History*, 11:4 (1988), 512.

28 *Ibid.*, 512 and 515.

7

'THOROUGHLY EMBUED WITH THE SPIRIT OF ANCIENT GREECE': SYMBOLISM AND SPACE IN VICTORIAN CIVIC CULTURE
Kate Hill

> My good Yorkshire friends, you asked me down here among your hills that I might talk to you about this Exchange you are going to build . . . I do not care about this Exchange – because you don't . . . But you think you may as well have the right thing for your money. You know there are a great many odd styles of architecture about; you don't want anything ridiculous; you hear of me, among others, as a respectable architectural man-milliner; and you send for me, that I may tell you the leading fashion; and what is, in our shops, for the moment, the newest and sweetest thing in pinnacles.[1]

Thus ran a lecture delivered by Ruskin in the Town Hall, Bradford, and published in 1866. However, it is the contention of this essay that Ruskin had misinterpreted the aims and intentions of provincial elites in improving their towns, particularly in the creation of civic buildings and, through this, an idea of the civic. They were not simply, carelessly, trying to get the best value for money. Victorian civic buildings, though implemented by architects and designers, were the expression of a particular vision of the city and its citizens. Moreover, civic architecture was used in such a way as to separate the elite from the rest of the town, and to enhance their status within the town itself and in relation to the rest of the country. In showing this it will also be suggested that the analysis of discourse, rhetoric and narrative needs to be situated within an examination of the way in which discourse was used, and the way in which control of the arenas of discourse limited its use.[2]

The second half of the nineteenth century saw an expansion, on a dramatic though usually uneven scale, of the powers, responsibilities and roles of municipal government.[3] Many aspects of this expansion have already been thoroughly investigated,[4] but there has been less coverage of the civic and cultural aspects of town and city councils.[5] These new civic amenities were symbolically loaded. They constituted an encoded vision of the ideal city and the ideal citizen. It was not, however, a universal vision, but one deployed by the elite of the municipality. How far was this vision realised? It is frequently summarised as 'civic pride', but I would like to explore some of the associated ideas and issues involved here further.

Broadly, I want to make two points. First, it is useful to look at civic culture and the rhetoric surrounding it as constituting a text, a discourse on the meaning of the city, presenting it as a spiritual legacy from the ancient world, and stressing the inheritance of that civilisation, and of the responsibilities attendant upon it.[6] In fact, one can even discern the development of a specific myth of historicity and progress being linked to the provincial urban environment, in opposition to the metropolis and other loci of a traditional elite. Secondly, an examination of the use of space reveals attempts to limit and control the behaviour that was possible within the civic complex and to disseminate new ideals of citizenship through civic institutions.[7] In this way the change from private institutions to public ones was engineered so as to retain middle-class control and dominance.[8]

However, middle-class hegemony has been described as fragile.[9] The elite were not able to eliminate challenges to their concept of the 'civic' altogether because of their invocation of the principles of universality and democracy, and were forced to negotiate with both lower-middle-class groups, who wanted a smaller, more 'respectable' civic sphere, and working-class groups, who wanted a civic sphere more attuned to their wishes, and less to their perceived needs.[10]

This chapter will concentrate on municipalities where civic improvement was consciously and enthusiastically undertaken as it is in these places that the most revealing public debates and rhetoric are to be found. Liverpool and Birmingham are obvious examples; Liverpool obtained no less than nine Improvement Acts between 1858 and 1883, and Birmingham was home to the most prominent exponents of the 'municipal gospel' from about 1860. Preston has also been examined, as a smaller town that redeveloped its civic centre later, and with more conflict. Central government legislation tended to provide for upkeep of amenities only through the rates, and so councils were generally dependent for their larger projects on bequests and donations from wealthy citizens, who thus became important leaders and initiators of civic improvement. Initially, therefore, we can examine the characteristics of benefactors and councillors, civic leaders in a broad sense. Examples of benefactors include Richard Tangye, manufacturer, who donated to Birmingham Art Gallery and Museum; William Brown, merchant, who donated the site and building for the Liverpool Museum; Edmund Harris, lawyer, who bequeathed a very large sum of money for charitable projects in Preston; and Richard Newsham, who donated his art collection to Preston Council. For some of these we can scrutinise their own avowed motives for their donations; and they are overtly utilitarian. Civic benefactors, however, also presented their actions in terms of democracy, intellectual and spiritual improvement, and of the town or city as a transcendent social organisation that could take humanity to a higher state of being. Thus Richard Tangye, writing about his gift to Birmingham of a building for the Art Gallery and his donation to a School of Art, pointed first to the lack of facilities for 'the artisans of Birmingham' to study good practice in art and design compared to other European countries, but added that 'in no town in England has there been such an advance in everything that tends to raise the intellectual level and to elevate the taste of every class, and the inhabitants of Birmingham, whether they are native born or "adopted sons", feel that they are indeed "citizens of no mean city"'.[11] The will of Richard Newsham read:

> If we of this generation were ardent mainly in mercantile pursuits, we also felt, and shared in some degree, the loftier passion for beauty and knowledge, and

set store on those things which embellish life, give present dignity to communities, and furnish, as all history teaches, their most enduring title to be held
in future remembrance and good fame.[12]

A second point to be made about such civic benefactors is that they were
commonly involved in local government, and moreover tended to be enthusiastic advocates of improvement in the council. For example, Tangye was
energetically involved in Birmingham Council's educational work.[13] So their
more spectacular donations can be seen as an extension of existing interests in
local improvement.

In Birmingham, the expansion of the municipal sphere led to an increase
in the status of councillors, peaking in 1890.[14] In Liverpool and Preston, this
pattern was not followed; there seems to have been a drop in the average social
status of councillors in the second half of the nineteenth century.[15] However, on
those committees which dealt with amenities such as parks, libraries and town
halls, high average social status seems to have been maintained.[16] The involvement of people such as the Tangyes, wealthy successful manufacturers with
Liberal leanings, may be viewed as typical of the kind of councillors who became
concerned with the improvement and creation of a set of civic buildings.
However, what characterises these high-status councillors on certain committees is that all political, religious and occupational groups are represented. In
Preston, it is noticeable that lawyers and cotton-mill owners are present in about
equal numbers, and in Liverpool, merchants share the committees with architects, lawyers and a few manufacturers. Of course, one would on the whole
expect this, and expect that members of the lower middle class, being generally
more hostile to municipal spending, would not sit on committees devoted to
creating and maintaining huge demands on the municipal purse. Within this
broad picture, professionals became increasingly important over time. Lawyers
particularly seem to have been heavily and increasingly involved with civic
improvement.[17] If any conclusions can be drawn from a study of those involved
in civic undertakings, then, it is that they formed the elite of the urban environment, they were concerned with practical improvements, but also they
wanted to advance their claims, as a group, to being cultured and civilised.

This is further confirmed if we turn to an analysis of the discourses
produced around the idea of the civic. The rhetoric surrounding the creation of
a civic culture focuses on several interrelated narratives or symbolic images of
the town. First, there is the town or city as a descendant of the city-states of the
ancient and Renaissance worlds. This is a very potent and pervasive metaphor
and can be seen in a good example from Liverpool, where an influential advocate of town improvement wrote:

> The commercial cities of antiquity, Carthage, Tyre, Palmyra, Alexandria,
> erected magnificent monuments, many of which remain to this day, to attest
> their greatness. The cities of the Middle-Age commerce, Venice, Florence,
> and Genoa, expended their wealth in vying with each other in adorning their
> cities in the spirit of honourable rivalry ... The inhabitants of the modern
> Tyre are not called on to make those heroic efforts which the citizens of
> former times were.[18]

Of course this was particularly appropriate for a commercial city like Liverpool, but was not restricted to it. In Birmingham too, civic promoters referred to 'the glories of Florence, and of other cities of Italy in the Middle Ages, and suggest[ed] that Birmingham too might become the home of a noble literature and art'.[19] Joseph Chamberlain spoke of the city-states of medieval Belgium, Germany and Italy, and how their independent burghers had 'left behind them magnificent palaces and civic buildings – testimonies to their power and public spirit and munificence'.[20] Preston's new Town Hall, it was claimed, would 'vie with the much admired civic palaces of Belgium'.[21] This theme is important because it glorifies local, democratic self-government and positions it in opposition to tyranny, implying a self-governing community rather than national government, or government by landed oligarchy, thus serving to enhance the power base of local councillors.[22] Simultaneously, democracy could by definition be limited to male householders. A tradition of local self-government, however, as Vernon has shown, did not necessarily preclude the existence of other traditions such as an aristocratic one.[23]

Hence, there is a presentation of commerce as glorious, honourable and noble, and as inextricably linked with magnificent and lasting architecture and civic virtue. Other forms of urban money-making, especially industry, are similarly represented, if somewhat apologetically, as an important foundation for civic greatness. The foundation stone of Birmingham Museum and Art Gallery is inscribed: 'By the Gains of Industry We Promote Art'. This discourse emphasised the spiritual nobility of a town, however individuals made their livings, and placed these towns firmly as inheritors of western civilisation. It was said of the building for the Harris Free Public Library, Museum and Art Gallery in the *Preston Guardian* of 1892 that 'The architect [coincidentally a councillor and chairman of the Free Public Library Committee] has been thoroughly embued with the spirit of ancient Greece when that country had reached the high-water mark of its civilisation.'[24] A further theme was the universal access to civic amenities, stressing the organic wholeness of the city.[25] In Liverpool it was said of the Corporation, 'they have uniformly resisted the idea of catering for any particular class in a great public institution'.[26]

At the same time as the ancient inheritance of civic culture was stressed, its forward-looking modernity was heavily emphasised. It was rational and progressive. Sir William Forwood spoke in Liverpool in 1907 of his ideas for a huge kind of civic education complex, comprising university, libraries, museums and art galleries, where a centre for literary and scientific advances could be developed. He was speaking at the opening of the museum extension, and maintained that such new buildings promoted 'public morality as well as the material prosperity of the people'.[27] In Birmingham too, J. T. Bunce, writing under the significant heading 'Progress and Spirit of Municipal Work', spoke of 'a deeper sense of responsibility, a higher tone and quality of debate, a fuller capacity for public work, and an increase of dignity, in keeping with the augmentation of powers and the advancing importance of the town' since 1850.[28] Leadership was being identified with a set of responsibilities towards the populace of a town, primarily to educate them in ideals of citizenship. So Thomas Greenwood, asking in 1888 'Why Should Every Town Have a Museum and Library?', gave the answers: 'Because a Museum and Free Library are as necessary for the mental and moral health of the citizens as good sanitary arrangements [and] because the existence or absence of a Museum and Free Library in a town is a standard of the intelligence and public spirit manifested in that town.' He stressed the responsibility of civic leaders and went on to argue that libraries and museums 'deepen the sense of the duties and privileges of citizenship', focusing on the improvement of the rest of society.[29]

This can usefully be seen in terms of the construction of industry and commerce as a romantic narrative, as examined by Nenadic and Joyce. Nenadic shows how important such narratives could be even where manufacturers were not particularly numerically significant.[30] Joyce's analysis of the themes and structure of such romances is, on the whole, borne out by the development of the civic sphere charted here, as well as in the educational institutions he examines. Modernity and progress were embodied in the commitment to improving public morality, the level of culture and civic responsibility. We can see the same discursive link being forged between commerce and industry on the one hand, and science, learning and art on the other, that Joyce finds in the *Proceedings* of the Manchester Athenaeum.[31]

Yet the invocation of the past in the romance of commerce is, I would argue, much greater than has previously been made clear.[32] Commerce and industry were simultaneously paving the way to a more cultured, civilised and progressive future guaranteed or vouched for by their connection with the transcendent greatness of classical, medieval and Renaissance civilisation. This may be interpreted as an appropriation of the past from those who had used it to attack commerce, industry and even democracy. It was a rejection of the distinction between utility and the spiritual, the new and the old, which had been developed by, among others, Ruskin, who described fondness for the new as originating in 'selfishness, shallowness and deceit', and as 'the result of everything being made a matter of trade'.[33] The discourse of civic culture as put forward in Liverpool, Birmingham and similar places, reintegrated these dislocated concepts. As was fitting for commercial and industrial towns, utility, progress, the new, the practical were valorised; but this did not mean rejection of the ancient, the spiritual, the purely intellectual. As Dellheim has argued in a more general context, progress and continuity were balanced.[34] The opposites were reconciled in an overarching romance, that of the town or city. If humanity was transcending its limitations by means of art, science, trade, industry, democracy and public life, this was, and had always been, a result of the urban environment, which brought out and nurtured the best human qualities.

This brings us back to the rhetoric surrounding the construction of new civic buildings. Underlying this was a sense of the city as the ideal form of social organisation, which to a certain extent had transcendent, even spiritual qualities. Thus it is that the architectural styles adopted not only invoked the past, but utilised, to a greater or lesser degree, the sacred idioms of the temple and the cathedral.

The qualities of the citizen that would be produced by such a civic culture were appropriate for the ideal city: male, rational, 'active', self-improving and valuing knowledge, especially of art and science, that could be put to use in commerce and manufacture.[35] This citizen conducted his business in public, ordered spaces and believed in progress. Tony Bennett has suggested that the aim of nineteenth-century museums was to create an identity of universal citizenship while simultaneously differentiating the population, and this may be extended to much of the civic redevelopment.[36] It was achieved through differential access to 'civic' space.

The sense of citizenship and of the behaviour appropriate to a citizen was to be instilled by enhancing and emphasising the dignity of the municipality. As Chamberlain said in 1874:

> I have an abiding faith in municipal institutions, an abiding sense of the value and importance of local self-government, and I desire therefore to surround them by everything which can mark their importance, which can show the place they occupy in public estimation and respect, and which can point to their great value to the community ... It behoves us to find a fitting habitation for our local Parliament.[37]

It becomes clear that architecture was the primary means by which a new kind of civic culture, for the brave new city-state, was to be achieved. Architecture came very much to be seen as testifying to the moral worth of the culture that produced it.[38] Rebuilt city centres were linked by their monumentality, to show the importance and respect due to the municipality.[39] The architect of the Harris building spoke of the need for a noble building in a prominent site, and said that: 'Such a disposition will give external dignity and importance to the structure, and indeed is required to prevent its domination by the neighbouring Town Hall.'[40] In Liverpool and Preston the dominant style for civic buildings was classical; in Birmingham Gothic, especially Ruskinian Gothic, was more prominent.[41] Although it has been argued that Gothic architecture was generally aligned with Tory circles in the mid-nineteenth century, and classical with Liberal, at the municipal level at least this was not the case.[42] Birmingham Council was largely Liberal throughout its period of municipal building, and in Liverpool a Tory majority was secure for all but nine years of the second half of the nineteenth century.[43] What mattered was that the style of architecture made plain the municipality's inheritance of the legacy of the city-state, either classical or medieval/Renaissance. Both embodied the virtues of self-government, democracy, and high civilisation founded on commerce and manufacture, as well as the spiritual, transcendent qualities suggested by the cathedral and temple idioms.

Moreover, the new city centre was ideally extremely spacious, allowing and encouraging the citizen to behave as a model of public virtue while going about his public duties and pleasures.[44] In Liverpool the library, museum and art gallery complex, opposite St George's Hall, was built where slum housing had formerly stood, and James Picton spoke of new wide streets bringing 'health and salubrity to the abodes of disease, and converting the foulest blot on the town's escutcheon into a means of usefulness and adornment'. It was also felt to be necessary to open up the town to enable the free flow of commerce through it.[45] This is reminiscent both of the kind of language surrounding and preceding Haussmann's remodelling of Paris, with a vocabulary of hygiene, and also of

Sennett's analysis of this remodelling as a coercive use of space, where new roads are provided to carry high volume, high speed traffic into and out of the city, fragmenting and blocking off poor districts.[46] It was as if the movement of commerce was being privileged above the movement of people and the new central civic areas were intended for model citizens. Through the movement of traffic, and the opening up of civic space, individualised citizens were distinguished from the teeming, unimproved inhabitants of the slums.

So in the discourse or narrative that was developed and expressed in the construction of a civic sphere, both symbolism and space were deployed to reinvent the notions of the city, the citizen, and the links between commerce and industry and civilisation. This was, moreover, a reinvention that took issue with a traditional intellectual interpretation of ancient civilisations, and one that asserted the claims of provincial cities over the metropolis as the seat of the virtues of ancient civilisations. Yet this was not merely a discourse embodied in buildings and rhetoric; it formed town centres which were used daily by a variety of citizens, and thus it is appropriate to examine questions of access and control. The issue of class becomes clear in the way the civic actually worked. The uses made of the new civic buildings most clearly reveal the middle-class elite's symbolic ownership of them. First of all, it is striking just how full they were of busts and portraits of local notables. In 1869 a statue of Joseph Mayer and a bust of William Rathbone were installed in Liverpool Museum;[47] and in 1907 Sir W. E. M. Tomlinson, Member of Parliament for Preston, presented a picture of himself to the Harris Library, Museum and Art Gallery.[48] The various new buildings and extensions to them gave ample opportunity for numerous ceremonial occasions, with endless dinners, speeches and conversazioni, exhaustively reported in the local press and recorded for posterity in ornate scrapbooks. In Liverpool alone we have the opening of the Public Library and Museum in 1861, at which speeches were given by members of all the learned and commercial societies, the opening of the Walker Art Gallery in 1877, the opening of the Picton Reading Room in 1880 and the opening of the Museum Extension Galleries in 1906. Invariably a special committee was set up to make the arrangements for the ceremonial opening.[49]

The new civic buildings were also very important in providing a meeting place for the various learned societies of respective towns and cities. Since in several instances, museums and art galleries were formed from the nucleus of Literary and Philosophical Societies' collections, the continuation of this other function is not very surprising, but the relationship between civic institutions and voluntary societies was changing.[50] By the 1900s, not only were local societies holding meetings in civic buildings, but so also were larger organisations, like the British Medical Association (annual meeting in the Harris building, Preston, 1913) and the Association of Chambers of Commerce (annual meeting in the Liverpool Museum, 1907).[51] Generally one of the council sub-committee concerned was a member of the organisation holding its meeting in a civic building. Guardianship brought with it privilege; the elite who were carrying out the duties and responsibilities of a civic leadership were also entitled to reap some reward. Thus the population of the urban democracy was differentiated as either providers or receivers of civic culture.

Members of the middle-class male elite used civic institutions as an extension of their own social arena, for mutual appreciation and convenience, and to consolidate their own class or group identity. Other groups in society were allowed in freely, but not on the same terms: they were only to absorb lessons in municipal citizenship while there, lessons which were firmly middle-class in origin.[52] Civic space was available on different terms and for different functions for different sections of society. The rhetoric of universal access was balanced in practice by exclusion and exclusivity in the social uses of the civic. There are some signs that access to civic space was a contested issue, although the nature of the evidence tends to obscure any conflict; and of course the winners tended to be the elite, who could suppress the traces of opposition. Certainly within municipal museum and art-gallery buildings, ordinary visitors were inclined to use the space for socialising and promenading, as well as, if not instead of, self-improvement. In Liverpool it was reported that 'increasing numbers of young people continue to visit the museum on Monday evenings for the purpose of promenading and conversation rather than for the inspection of the objects exhibited'. The authorities took a strict line with such frivolity and stopped Monday evening opening until a suitable educational tone re-established itself.[53]

The very development of a civic culture itself was not uncontested. Liverpool, Birmingham and Preston all had vigorous ratepayer lobbies. In Liverpool, they managed to hold the Library and Museum Rate at one penny in the pound up to the end of the nineteenth century (it was at least twopence in the pound in most comparable towns).[54] There were alternative attempts to create public amenities – for example, in Preston in the 1850s a Working Men's Committee raised £476 4s 6d towards the setting up of a free public library and museum.[55] Yet without middle-class support, which was generally unforthcoming, working men were unable to fund the project. The middle class had effectively prevented them from gaining a stake in the civic arena. When the library and museum were set up in Preston, decades later, it was with such a large capital, around £100,000, that the working-men's fund of a few hundred pounds was a mere drop in the ocean.[56]

Because of its relatively small size, Preston shows the challenges and negotiations in the civic sphere particularly clearly. In 1902 the Operative Cotton Spinners Society forwarded a resolution to the Free Public Library Committee, that the Library, Museum and Art Gallery be open on Sundays, because 'such opening would be of advantage to the whole of the municipality'.[57] They took on the rhetoric of municipal well-being and responsibility and used it against the Council. The narratives surrounding the progressive city gave them the opportunity to challenge civic leaders on their own terms: democracy, universal access, self-improvement and so on. In the months following this, more resolutions were forwarded. Labour groups were in favour of Sunday opening, church groups, naturally, against.[58] As well as a straightforward issue of Sabbatarianism, this seems to be a clash also in ideals of citizenship, with the more autonomous working-class organisations opposing the Council's view. Within the Free Public Library Committee itself, it was swiftly resolved not to open on Sundays. But in the Council as a whole, the issue was reopened (though defeated) by

H. Cartmell, a 'Progressive', one of a group of employers and professionals from the distant suburbs who favoured a bigger role for the Council.[59]

In 1904 Sunday opening was re-examined, with the Independent Labour Party forwarding a resolution in favour passed at a meeting in the marketplace. This time the Library Committee resolved to open for two hours on Sundays, and despite letters against such an opening from a few church groups, the resolution was upheld in the full Council. Significantly, by 1904 there were now two Labour councillors.[60] So in this instance, although working-class groups could legitimately argue for Sunday opening in terms of the very discourse used by civic leaders, they could only carry their case once they had already achieved a position of greater power in local government. And, despite the fact that civic leaders on the council avowed an ideal of universal access and democracy, this was not necessarily Council policy.

In 1894 a special meeting of Preston's Library Committee took place to consider the question of the exhibition of a reproduction of Michelangelo's *David*. Six members of the committee objected to the public display of nudity and succeeded in having the *David* removed to a remote upper room, rather than prominently displayed in the ground-floor hall leading to the reading rooms as it had been.[61] It would appear that universal access to the art of ancient civilisations was not always and by everyone believed to lead to self-improvement, citizenship and higher public life. In this case, it is not possible to identify any common links in the groups opposing and supporting the change, but the division would appear to have been *among* the middle-class elite.

All this indicates considerable variations in ideas of what the civic arena should be. The idea of the civic as grand, imposing and embodying the best in classical civilisation was challenged by the ideal of economy and minimum government, by the ideal of respectability and high moral tone, and by the ideal of truly universal access and utility. These kinds of disputes could be found anywhere, though in the larger municipality of Liverpool there was already a greater emphasis on universality, more concern with including the working class, which may have forestalled some conflict.[62] It seems to be the case, though, that the various lobbies put forward their case in the rhetoric of the town or city viewed as the environment best suited to the overall improvement of humankind.

Importantly, these lobbies were rarely successful unless they came from within the council or a comparable power base. For at least the bulk of the second half of the nineteenth century, the 'big men' were able to impose their view of the civic sphere, though were forced into more negotiation by 1900. By this time the dominant view of the civic seems to have changed, with the growth of what has been termed municipal socialism,[63] with a lowering in the social status of councillors,[64] and with the beginnings of the labour movement.

The new discourse of civic culture that appeared in the second half of the nineteenth century was not consistent, though the emphasis tended to be on the provincial town as a manifestation of the best in human nature, and its ability to reconcile the progressive and the ancient, the monumental or spiritual and the useful. This new discourse was put forward by energetic advocates of civic culture who came overwhelmingly from the ranks of the middle-class elite – merchants, manufacturers and professionals – and was used at least partly as a reply to the accusations of philistinism that came from intellectuals such as Ruskin. They could also refute the accusations of Arnold that: 'They [the middle classes] want culture and dignity; they want ideas', and, while showing that they did not consider the ancient world to be 'so much lumber', attempted to instil it with a different set of meanings linked to commerce and manufacture.[65] This discourse provided a set of symbols, meanings and values surrounding the civic which could be reinterpreted by other groups, and to a certain extent could validate alternative demands for the civic. However, civic leaders by and large managed to set the limits within which meanings could be produced because of their control of the institutions of, and access to, public life. In the architecture and behaviour associated with the 'civic', elite control was more apparent and coherent. 'Civic pride' created temples of high culture, commerce and citizenship, within an open and policed space. Simultaneously, these were meeting places, self-justifying arenas for the middle-class elite who had, frequently, funded them. This is all a long way from the crude and unimaginative civic development imputed to the provincial, and especially industrial, middle classes by Ruskin and Arnold. Some concessions were made as public life and the municipality were invaded by a variety of interests, initially lower-middle-class but increasingly labour. This brought restrictions on rate levels, a privileging of moral over aesthetic judgement and finally, under increasing working-class pressure, Sunday opening.

The nature of the civic was subject to such challenges and negotiation because of the implications it held for the understanding of citizenship and of urban society in general. Different civic cultures could produce a more or less egalitarian or hierarchical city; a more or less disciplined populace; public spaces safe for the middle classes or useful to the working classes. The elite of the middle classes were in a privileged position to determine the outcome of these debates, and to undermine other concepts of the civic, but nevertheless achieved only partial success. This reinforces the need for an understanding of the complexities and negotiated nature of power in the nineteenth-century city, and of cultural and social reproduction among the middle classes. More especially, it indicates that while discourse and narrative were very important in structuring consciousness and creating meaning, they did not operate in an autonomous way upon social formations. Rather, the subject positions from which such discourses were articulated determined their success. Similarly, discourse cannot be seen as directly shaping action. A discourse of universal access and democracy could co-exist with mechanisms of control that worked to distinguish social groups through differential access. Neither the social configurations nor the discourses should be privileged as determining factors. What we are seeing in the creation of civic culture is a process of mutual 'becoming' (in Daniel Miller's phrase).[66] Each is constantly constituting the other. The romance of the city constitutes civic leadership: the provincial urban elite, as the guardians of classical heritage and guarantors of progress. It allows that civic leadership to assert itself against the intellectuals, traditional custodians of the ancient world, and in opposition to metropolitan dominance. However, the social formations of that city constrain and shape the stories that can be told about it.

NOTES

1 From John Ruskin, 'The crown of wild olive', quoted in K. Clark (ed.), *Ruskin Today* (London, John Murray, 1964), p. 254.

2 The related concepts of discourse and narrative are becoming increasingly central to historical analysis, and more and more the case is made for the investigation of discourse as an autonomous field creating meaning and therefore prior to social action. In this case I am arguing for a slightly altered emphasis in the 'linguistic turn', albeit one that is already present by implication. Cf. James Vernon: 'Cognition is always a social process, *inseparable* from relationships of social power, just as the real is as much a discursive construct as the subjectivities through which we seek to understand and make sense of it' (my emphasis). 'Who's afraid of the "linguistic turn"? The politics of social history and its discontents', *Social History*, 19:1 (1994), 96.

3 This has been examined by many historians; see for example G. Best, *Mid-Victorian Britain 1851–1870* (London, Fontana, 1979), ch. 1; A. Briggs, *Victorian Cities* (Harmondsworth, Penguin, 1968), Introduction; R. J. Morris and R. Rodger, 'An introduction to British urban history 1820–1914', and H. Fraser, 'Municipal socialism and social policy', both in Morris and Rodger (eds), *The Victorian City: A Reader in British Urban History 1820–1914* (London, Longman, 1993).

4 See H. Meller, *Leisure and the Changing City, 1870–1914* (London, Routledge and Kegan Paul, 1976), ch. 5, and R. Hartnell, 'Art and civic culture in Birmingham in the late nineteenth century', *Urban History*, 22:2 (1995), 229–37. There is also some consideration of the civic in Morris and Rodger, *The Victorian City*, 'Introduction', and Briggs, *Victorian Cities*, chapters 4 and 5.

5 However, see the very important work by James Vernon, *Politics and the People: A Study in English Political Culture c. 1815–1867* (Cambridge, Cambridge University Press, 1993), especially ch. 2, 'Power imagined'.

6 Cf. Vernon, *Politics and the People*, p. 49.

7 This draws on ideas about the manipulation of space as an exercise of power; see Foucault's comment in P. Rabinow (ed.), *The Foucault Reader* (Harmondsworth, Penguin, 1991), p. 252: Architecture produces 'the coding of . . . reciprocal relations'. Tony Bennett suggests, following Foucault, that in the nineteenth century there were attempts to modify behaviour by making the public self-regulatory, especially in museums: 'Relations of space and vision are organised not merely to allow a clear inspection of the objects exhibited but also to allow for the visitors to be the object of each other's inspection – scenes in which, if not a citizenry, then certainly a public displayed itself to itself in an affirmative celebration of its own orderliness in architectural contexts which simultaneously guaranteed and produce that orderliness.' T. Bennett, *The Birth of the Museum* (London, Routledge, 1995), p. 52.

8 See R. J. Morris's work on the middle classes and voluntary societies, which covers the period up to 1850. He identifies the main imperative as a search for order, stability and hierarchy, and argues that the universalising claims of middle-class culture are further developed after 1850. R. J. Morris, *Class, Sect and Party: The Making of the British Middle Class* (Manchester, Manchester University Press, 1990), pp. 325, 331.

9 J. Garrard, 'Urban elites, 1850–1914: the rule and decline of a new squirearchy?' *Albion*, 27:3 (1995), 590–2.

10 Fraser discusses working-class attitudes towards the municipality around the turn of the nineteenth century (Municipal socialism', pp. 276–80). Morris and Rodger suggest working-class collective visions and identities centred on the neighbourhood rather than the city (*The Victorian City*, 'Introduction', p. 35). The characteristically frugal approach of the lower middle class to local government is discussed by G. Crossick, 'Urban society and the petty bourgeoisie in nineteenth-century Britain', in D. Fraser and A. Sutcliffe (eds), *The Pursuit of Urban History* (London, Edward Arnold, 1983).

11 Sir Richard Tangye, *One and All: An Autobiography* (London, S. W. Partridge, 1889), p. 135.

12 Will of Richard Newsham, quoted in *Preston Corporation Art Gallery Illustrated Catalogue* (1907).

13 Tangye, *One and All*, p. 147.

14 E. P. Hennock, 'The social composition of borough councils in two large cities 1835–1914', in H. J. Dyos (ed.), *The Study of Urban History* (London, Edward Arnold, 1983), p. 324.

15 See K. Hill, 'Municipal museums in the north-west 1850–1914: social reproduction and cultural activity in Liverpool and Preston', unpublished Ph.D. thesis, Lancaster University, 1997, ch. 3.

16 *Ibid.*, appendices 1 and 2.

17 *Ibid.*, p. 152.

18 J. A. Picton, *Liverpool Improvements and How to Accomplish Them* (Liverpool, E. Howell, 1853), p. 24. See also Arline Wilson's essay (ch. 3) in this volume.

19 H. W. Crosskey, Unitarian minister, quoted in Hartnell, 'Art and civic culture', p. 231.

20 Quoted in B. I. Coleman, *The Idea of the City in Nineteenth-Century Britain* (London, Routledge and Kegan Paul, 1973), p. 160.

21 W. A. Abram, *Memorials of the Preston Guilds* (Preston, 1882), p. 145. I am indebted to Dr Andrew Walker for supplying this reference.

22 In a similar way, Dellheim points out that Cobden and Bright invoked the Hanseatic League as an example of medieval struggle against aristocratic tyranny. Charles Dellheim, *The Face of the Past: The Preservation of the Medieval Inheritance in Victorian England* (Cambridge, Cambridge University Press, 1982) p. 30.

23 Vernon, *Politics and the People*, p. 54.

24 *Preston Guardian*, 17 December 1892.

25 For a more detailed examination of organic metaphors for the city, see G. Davison, 'The city as a natural system: theories of urban society in early nineteenth-century Britain', in Fraser and Sutcliffe, *The Pursuit of Urban History*, pp. 354-66.

26 J. A. Picton, *Notes on the Free Library and Museum of the Borough of Liverpool* (Liverpool, n.d.), p. 692.

27 *Liverpool Daily Post and Mercury*, 16 November 1907.

28 J. T. Bunce, *History of the Corporation of Birmingham*, 2 vols (Birmingham, Cornish Brothers, 1885), 2, p. xxii.

29 T. Greenwood, *Museums and Art Galleries* (London, Simpkin, Marshall, 1888), p. 389.

30 S. Nenadic, 'Businessmen, the middle classes, and the "dominance" of manufacturers in nineteenth-century Britain', *Economic History Review*, 2nd series, 44:1 (1991), 66–85.

31 P. Joyce, *Democratic Subjects: The Self and the Social in Nineteenth-Century England* (Cambridge, Cambridge University Press, 1994), ch. 13.

32 A similar point is made by Vernon, who writes, 'local ruling elites sought to endow their institutions with new identities by inventing civic traditions which appropriated a select- ive past in order to emphasise the progress of the present' (*Politics and the People*, p. 63).

33 Clark, *Ruskin Today*, p. 203; J. Evans (ed.), *The Lamp of Beauty: Writings on Art by John Ruskin* (Oxford, Phaidon, 1959) p. 179.

34 Dellheim, *The Face of the Past*, p. 31.

35 These qualities have been noted by Davison as appearing in theories of the city earlier in the century; according to him Vaughan's *The Age of Great Cities* 'exemplified the triumph of liberty, intelligence, commerce, the family and the Protestant religion over the forces of barbarism, militarism, feudalism, "domestic slavery" and superstition, a progression which Vaughan illustrated with a synoptic account of the European city from the Greek city-state to the manufacturing metropolis', ('The city as a natural system', p. 355).

36 Bennett, *The Birth of the Museum*, p. 28.

37 Quoted in Coleman, *The Idea of the City*, p. 159.

38 M. W. Brooks, *John Ruskin and Victorian Architecture* (London, Thames & Hudson, 1989), p. 242, gives as a principle of J. H. Chamberlain, the architect of many of Birmingham's civic projects, 'that architecture testifies to the moral worth of the culture that produced it'.

39 Morris and Rodger, *The Victorian City*, 'Introduction', p. 21.

40 Minutes of the Free Public Library Committee, Preston Council, 18 August 1882, Lancashire Record Office, CBP 55.

41 Brooks, *John Ruskin*, ch. 11.

42 *Ibid.*, p. 234. He goes so far as to say that Ruskinian Gothic became 'an essential instrument of the Liberal social program', p. 234.

43 P. J. Waller, *Town, City and Nation* (Oxford, Clarendon Press, 1983), p. 294; Hartnell, 'Art and civic culture', p. 233.

44 Cf. R. Sennett, *Flesh and Stone: The Body and the City in Western Civilisation* (London: Faber and Faber, 1994), p. 296: 'Crowds of citizens became increasingly pacified in the great open volumes where the Revolution staged its most important public events.'

45 Picton, *Liverpool Improvements*, p. 10.

46 A. Corbin, *Time, Desire and Horror: Towards a History of the Senses*, trans. J. Birrell (Cambridge, Polity Press, 1995) ch. 12; Sennett, *Flesh and Stone*, pp. 329–31.

47 Minutes of Museum Sub-Committee, Liverpool Corporation, 7 January 1869, National Museums and Galleries on Merseyside Archive, MM/1.

48 Minutes of Free Public Library Committee, Preston, 18 February 1907.

49 *Ceremonies connected with the Opening of the Building for a Free Public Library and Museum presented by William Brown Esq. to the Town of Liverpool* (Liverpool, 1861); *Liverpool Daily Post and Mercury*, 16 November 1907. See also the opening ceremony of the Harris Free Public Library, Museum and Art Gallery as reported in the Minutes of the Free Public Library Committee, Preston, 17 November 1893. Cf. the importance of ceremony and special committees in the presentation of portraits as discussed in Louise Purbrick's chapter in this volume.

50 See Minutes of the Museum Sub-Committee, Liverpool, between 1860 and 1880 for countless examples.

51 Minutes of the Free Public Library Committee, Preston, 20 January 1908, 16 June 1913.

52 Members of various sub-committees were in correspondence with national museums and art galleries, and belonged to various national societies and institutions.

53 Minutes of the Museum Sub-Committee, Liverpool, 20 January 1870, 8 December 1870.

54 Museums Sub-Committee, Liverpool, *Annual Report 1898*, National Museums and Galleries on Merseyside Archive, MM/5.

55 M. Whittle, 'Philanthropy in Preston: the changing face of charity in a nineteenth-century provincial town', unpublished Ph.D. thesis, Lancaster University, 1990, p. 258.

56 *Ibid.*, p. 261.

57 Minutes of the Free Public Library Committee, Preston, 18 August 1902.

58 Minutes of the Free Public Library Committee, Preston, 15 September 1902, 20 October 1902.

59 Minutes of the Free Public Library Committee, Preston, 30 October 1902. On the 'Progressives' see M. Savage, *The Dynamics of Working-Class Politics: The Labour Movement in Preston 1880–1940* (Cambridge, Cambridge University Press, 1987), p. 149.

60 Minutes of Free Public Library Committee, Preston, 18 July 1904, 28 July 1904; Savage, *Dynamics of Working-Class Politics*, p. 147.

61 Minutes of the Free Public Library Committee, Preston, 22 June 1894.

62 Liverpool was certainly doing much more in the way of welfare provision than Preston; in the early twentieth century it was described as an agency for 'cradle to grave welfare': D. Fraser, *Power and Authority in the Victorian City* (Oxford, Basil Blackwell, 1979), p. 49.

63 *Ibid.*, p. 172; J. R. Kellett, 'Municipal socialism, enterprise and trading in the Victorian city', *Urban History Yearbook* (1978), 36–45.

64 J. Walton, *Lancashire: A Social History 1558–1939* (Manchester, Manchester University Press, 1987), p. 232.

65 M. Arnold, *Culture and Anarchy and Other Writings*, ed. S. Collini (Cambridge, Cambridge University Press, 1993), pp. 20, 21.

66 D. Miller, *Material Culture and Mass Consumption* (Oxford, Blackwell, 1987), p. 33.

8

THE MIDDLE CLASS, MODERNITY AND THE PROVINCIAL CITY: MANCHESTER c. 1840–80

Simon Gunn

The nineteenth-century city was both progenitor and locus of the experience of modernity, 'the modes of experiencing what is "new" in "modern" society' in David Frisby's words. For Michel de Certeau the city was 'simultaneously the machinery and the hero of modernity'.[1] Modernity is an elusive and contested term. It has been applied to a range of diverse, if related, phenomena, from forms of urban organisation and design to modes of experience frequently registered as 'shock' or dislocation.[2] In this latter sense, modernity signifies both a liberation from traditional ways of life and modes of perception, and a profound anxiety at the consequences of this liberation, a condition marked by contingency, flux and disjuncture.

Both the spatial and experiential dimensions of modernity found their fullest expression in the urban context. Urban modernity thus implied simultaneously the remaking of the city and the ways it was experienced, handled or managed. Recent studies of the emergence of the modern city have concentrated on metropolitan centres: London, Vienna, Paris, New York.[3] However, in the early nineteenth century it was the provincial capitals of industrial England – Birmingham, Liverpool and, above all, Manchester – which attracted attention as exemplars of urban modernity. Unprecedented creations giving rise to novel forms of production, circulation and social relations, they served as the privileged object of new kinds of urban tourism and social reportage. In a seminal study, Steven Marcus observed how the impact of Manchester strained the language of writers of the 1830s and 1840s to its limits, in the effort not only to communicate the phenomenological character of the city but to control the anxiety it provoked. While Disraeli and Carlyle resorted to the conventions of literary romanticism to domesticate the unfamiliar and disturbing, Engels took the diametrically opposite course: confronted by the horrors of the slums, he began to specify in grim, laborious detail. What united these different responses, according to Marcus, was the 'distinctively modern conscious experience of the extreme'.[4] The double sense of the extraordinary and ominous import of the new industrial city was evoked in a speech by Sir James Stephen, leading civil servant and evangelical, at the opening of the Manchester Free Library in 1852. 'Manchester is a name of deep and even of awful significance', he began, 'for here is the metropolis of that Titanic industry on the continued success of which England has deliberately pledged her station and her authority among the nations of the world.' Praising the technological 'miracles', the 'great and tremendous experiment' here enacted, Stephen nevertheless ended on an apocalyptic note: 'These mighty discoveries and strange inventions, these gigantic revelations, these unheard-of migrations, this heaving of the lower strata of society, this increasing power of the popular voice – all these things testify that we have reached the accomplishment of the prophecy of that time "when men shall run to and fro on the earth, and knowledge shall be increased" – and therefore that we are approaching a great crisis and catastrophe in human affairs'.[5]

The 1850s are generally seen as the watershed of this kind of anxiety-laden panegyric. After mid-century, so the historical orthodoxy goes, Manchester, Birmingham and the other English provincial centres were displaced by London as the epitome of the modern city.[6] However, this chronology is problematic. In the first place, it directs attention away from the provincial industrial cities at a critical period. It was in the decades between 1840 and 1880, I will argue, that the urban form of these cities was fundamentally reshaped. Manchester in the 1860s and Birmingham in the 1880s were bywords for architectural progressiveness and spatial modernity. London was able only to rival the provincial centres on these terms from the 1880s.[7]

Secondly, the switch of focus from the provinces to the metropolis in urban historiography coincides with recent arguments in the interpretation of the nineteenth-century middle class. The 'revisionist' historiography, which has emphasised the subordination of the northern industrial middle class to the inherited influence of land and the City of London, has also perceived the mid-century as a pivotal moment, determining or confirming this subaltern status.[8] As a result, not only has the architectural and spatial modernity of the industrial city been obscured, but also its connection with the provincial middle class. Yet, as R. J. Morris observed some years ago, there exists a 'fundamental relation between urbanisation and the middle class'. While it was property-owners – merchants, manufacturers, professionals – who were the principal agents of urban development, the identity of the 'middle class' itself was historically tied to the notion of urbanism and of specific urban locales.[9] The different forms this relation took, however, and how they changed over time, have not received systematic attention. There is a need, therefore, to examine the middle class and the provincial city at a critical point of transformation as suburbia took shape from the mid-nineteenth century. What means did a suburban middle class employ to sustain relations with the city in which it was no longer resident? How were 'middle-class' identity, and authority, upheld in the fluid, impersonal conditions of modern city life?

This chapter examines the links between urban modernity and the provincial middle class. The context is mid-Victorian Manchester, with side glances to Birmingham and other provincial capitals. Manchester was not necessarily typical of such cities, but it is an important example given its metropolitan status as the hub of Britain's most developed industrial sector in the mid-nineteenth century, and its reputation as the model of a new kind of urban civilisation. In the first part of this chapter I shall examine how the new urban civilisation was expressed in the architecture and design of the city centre, and especially the ways in which it was represented in terms of monumentalism and morality. Part

II develops this analysis, suggesting the emergence of a new politics of space by the 1860s in which ideas of the city centre as a moral space co-existed with its representation as a place of danger and transgression. In this period the city centre was recast as a focus for consumption and display, performance and ritual. Part III analyses some of the stylised forms, such as the journey to work, the activity of High 'Change and the promenade, through which a suburban middle class negotiated the experience of the city and gave symbolic expression to a collective identity. By way of conclusion, I shall argue that the forms of civic culture which developed in the later nineteenth century were the products of this new conception of the city and of the centrality of symbol and ritual in middle-class responses to urban modernity.

I

Most commentators are agreed that the key moment in determining Manchester's urban form was the withdrawal of the city's business elite from their warehouse residences in the narrow streets of the central area to suburbs on the fringes of the city. According to the geographer Robert Fishman, this process occurred very rapidly between 1835 and 1845. Its impulses were twofold: on the one hand, growing class tension in the city, on the other, the combination of escalating land values in the central district and the availability of plentiful cheap building land on the periphery. As Fishman wryly puts it, in promoting suburban development early speculators like Samuel Brooks 'merely fulfilled the imperative of all Manchester merchants: to sell in a dear market and buy in a cheap one'.[10] The result was the well-known configuration noted by Engels in 1844, and publicised in guidebooks in the 1850s, consisting of a central business district surrounded by a zone of factories and workers' housing, with bourgeois suburbs providing an expanding outer ring.[11] In the work of the Chicago School of the 1920s, Manchester's development became the model of the modern industrial city, whose organising principle and decisive feature was social segregation.

This model of urban form needs treating with some caution. In particular, historians and geographers have found substantial differences in timing and degree of residential segregation in English cities. Research on Leeds, Birmingham and Liverpool has suggested that social segregation by residence was limited before 1850, tending to be by street and to apply mainly to the richest and poorest sections of urban society. Clear segregation of social classes by district became a feature of provincial cities only in the last quarter of the nineteenth century.[12] In Manchester there was evidence of social segregation by residence within the town before the 1830s, yet significant movement to the exclusive outer suburbs such as Bowdon and Alderley only occurred from the 1850s. Meanwhile, suburbs closer to the city became if anything more socially mixed due to the continuous pressure of population from the centre. Thus the *Manchester City News* commented on the formerly semi-rural suburb of Greenheys in 1871: 'The district known as Greenheys will be found to contain as complete a combination of wealth and poverty, respectability and vice, as could well be got together in a single suburb.'[13]

Nevertheless, the complexity of the suburbanising process does not alter the fact that the central district of Manchester saw a continuous outflow of population from very early. A number of the central wards were losing population in the 1820s, while by the 1850s this applied to the township as a whole.[14] The tendency to create a non-resident centre, an empty public space in the middle of the city at night, was thus more advanced in Manchester than elsewhere. Similar processes did not seriously affect the City of London or other provincial centres until the 1860s, while the continental bourgeoisies remained resident in the centres of cities like Paris, Berlin and Vienna despite the growth of manufacturing industry.[15]

It is possible to argue, then, that the spatial modernity of Manchester lay less in the precocious development of suburbs than in the creation of an empty, functional heart. For the moment of bourgeois withdrawal, the 1840s, was also the point at which the central area of the city underwent a process of massive rebuilding and redesign, lasting until at least the 1880s. One index of this is the rise of the rateable value of property in Manchester and Salford, which surpassed all municipal boroughs outside London by 1882; another is the fact that building workers came to represent the second largest group of male workers by 1871, exceeding those employed in textiles, clothing or warehousing.[16] The majority of rebuilding occurred in the relatively small area which comprised the city centre. Perceptions of this centre seem to have changed little over time. Engels described the 'commercial district' in 1844 as a half-mile long and a half-mile wide. Fifty years later a local guidebook similarly defined the central area as commensurate with the business district of shops and warehouses, bounded by the city's four main railway termini.[17]

But the transformation was moral and aesthetic as much as physical. Cobden's comment in 1845 that Manchester was 'the shabbiest city in Europe for its wealth' merely echoed the views of other contemporary observers. 'There are no great boulevards or heights to aid the eye', wrote Faucher in 1844: 'It is distinguished neither by those contrasting features which mark the cities of the middle ages, nor by that regularity which characterises the capitals of recent formation. All the houses, all the streets resemble each other.'[18] By the 1850s, however, the city had become noted for its architectural progressiveness. 'Manchester is a more interesting city to walk over than London', the editor of the *Building News* commented in 1861: 'One can scarcely walk about Manchester without coming across frequent examples of the *grand* in architecture. There has been nothing to equal it since the building of Venice.'[19] It was the *palazzo* warehouses, of course, developed from 1846 and imitated nationally, that attracted attention for their scale, architectural design and decorative display. 'Babylonian monuments', the *palazzo* warehouses lined roads such as Fountain St and Portland St in the 1860s, forming what Girouard has termed, in a telling phrase, an 'architectural parade'. What caught the eye of *The Builder* were the frontages, 'containing decorative work extraordinary in amount as compared with what was formerly thought necessary'. It was noted that decoration was most elaborate on wholesale warehouses, whose facades were depicted as 'equivalent to ornamental and fantastic advertisements'.[20] Here display was used to flaunt wealth and attract customers, a strategy subsequently used by joint-stock banks and insurance companies.

Monumentalism was indeed a major feature of Manchester's architecture from the 1850s, whether the buildings were defined as 'commercial' or 'public'. With this went a strong emphasis on the moral aspects of architecture and design, the built environment itself becoming directly expressive of moral order. Inscriptions to public and private virtue littered monuments and statues, and were to be found likewise in warehouses and the Royal Exchange, a custom which attracted the ire of *The Builder* in 1874: 'One gets rather tired of this cant of painting up such texts in places of business. Every one on the floor of the room will be occupied in the pursuit of riches, so what is the point of denying it on the ceiling?'[21] But the invocation of moral order also took sharper forms. It was significant that between 1849 and 1872 the main investment in public buildings went into disciplinary institutions: courts, prisons, work-houses, asylums.[22] For the most part these were strategically placed on the outer fringes of the working-class districts. Yet the connection between the disciplinary complexes and 'improving' institutions in the centre was not missed by contemporaries. As a visitor to the public library in King St speculated in 1872: 'The kind friend who accompanied me subsequently drove me to the Assize Courts – from a building calculated to prevent crime to a palace devoted to its punishment. What is the bearing of the former on the latter?'[23] Or, one might wish to add, the latter on the former, the museum (or public library) and the penitentiary representing, in Tony Bennett's phrase, the 'Janus face of power' in the mid- to late nineteenth-century city.[24] Certainly, contemporary commentators saw a clear link between architecture and moral order, one such conceiving the warehouses as 'huge stone guardians watching over the health and morals of the city'.[25]

A similar mix of imperatives lay behind the drive to build, widen and cleanse streets. Action was already under way before incorporation, with the widening of Market St from 1822, subsidised from the profits of the municipal gas company. But the whole programme was greatly expanded after the passing of the various Police and Improvement Acts from 1844. By 1862 it was claimed that 60 miles of streets had been paved and drained.[26] The priorities of traffic flow and sanitation, clearly important here, linked the contemporary notion of circulation to the principle of the city as a 'system' analogous to the human body. Urban reconstruction in the mid-nineteenth century thus appropriated and elaborated an earlier imagery of the city as an organism, new roads being conceived as 'veins' and 'arteries', parks as 'lungs', and so on.[27] At the same time, the idea of 'cleansing' had its larger purposes, clearing the streets not only of mud and debris, but of undesirable social elements associated with a 'residual' population in back streets and slums. Street 'improvements' in the 1850s and 1860s contributed to the displacement of an estimated 30,000 people in the vicinity of Deansgate, Market St and London Rd, testimony to the determination to clear population from the central core. Improvement raised rates and property values: between 1862 and 1871, with clearance in full swing, land values in the central area more than doubled, and increased sixfold in some parts.[28] This, in turn, allowed particular streets to be recreated as sites of consumption and display. The widening of Market St enabled it to be acclaimed as Manchester's 'principal street' by the 1840s, while the rebuilding of disreputable Deansgate from 1869 saw it reincarnated as the city's most 'fashionable thoroughfare' in the 1880s.[29]

A further aspect of urban reconstruction, the provision of open civic spaces, was constrained by the density of building and commercial pressures. Nevertheless, efforts were made. While William Fairbairn's ambitious proposal in 1836 to remodel Piccadilly as a neo-classical forum did not materialise, the area was redesigned in the 1850s to create an esplanade including public statuary.[30] Yet Piccadilly did not develop as a civic square on the desired lines. Critics noted the volume of traffic and the presence of beggars and 'loungers of the poorer class' as obstacles to the achievement of the requisite 'metropolitan grandeur'.[31] Piccadilly was therefore rejected as a site for both the Albert Memorial and the new Town Hall. Instead, attention turned westwards to Albert Square, developed from the 1860s. Here it was possible to create, in *The Builder*'s words, a modern 'architectural centre', dignified and secluded from the main commercial streets, a fit setting for public monuments and civic ceremonial.[32]

The reconstruction of Manchester during the mid-Victorian decades was a major enterprise, paralleling developments carried out in cities such as Birmingham, with the creation of New St Station, itself an embodiment of modernity, and wide thoroughfares such as Corporation St, modelled on Haussman's Parisian boulevards. The city centre came to represent a new form of urban organisation, focused on the exigencies of distribution, exchange and, increasingly, consumption. In the 1840s Faucher had noted how, despite its 'apparently indifferent combination', Manchester's business district was already organised around the circulation of capital and commodities, creating 'an economy both of time and wealth in production'.[33] Street construction between 1840 and 1870 continued to order the flow of traffic and people in new ways. In 1870 the French critic, Hippolyte Taine, observed that slum clearance had made way for 'symmetrical streets ... mathematically laid down'. This contrasted with the streets in older, adjacent slum areas like Ancoats, described by the Medical Officer of Health in 1884: 'With a population equal to that of a large city, [Ancoats] has not a single road or street enabling that vast population to communicate in a fairly straight line with the city with which its business chiefly lies. A series of zig-zags, along narrow streets, forms its avenues to the city.'[34]

As Richard Sennett has commented, the layout of new streets in the nineteenth-century city privileged motion over assembly, individuals in a crowd over organised groups.[35] This, in turn, facilitated the street as a focus for shopping and spectating, the development of department stores, arcades and window displays acting as principal attractions. 'The blaze of light, the glitter, the dazzle, the many colours and the soft strains of harmony which come from invisible quarters, blended together, make ... for an attractive and cheerful spectacle', a contemporary noted of Manchester shop windows in the 1870s, evoking at once the artifice and magnetic appeal of such displays.[36] Through the accounts of local journalists, as well as of visitors such as Taine, Manchester became defamiliarised and exoticised. In the 1870s the city was projected by day as a 'spectacle' or a 'giant bazaar', by night as a 'mausoleum of the dead', its warehouses comparable to 'the deserted temples of a forgotten hierarchy'.[37] Such descriptions represented the city as a giant stage set in which buildings, events and individuals appeared to take on dramatic significance. In these ways the modernity of spatial forms in the city was accompanied by representations which worked to heighten distinctions between centre, slum and suburb, and gave these distinctions moral and imaginative force.

II

The suburban middle class of cities such as Manchester were implicated in these processes in multiple ways. As property-owners, investors, speculators, architects and councillors, the city's male bourgeoisie were to a very large extent the agents of the new cityscape. In turn, the identity of the bourgeois elite was affirmed by the re-creation of the city itself, reinforcing the status of the elite as 'our representatives', 'our leading merchants, capitalists and public men'.[38] But, if the central area of Manchester had been designed as an empty space, a space of authority, this did not render it unproblematic for the elite or a wider suburban middle class.

In the first place, it was a bounded yet permeable domain. While the central area was surrounded by working-class districts, some of the city's worst slums impinged directly on the city's main streets, notably Deansgate and Shudehill. 'The town is encircled by a huge cordon of beastliness and filth, enough to strike terror into the hearts of every civilised inhabitant', a local journal complained in 1870.[39] This fear was exacerbated by ignorance of working-class districts. Cooke Taylor claimed in 1842 that Manchester merchants knew less about Ancoats than about China, and visits to the district continued to be framed in the language of social 'exploration': 'When we have penetrated into the heart of this factory city we become conscious that we have left the Manchester of our everyday acquaintance completely behind us, and have entered upon a new order of things.'[40] From the late 1860s, the Manchester press ran regular features not only on 'rookeries' and 'dens of vice', but on the city centre at times when a suburban middle class was absent, at night and weekends.[41] What such reports revealed was a working class taking over central streets such as Deansgate and Oldham St on Saturday and Sunday evenings. Particularly disturbing was the case of Oldham St, whose clothes shops attracted middle-class women ('our wives and sisters'), but which on Sunday evenings was 'given over to the carnival revels of Manchester's vagabonds', a saturnalia of drink, promiscuity and juvenile crime which spilled out into Market St and Piccadilly. These occasions were by no means ephemeral; the Sunday night entertainments in Oldham St continued to act as the focus of popular revelry and 'respectable' concern into the early twentieth century.[42]

Such events provide some evidence of the popular appropriation of the city and the subversion of bourgeois codes of street conduct. For a bourgeois audience, and certain sections of it in particular, they could only serve to reinforce perceptions of the city as a place of danger. Social surveys, like those of Ancoats and Deansgate in the 1860s, as well as police reports, may have encouraged a more nuanced view of plebeian Manchester, separating the 'criminal' and 'dangerous' classes from the 'upright' working class, but it is by no means clear how far such views permeated wider propertied opinion. A visceral anxiety regarding poorer sections of society continued to mark reportage in the 1860s and 1870s. Commenting on Deansgate, a journalist observed that 'although one does sometimes come into rather close contact with certain repulsive forms of vice and squalor, . . . one is less likely to be molested there than by the roughs in Ancoats, or even more in passing down Market St at a late hour'.[43] While the numbers apprehended for crime actually decreased in central wards like St Ann's and Exchange between 1847 and 1865, fears of a 'crime wave' in the later 1860s did little to reassure propertied opinion of the safety of central streets, especially at night.[44] In response, prompted by the Watch Committee, police strategy was redirected towards the regulation of 'immoral' forms of street behaviour, such as drunkenness, prostitution and begging.[45]

The city centre was considered especially hazardous for middle-class women. Quite apart from the treacherous condition of the streets, the mud and volume of traffic, there were the familiar problems associated with maintaining respectability. If the two key figures to be decoded in the mid- and later Victorian period were the 'gentleman' and the 'loose woman', such decoding became increasingly necessary and difficult as forms of dress no longer instantly disclosed social class. Elizabeth Wilson has observed how complex dress codes became in the mid-nineteenth-century city, since 'everyone was in disguise, incognito, and yet at the same time an individual more and more *was* what he [or she] wore'.[46] More specifically, Christopher Breward has argued that the introduction of crinolines and aniline dyes for women, and of increasingly sophisticated ready-made suits for men, made for a 'quantifiable change' in street dress in the 1860s.[47] The fashionable figures of the 'swell' and of 'shopping ladies' were well-established archetypes in Manchester by the 1870s, and the ironic attention paid in the local press, especially to the former, was suggestive of the concern registered at the difficulty in judging respectablity on the basis of appearance alone.[48]

Changes in dress marked an increase in expressiveness and freedom, but they were not without attendant problems, especially for middle-class women. Deborah Gorham has rightly observed that 'women, not men, managed the outward forms that both manifested and determined social status'.[49] Heightened visibility rendered appearance in public all the more hazardous given the mid-Victorian proclivity for associating women and the city centre with prostitution. Faucher estimated that there were between 500 and 600 prostitutes in Market St at dusk in the 1840s, a focus for wealthy men not only from Manchester but the cotton towns, and the numbers appear to have grown until at least the early 1860s.[50] Prostitutes were regularly reported at such 'respectable' events as the Hallé concerts, the theatre and society balls in the 1860s and 1870s, quite apart from their presence on the street.[51] Such were the resultant difficulties for 'respectable' women in town that there were calls in 1875 for the creation of a Ladies Club, where women could find refreshment during shopping, safe from the suspicious looks and unwelcome attentions of men.[52] The 'question' of prostitution thus deflected on to women as a group the problem of the licence which middle-class men granted themselves in public places.

The 'moral city' evoked in Manchester's design and architecture was therefore always an unstable construct, existing in uneasy relation with the perception of the city as a place of vice and disorder. Bourgeois representations of the modern city evinced not only civic pride, but also anxieties connected with the difficulties of social mixing and the vicissitudes of the street. From the vantage point of the middle class the key problems of urban social life were increasingly associated with upholding collective social identity in a fluid and anonymous public sphere. Closely tied to this, and fundamental to middle-class identity, was the question of making authority visible.

III

How, then, did a suburban middle class negotiate relations with the city centre? The question is especially germane in the case of Manchester, since by the 1860s many of the city's wealthier families lived at a distance of up to 12 miles from the centre, in suburbs such as Prestwich, Sale and Bowdon. For many middle-class London families of the period, by contrast, work was often an omnibus ride away, while residence in the West End meant that fashionable shopping areas could be visited on foot.[53] The issue is a complex one, not least because so much of the relevant literature assumes that suburbanisation involved a physical and psychic withdrawal from the city.[54] One striking feature was the highly ritualised or stylised aspect which marked much of middle-class behaviour in transacting urban relations. Ritual is, of course, a source of contested definitions; here it is used to designate 'rule-governed activity of a symbolic character' which is expressive, repeated, and contains an element of performance.[55] The idea of ritual, in this sense, encompasses a variety of behaviours, from routine at one end of the spectrum to highly formalised ceremonial at the other.

Some of the features of middle-class ritual were evident in the act of commuting from suburb to city. From the 1820s, employers often used the occasion as a symbolic demonstration of moral virtues: punctiliousness, abstinence, self-discipline. The carriage which took the cotton master Joseph Leese from Ardwick to his warehouse in Portland St was known as the 'Polygon Diligence' by virtue of its unvarying punctuality. It was a trait that Leese elevated to a canon of business practice, going so far as to suspend dealings with manufacturers who failed to have their goods ready by 7 a.m. 'until they came to their senses and amended their manners'.[56] The transition to commuting by train from the 1850s left less scope for such performative moral display, but the element of routine remained. Observers noted the 'wonderful regularity' which the act of commuting imposed on business travellers, and the customary seating arrangements which ensured that no passenger would 'occupy any corner of which he did not feel quite sure'.[57] The railway compartment also imposed on travellers a new regime of silence in public and, with it, a 'territoriality of the self' which the sociologist Georg Simmel considered fundamental constituents of nineteenth-century urban modernity.[58]

Such behaviour was more than merely Pooterish, involving a wide social constituency and playing a normative role in negotiating the transition between different social spaces: home and work, suburb and city. It represented a formal-isation of new codes of public etiquette, comprehension of which was essential to middle-class status. Once in the city, middle-class behaviour was subject to other kinds of regulation. For businessmen, the most important forum was the Exchange: High 'Change on Tuesday and Friday was a weekly rite when cotton merchants, manufacturers and a host of other traders from across the textile districts converged on Manchester. A visit to the Exchange was an essential part of the 'spectacle' of Manchester, guidebooks insisted.[59] Listless for much of the week, the hall was transformed at the hour of High 'Change into a 'beehive', a sea of 'dancing dervishes' as bargaining began and deals were struck.[60] Transactions were conducted by gesture – 'nods, winks, shrugs, or brief phrases' – in an atmosphere of 'silence and perpetual motion'. Chaotic to the uninformed observer, High 'Change was in fact governed by a grid system and a strict code of business conduct. As contemporaries consistently affirmed, the drama enacted on Exchange was underpinned by 'laws'; it represented the physical embodiment of the ideas of political economy.[61] Yet High 'Change was more than a visual symbol for the abstract workings of economic laws. It was also, no less fundamentally, a public demonstration of the ordered, regulated character of the world of business itself. It gave symbolic embodiment to the idea that the search for profit was not a random process of chance, but a structured, rule-governed activity.

For bourgeois actors spectacle and ritual were involved in the pursuit of pleasure as well as the world of work. One important example in Manchester was the Saturday morning promenade in which St Ann's Square was briefly 'metamorphosed into a full-dress parade ground' by fashionable youth.[62] At midday carriages would arrive at the square, disgorge their occupants, mainly consisting of young men and women, whereupon the promenade would 'take shape of its own accord'. Watched by a substantial crowd in and around the Exchange, the promenade was 'outwardly an extremely simple ceremony': 'It consists of a saunter past certain aldermanic art repositories, a measured pacing of the Square flags, a leisurely crush through the Passage, and a lounging survey of the millinery of King St.' The promenade was also of short duration; within half an hour the participants returned to their carriages and the suburbs.[63]

Outwardly simple, again more was at stake in 'Doing the Square' than a mere display of fashion. Repeated at the same time throughout the year, the event was constructed as an 'institution', observers claiming that the Square had been used by 'the gentle blood of Cottonopolis . . . to air its gentility' since the eighteenth century.[64] Like the act of commuting, therefore, the Saturday morning promenade represented an adaptation of older forms of social behav-iour to new settings. The promenade itself was strongly territorial. Coalescing spontaneously, as it were, according to custom, it followed a more or less invari-able route. King St, it was explained, was the procession's 'extremest limit': 'Once it rubs shoulders with the commonalty of Cross St., or profanes its garments with Deansgate mud, it is lost.'[65] At the same time as appropriating the Square from the business men and prostitutes who frequented it, therefore, the promenade also marked the bounds dividing the 'respectable' city from the slums of Deansgate. By extension, the purpose of the promenade, as David

Scobey has observed, was to 'stabilize the play of appearances.'[66] It sought to achieve this, first, by making wealth, gentility and leisure conspicuous on the street; as a form of symbolic address, it made 'class' and social distinction visible. Inclusion in the event was determined not only by dress, but by the ability to master the composite range of gestures – bowing, removal of the hat, nodding, looking –, and confirmed by the act of mutual 'recognition'. Women's role in controlling the play of inclusion and exclusion by acknowledging or ignoring the other was crucial in maintaining the promenade as a social and moral collectivity, and a rite of gender as well as of class. Moreover, as a generic social form, the promenade incorporated wide sections of the middle class, transcending divisions of politics, religion and (in a limited sense) status. Observing the parade at the 'fashionable day' of the flower show in 1878 (entrance half a guinea), a commentator remarked on the variety of the crowd: 'the immensely rich arm in arm with the comparatively poor; Tory and Liberal, Churchman and Dissenter, tradesman and professor, banker and merchant – all sorts of people, in all styles of dress, from the very pink of fashion to the plainness of a Quaker'.[67]

This visualisation of social position, and with it the affirmation of collective identity, was important in a city such as Manchester, where, as a commentator put it, there was 'more room for the display of the ever-shifting chances and changes of life' than in older-established urban centres.[68] Partly as a response to the social mixing and fluidity of the city centre, an alternative bourgeois promenade was established in the late 1860s at the Botanical Gardens on the suburban fringe of Old Trafford. Here it was possible to maintain exclusivity by charging an entrance fee, and to affirm the traditional associations of the promenade with health and morals by locating the bourgeois family in a park-like setting.[69] However, the Botanical Gardens did not displace St Ann's Square as the focus for promenading or for other rituals whose function was to give symbolic form to the idea of class identity and difference. The city centre remained the principal site for important elements of bourgeois ritual until the First World War. For married women, Tuesday and Saturday were customarily designated as days for shopping in the fashionable environs of King St, St Ann's Square and, from the 1870s, Barton Arcade. For both sexes from the late 1850s, there was the institution of Thursday as 'Hallé night', the city's most prestigious social occasion, attracting the wealthy from the suburbs and the cotton districts.[70]

IV

What this suggests is that stylised, ritualistic forms of conduct were one of the more important ways in which a suburban middle class handled the conditions of urban modernity in the provincial city. They were, of course, not the only ways. There also existed a flourishing, long-established culture of conviviality, lived out by men in the city's clubs, restaurants and less salubrious locations.[71] But the consistent reference to the deliberate absence of formality in such settings, to the abundance of drink and bonhomie, suggests that this culture did not exist separately from the world of etiquette, but was indissolubly linked to it as a form of psychic release. From this perspective, 'a night in bohemia' was merely the obverse of a day spent 'keeping up appearances'.[72]

The regulated and the habitual were normative codes of middle-class presentation in public. Together with the redesign of the city itself they formed part of the politics of authority in the mid- to late nineteenth century. The most conspicuous feature of this was the cult of civic pride, closely identified with urban Liberalism. The monumental town halls built from the 1850s were part of the larger reconstruction of the city, intended to create a symbolic centre at the heart of an emptied public space as well as to affirm the collective power and presence of the provincial bourgeoisies. In Birmingham, the building of Chamberlain Square from the 1870s, housing the town hall, Liberal club, museum, art gallery, reference library and educational institutions, created a politico-cultural complex of unprecedented scale and magnificence.[73] In Manchester, the development of Albert Square in the 1860s, with its Memorial Hall and monuments to Prince Albert and departed Liberal heroes, suggests how the creation of dead, empty space was used to lend moral authority to the building of the new town hall as the embodiment of architectural modernity and civic virtue.

Civic squares acquired substantive symbolic importance, and not only for local notables. R. J. Morris and Richard Rodger have noted how George Square and Municipal Buildings in Glasgow, constructed in 1883, became a symbol of the city, 'so much so that by the end of the century every labour and trades union leader knew that to hold a demonstration in George Square was to lay symbolic claim to power within the city'.[74] It was natural, therefore, that such squares and open spaces became the setting for the most highly formalised rituals of later nineteenth-century provincial civic culture: ceremonials and processions, funerals of local worthies, Liberal and Conservative party marches. The celebrations surrounding the opening of Manchester Town Hall in 1877 or the birthday of John Bright in Birmingham in 1883 are suggestive of the highly stage-managed character of such events, the effort to make power (including popular power) visible in an orderly as well as a theatrical manner.[75]

Yet these ritual occasions were not the product of party politics or civic pride alone. They developed in the context of a wider politics of urban space, encompassing the reconstruction of the provincial cities in the decades after mid-century and the creation of new ways of visualising identity and authority in public life. In this politics of space, ritual and symbol were two of the key codes through which the middle class manifested its identity and defined its relations with the modern city. Ritual and symbol gave order to the freedom and flux of the city, and provided a means of containing the anxieties to which the conditions of urban modernity gave rise.

NOTES

1 D. Frisby, *Fragments of Modernity: Theories of Modernity in the Work of Simmel, Kracauer and Benjamin* (Cambridge, Polity, 1985), p. 1; M. de Certeau, *The Practice of Everyday Life* (Berkeley, University of California Press, 1984), p. 95.

2 M. Berman, *All That is Solid Melts into Air* (London, Verso, 1983); M. Savage and A.

Warde, *Urban Sociology, Capitalism and Modernity* (London, Macmillan, 1993), ch. 6; D. Harvey, *The Condition of Postmodernity* (Oxford, Blackwell, 1990), ch. 2; H. Lefebvre, *Writings on Cities* (Oxford, Blackwell, 1996). The idea of modernity is developed in slightly different ways by social theorists such as Habermas, Lyotard and Giddens, though in his use of concepts such as the 'emptying out of space and time', the 'disembedding of social institutions' and 'reflexivity' Giddens comes close to some of the ideas pursued in this chapter. See J. Habermas, 'Modernity: an incomplete project', in H. Foster (ed.), *Postmodern Culture* (London, Pluto, 1985); J.-F. Lyotard, *The Postmodern Condition* (Manchester, Manchester University Press, 1986); A. Giddens, *Modernity and Self-Identity* (Cambridge, Polity, 1991), pp. 14–21.

3 D. Olsen, *The City as a Work of Art: London, Paris, Vienna* (New Haven, Yale University Press, 1986); C. Schorske, *Fin-de-Siècle Vienna: Politics and Culture* (London, Weidenfeld and Nicholson, 1980); S. Buck-Morss, *The Dialectics of Seeing: Walter Benjamin and the Arcades Project* (Cambridge, Mass., M.I.T. Press, 1991); J. Walkowitz, *City of Dreadful Delight: Narratives of Sexual Danger in Later Victorian London* (London, Virago, 1992); P. Rabinow, *French Modern: Norms and Forms of the Social Environment* (Cambridge, Mass., MIT Press, 1989); E. Spann, *The New Metropolis: New York City 1840–1857* (New York, Columbia University Press, 1981); D. Schuyler, *The New Urban Landscape: The Redefinition of Urban Form in Nineteenth-Century America* (Baltimore, Johns Hopkins University Press, 1986).

4 S. Marcus, *Engels, Manchester, and the Working Class* (London, Weidenfeld and Nicholson, 1974), pp. 38–41, 98, 181.

5 Cited in *The Builder*, vol. 10 (1852), 580.

6 The classic statement of this argument is A. Briggs, *Victorian Cities* (Harmondsworth, Penguin, 1963), ch. 8. See also Olsen's assertion that 'London offered possibilities of conspicuous self-indulgence and significant display that would have been out of place in the industrial city', *The City as a Work of Art*, p. 6.

7 A point implicitly accepted by Judith Walkowitz in *City of Dreadful Delight*, p. 24. This chapter owes a considerable debt to the ideas she develops on the city and urban spectatorship in chapters 1 and 2 of her study.

8 The historiography is too extensive to cite in full but see *inter alia* W. D. Rubinstein, *Elites and the Wealthy in Britain since the Industrial Revolution* (Brighton, Harvester, 1987); M. Wiener, *English Culture and the Decline of the Industrial Spirit* (Cambridge, Cambridge University Press, 1981); P. J. Cain and A. G. Hopkins, *British Imperialism: Innovation and Expansion 1688–1914* (Harlow, Longman, 1993). There are differences of emphasis within this historiography, Wiener seeing the 1850s as heralding 'a counter-revolution' in which industrial ideals were supplanted by gentry values, Cain and Hopkins arguing for the long-term predominance of the service sector and 'gentlemanly capitalism' over industry and the manufacturing interest.

9 R. J. Morris, 'The middle class and British towns and cities of the industrial revolution', in D. Fraser and A. Sutcliffe, *The Pursuit of Urban History* (London, Arnold, 1983) p. 286.

10 R. Fishman, *Bourgeois Utopias: The Rise and Fall of Suburbia* (New York, Basic Books, 1987), pp. 84–6.

11 For this kind of description in guidebooks see T. Bullock, *Bradshaw's Guide to Manchester* (London, 1857), pp. 7–8.

12 D. Ward, 'Environs and neighbours in the "two nations"; residential differentiation in mid-nineteenth century Leeds', *Journal of Historical Geography*, 6 (1980), 133–62; Ward, 'Victorian cities: how modern?', *Journal of Historical Geography*, 1 (1975), 135–51; R. Lawton, 'The population of Liverpool in the mid-nineteenth century', *Transactions of the Historical Society of Lancashire and Cheshire*, 107 (1985), 89–120; R. Dennis, *English Industrial Cities of the Nineteenth Century* (Cambridge, Cambridge University Press, 1984), ch. 7.

13 S. Gunn, 'The Manchester middle class, 1850–80', unpublished Ph.D. thesis, University of Manchester, 1992, ch. 4; 'Round about Manchester', *Manchester City News* (henceforth *MCN*), 18 November 1871.

14 For comments see H. B. Rodgers, 'The suburban growth of Victorian Manchester',

Journal of the Manchester Geographical Society, vol. 58 (1962), 4; H. Baker, 'On the growth of the commercial centre of Manchester, movement of population and pressure of habitation', *Transactions of the Manchester Statistical Society* (1872–3), 88 ff.

15 Fishman, *Bourgeois Utopias*, pp. 11–14.

16 For figures see Gunn, 'Manchester middle class', p. 48; M. Hewitt, *The Emergence of Stability in the Industrial City: Manchester 1832–1867* (Aldershot, Scolar Press, 1996), p. 42.

17 F. Engels, *The Working Class in England in 1844* ([1844,] London, Allen and Unwin, 1968), p. 46; J. Mortimer, *Mercantile Manchester Past and Present* (Manchester, 1896), p. 78.

18 L. Faucher, *Manchester in 1844* (London, 1844), p. 16.

19 Cited in C. Stewart, *The Stones of Manchester* (London, Edward Arnold, 1956), p. 13.

20 'Adrift in Manchester', *MCN*, 3 February 1872; M. Girouard, *The English Town* (New Haven, Yale University Press, 1990), p. 239; *The Builder*, vol. 16 (1858), 98, and vol. 18 (1860), 643.

21 *The Builder*, vol. 32 (1874), 889.

22 For example: Manchester Royal Lunatic Asylum, 1849; City Gaol, 1850 (extended 1858); Workhouse, Crumpsall, 1855; Assize Courts, 1865; County Gaol, 1866; City Court House, 1872.

23 'Adrift in Manchester', *MCN*, 6 January 1872.

24 T. Bennett, 'The exhibitionary complex', in N. Dirks, G. Eley and S. Ortner (eds), *Culture/Power/History* (Princeton, Princeton University Press, 1995), p. 151.

25 'Adrift in Manchester', *MCN*, 3 February 1872.

26 T. S. Ashton, *Economic and Social Investigations in Manchester, 1833–1933* (London, King, 1934), ch. 4.

27 For the history of this imagery and of the profound connections between the human body and urban design see R. Sennett, *Flesh and Stone: The Body and the City in Western Civilisation* (London, Faber and Faber, 1994).

28 Baker, 'On the growth of the commercial centre'.

29 Love and Barton, *Manchester as it is* (Manchester, 1839), p. 20; *Manchester of Today: An Epitome of Results* (London, 1888), p. 34. For the rebuilding of Deansgate see *Momus*, 21 July 1881.

30 W. Fairbairn, *Observations on the Improvements of the Town of Manchester, Particularly as Regards the Importance of blending in Those Improvements, the Chaste and the Beautiful with the Ornamental and Useful* (London, 1836); A. J. Pass, *Thomas Worthington: Victorian Architecture and Social Purpose* (Manchester, Manchester Literary and Philosophical Society, 1988), pp. 28–9.

31 'The lungs of Manchester', *The Freelance*, 1 September 1876; L. Grindon, *The Infirmary Sites Question* (Manchester, 1876), pp. 16 ff.; *Manchester Faces and Places*, 1 (1889–90), p. 14.

32 *The Builder*, vol. 24 (1876), 941–2.

33 *Manchester in 1844*, pp. 17–18.

34 H. Taine, *Notes on England* ([1870,] London, Thames and Hudson, 1957), pp. 226, 241; Reports of the Medical Officer of Health, March 1884, p. 120, Manchester Central Reference Library.

35 Sennett, *Flesh and Stone*, ch. 10.

36 'The land of toys', *Comus*, 10 January 1878.

37 'Adrift in Manchester', *MCN*, 20 January 1872; 'Manchester by night', *The Freelance*, 11 August 1876.

38 Charles Rowley provides an interesting example of these kinds of representations and reflections on them; see his *Fifty Years of Ancoats: Loss and Gain* (Manchester, 1899) and *Fifty Years of Work Without Wages* (Manchester, 1910).

39 'Manchester slums', *The Freelance*, 12 March 1870.

40 W. Cooke Taylor, *Notes of a Tour in the Manufacturing Districts of Lancashire* ([1842,] London, Cass, 1968), p.14; 'Out Ancoats way', *The Freelance*, 14 November 1873.

41 See for example 'Manchester by night', *The Freelance*, 11 August 1876; 'Sunday afternoons in Albert Square', *City Lantern*, 19 July 1878; and series such as 'Adrift in Manchester', *MCN*, 23 December 1871 and thereafter.

42 'Oldham St. on a Sunday night', *The Freelance*, 6 August 1870, and the subsequent letter,

'The state of Oldham St.', 16 August 1870; 'A Sunday promenade', *City Lantern*, 6 August 1874; 'Sunday night in Oldham St.', *Comus*, 14 February 1878; C. E. B. Russell, *Manchester Boys* (Manchester, 1905).

43 'Urban rambles II', *The Freelance*, 2 November 1867.

44 From tables 'Showing the number of apprehensions which have taken place within each ward of the borough . . .', Manchester Police Returns, 1847–65, Manchester Central Reference Library. Unfortunately, statistics do not appear to have been collected on a ward basis beyond this date. For the 'crime wave' of the late 1860s see A. Aspland, *Criminal Manchester* (Manchester, 1868); also the comments in S. J. Davies, 'Classes and police in Manchester 1829–1880', in A. J. Kidd and K. W. Roberts (eds), *City, Class and Culture: Studies of Cultural Production and Social Policy in Victorian Manchester* (Manchester, Manchester University Press, 1985), pp. 36–7.

45 Davies, 'Classes and police', pp. 37–8; see also D. Jones, *Crime, Protest, Community and Police in Nineteenth-Century Britain* (London, Routledge, 1982), ch. 6, for a useful analysis of crime and policing in Manchester during this period.

46 E. Wilson, *Adorned in Dreams: Fashion and Modernity* (London, Virago, 1996), p. 137. For additional comment on the meanings of nineteenth-century dress see R. Sennett, *The Fall of Public Man* ([1976,] London, Faber and Faber, 1993), p. 165.

47 C. Breward, *The Culture of Fashion* (Manchester, Manchester University Press, 1995), pp. 156–62.

48 For interesting comments on changes in middle-class clothing in Manchester in the early and mid-nineteenth century see 'On the Rialto II', *The Sphinx*, 15 August 1868; 'The square', *City Lantern*, 6 November 1874; 'Saturday morning on Market St.', *The Freelance*, 25 June 1875.

49 D. Gorham, *The Victorian Girl and the Feminine Ideal* (London, Croom Helm, 1982).

50 Faucher, *Manchester in 1844*, p. 41; Jones, *Crime, Protest, Community*, pp. 164–5.

51 See for example the references in *The Freelance*: 'Mr Hallé's concerts', 24 October 1868; 'The streets on Sunday evenings', 27 August 1870; 'At the Volunteer ball', 8 January 1875.

52 'A sanctuary for Manchester ladies', *The Freelance*, 25 February 1875.

53 Z. Shonfield, *The Precariously Privileged: A Professional Family in Victorian London* (Oxford, Oxford University Press, 1987), p. 44; Walkowitz, *City of Dreadful Delight*, pp. 48–50.

54 For Manchester see K. Chorley, *Manchester Made Them* (London, Faber and Faber, 1950), pp. 136–46. The classic statement of this argument in the national context remains Wiener, *English Culture and the Decline of the Industrial Spirit*.

55 P. Connerton, *How Societies Remember* (Cambridge, Cambridge University Press, 1989), pp. 44–5.

56 'Kershaw, Leese, Sidebottom and Co.', *MCN*, 21 January 1865.

57 'To and fro on the Bowdon line', *The Freelance*, 14 December 1867. See also Chorley, *Manchester Made Them*, pp. 147–69 for further comments on the act, and impact, of commuting.

58 See W. Schivelbusch, *The Railway Journey* (Leamington Spa, Berg, 1986), pp. 73–7 for an extended discussion.

59 Love and Barton, *Manchester as It is*, p. 192; Mortimer, *Mercantile Manchester*.

60 Cited in D. Farnie, 'The commercial development of Manchester in the later nineteenth century', *Manchester Review*, 7 (1956), 327–33.

61 Cooke Taylor, *Notes of a Tour*; R. Allen, *The Manchester Royal Exchange* (Manchester 1921); Mortimer, *Mercantile Manchester*.

62 'Manchester swells', *City Lantern*, 11 February 1876.

63 The St Ann's Square promenade was extensively reported in the Manchester periodical press. See in particular 'Doing the Square', *The Freelance*, 3 April 1869; 'On the Square', *The Freelance*, 9 January 1874; 'The Square', *City Lantern*, 6 November 1874.

64 'The Square', *City Lantern*, 6 November 1874.

65 *Ibid.*

66 D. Scobey, 'Anatomy of the promenade: the politics of bourgeois sociability in nineteenth-century New York', *Social History*, 17:2 (1992), 213. This section owes much to

Scobey's revealing analysis, although it is necessary to recognise the importance of context; New York was not Manchester.

67 'The flower show', *City Lantern*, 14 June 1878.

68 'In City Road', *City Lantern*, 21 May 1875.

69 See for example 'A musical promenade at the Botanical Gardens', *The Freelance*, 16 May 1868; 'The Botanical', *The Freelance*, 27 May 1871; 'The flower show', *City Lantern*, 25 May 1877.

70 'Shopping in St. Ann's Square', *The Freelance*, 5 November 1876; Faucher, *Manchester in 1844*, pp. 19–20; 'On 'Change', *The Freelance*, 30 March 1867. For a more critical view of the Exchange see 'On the Rialto', *The Sphinx*, 25 July and 15 August 1868. For the Hall, see 'Music in full dress', *The Freelance*, 5 January 1867; also S. Gunn, 'The sublime and the vulgar: music and the constitution of "high culture" in Manchester, c.1850–1890', *Journal of Victorian Culture*, 2:2 (1997) 208–28.

71 See *inter alia* J. S. Stancliffe, *John Shaw's 1738–1938* (Manchester, 1938); A. Darbyshire, *A Chronicle of the Brazenose Club*, vol.1 (Manchester, 1892); 'The dining rooms of Manchester', *The Freelance*, 16 February 1867 and thereafter; 'A night in Bohemia', *The Freelance*, 22 March 1878; 'A midnight dance', *Comus*, 17 January 1878.

72 The notion of psychic release may also be related to the strains imposed on men in the city. See for example Ruskin's speech 'Of Queen's Gardens' given at Manchester Town Hall in 1864, when he described men as requiring to be '*always* hardened' and the city itself as a 'furnace-ground'. The speech was published in *Sesame and Lilies* (London, 1893).

73 For a description of the construction of Chamberlain Square see Girouard, *The English Town*, pp. 221–2.

74 R. J .Morris and R. Rodger, 'Introduction', in Morris and Rodger, (eds), *The Victorian City* (London, Longman, 1993), p. 9.

75 W. E. A. Axon (ed.), *An Architectural and General Description of the Town Hall, Manchester* (Manchester, 1878); P. Joyce, *Democratic Subjects* (Cambridge, Cambridge University Press, 1994), pp. 137–8.

PART TWO

GENDER, IDENTITY AND CONSUMER CULTURE

PRELUDE

Like the earlier Prelude this one seeks to provide a brief introduction to the chapters which follow and readers wishing to pursue the issues can do so through the note references to each chapter and also via the selection of 'Further reading' at the end of the book. In the chapters that follow, issues of gender and class are related to legal constructions of identity, representations of the lower middle class, and the developing cultures of consumption and 'popular' musical taste. The private/public dichotomy is explored in the context of bourgeois culture(s) traditionally located in the former but repeatedly colonising the latter. The culture of the suburbs is a central theme in several of the chapters in Part Two.

Craig Young's chapter, 'Middle-class "culture", law and gender identity: married women's property legislation in Scotland, c. 1850–1920', deals with the traditional focus of gender studies in the nineteenth century – namely, the position of women, domestic ideology and the perpetuation of patriarchy. Young's analysis brings to the subject the perspective of the geographer interested in the spatial dimensions of power relationships. He deals with the inter-relationship between the law of married women's property rights and the construction of gender identity in Scotland between 1850 and 1920. The legislation is seen as a cultural construction carrying with it a middle-class and male interpretation of gender relations. From this it is clear that Young regards gender divisions as social constructs, enforceable through law but ultimately changing, negotiable and transient (the law of married women's property in Scotland was reformed in the 1920s). The view of socio-spatial relations enshrined in the law of property, however, was defended at the time as 'natural' in innumerable local cases in Scotland. The cultural category 'woman' with all it implied in the nineteenth century was legitimised in a case law which enacted an 'abstract vision' of separate-spheres ideology (an ideal type rather than universally observed practice). Nonetheless, the property law achieved a 'social closure around representations of a "proper" socio-spatial order', acting as a cultural mechanism replicating patriarchy in people's lived legal and social relations.

The evolution of gender identities is also explored in Christopher Hosgood's chapter entitled, 'Mrs Pooter's purchase: lower-middle-class consumerism and the sales, 1870–1914'. Hosgood deals with issues which also feature prominently in the following chapters by Hammerton and by Greenfield, O'Connell and Reid, namely the representation of the suburban middle classes

in contemporary journalism and fiction and the evolving sub-cultures of suburban female (and male) consumerism. His innovative study explores the
mechanics of consumerism, rather than its promotion, by focusing on the
shopper rather than the retailer. Most studies of consumer culture and the
'tyranny of fashion' have emphasised their conservative/conformist implications.
In the context of the later Victorian and Edwardian period it served to subordinate the lower middle class to prevalent notions of taste and reinforced a
bourgeois sense of cultural superiority in those immediately above the new
suburbanites. Gender and class were at the heart of representations of consumer
culture and the lower-middle-class female was consistently derided in newspapers and periodicals. The women from the suburbs who shopped in the new
department stores and frequented the 'sales' were depicted as frivolous, tragi-
comic creatures driven by desire; 'social climbers' whose compulsive 'bargain
hunting' was doomed by very definition to leave them a step behind the fashionable. However, Hosgood argues that shopping had more liberating, even
subversive, implications for women. Some of the women's magazines treated
'sale' shopping as a rational exercise in consumption and offered advice to the
would-be purchaser. Moreover, the invasion of the West End by suburban shoppers and the 'carnivalesque' atmosphere at sales time offered an escape from the
domestic routine plus the chance for the inversion of conventional norms of
respectable womanly behaviour. It was precisely the same culture of
consumerism at which the critics sneered that also created a sense of unease
when it seemed to challenge accepted codes of respectable behaviour both in
terms of class and gender.

The analysis of contemporary representations of the cultural habits of the
lower middle classes, this time of the suburban male, is continued with James
Hammerton's 'The English weakness? Gender, satire and "moral manliness" in
the lower middle class, 1870–1920'. Through his reading of some of the satirical constructions of petit-bourgeois masculinity prevalent in the late Victorian
and Edwardian eras, the private world of domesticity emerges as the stage on
which the imagined male, lower-middle-class and suburban, acted out his
'Pooteresque' existence. The Grossmith brothers' *Diary of a Nobody* is merely
the best known, and most affectionate, example of a genre of critical portraits
of the domesticated suburban clerk. This satirical genre was related to wider
anxieties about the nature of masculine identity in an increasingly complex
urban society. Ironically, the butt of the satire, the domesticated suburban male,
was later to represent the epitome of 'modernity'. By the interwar years the
servantless suburban household had become the middle-class norm (and an
ideal type for the rest of society). The representation of the domesticated
husband was now less class-specific and more positive as suburban living was
transformed into a cultural ideal. Hammerton's study thus lights upon a crucial
moment when a 'deeply gendered lower-middle-class masculine identity' was
forming in contrast to the idealised masculine norms characteristic of the earlier
satires. This was perhaps the moment when modern conditions of domestic life
and relationships were being created, although, as Hammerton acknowledges, a
study of other sources such as autobiographies would throw more light on this.

The chapter by Greenfield, O'Connell and Reid takes the analysis of the culture of the middle-class male and of consumerism into the interwar years. In 'Gender, consumer culture and the middle-class male, 1918–39', the suburban ideal is revisited and this time it is linked to the culture of consumption as middle-class male identity is explored through magazine constructions of the 'ideal type' of the male consumer. As in Hammerton's chapter, masculine identities associated with 'modernity' are portrayed as emerging in the 1920s and 1930s in contrast with older pre-1914 cultural norms. A key cultural instrument in this was the operation of a consumer society. The new forms of domesticity nurtured in a suburban culture created new markets for domestic and leisure goods aimed specifically at men including fashion, sport and motoring. The competent and capable male was often defined in gender as well as in class terms, notably in contrast to the 'dependent', 'submissive' female. In the 'new consumerism' of the interwar years, the world of goods increasingly came to underpin status and identity among the burgeoning middle classes. Previous attention amongst historians of consumption has focused upon the female as consumer of goods. Greenfield *et al.* argue convincingly that this was a male as well as a female market and that the identity of the middle-class male was constructed around the normative values of a consumer who owned a suburban house, drove a motor car and who was a competent exponent of what were regarded as distinctly masculine technologies.

The suburban culture of the interwar years is further explored in the last chapter in the collection, Lowerson's study of the life of the amateur operatic societies entitled 'An outbreak of allodoxia? Operatic amateurs and middle-class musical taste between the Wars'. 'Allodoxia' in the assessment of cultural 'taste' is a term borrowed from the work of the increasingly influential (among British social historians) French sociologist Pierre Bourdieu. For Bourdieu it represents petit-bourgeois cultural pursuits which are both 'authorised' and yet 'limited' by the 'high' art forms to which they are an alternative. The English term 'middle-brow' does not quite convey as much. For his own part, Lowerson argues against class-specific analysis and repudiates the notion of an inclusive 'middle-class culture' as too broad to be of value. For example, it neglects differentiation around loci of musical taste such as 'high' and 'low', 'elite' and 'mass'. Instead, Lowerson chooses to use the term 'middlebrow' (the first-known use of which was in *Punch* in 1925) as a focus to explore the canons and conventions of an ignored genre, the musicology of the suburban 'middle'. Lowerson's study provides further confirmation of the extent to which aesthetic categories are related to social and cultural hierarchies and serves to undermine the notion of a coherent and all-inclusive middle-class cultural sphere. Such a conclusion lends support to the idea that the history of the middle in the history of British society is best represented in terms of difference and dissonance rather than continuity and coherence.

9

MIDDLE-CLASS 'CULTURE', LAW AND GENDER IDENTITY: MARRIED WOMEN'S PROPERTY LEGISLATION IN SCOTLAND, c. 1850–1920
Craig Young

INTRODUCTION

It is by no means easy to define the nature of, or generalise about the experience of, the British middle class. Structural definitions are often not matched by clear expressions of class identity or action. Two processes, however, seem to have been important in defining the 'middle class' way of life and experience. These were the nature of their relationship to property and the development of an ideal view of the gendered nature of society. An important element of that ideal social view was the construction of masculine and feminine identities. The focus of this chapter is how the regulation of gendered property relations was influenced by, and helped reproduce elements of, what could be termed 'middle-class culture'. The creation, interpretation and operation of Scottish law relating to married women's property ownership are analysed to reveal this body of legislation as a social construct reflecting and reproducing an essentially 'middle-class' world-view. The nineteenth century was also a period of challenge to accepted social relationships, particularly legal and gender relations. Thus middle-class 'culture' can be seen as an arena within which meanings were created and contested to legitimate arguments in support of a particular legal and social future.

The law regarding married women's property rights in Scotland between c.1850 and 1920 is examined here to illustrate these general points. After defining how 'culture' is treated in this study, and discussing the inter-relationship of law, society, culture and identity, the legal background to the analysis is presented. The chapter then considers the relationship between 'middle-class culture' and law in three areas. First, the role of socially held concepts of the proper ordering of society in the construction of this legislation in Parliament is outlined. Then the construction of gendered identity in the courtroom is illustrated. Finally, the material implications of these symbolic constructions is analysed by considering the implications for middle-class women of the operation of this body of legislation.

'CULTURE', IDENTITY AND LAW

The use of 'culture' as an analytical term is problematic. 'Culture' can refer to descriptions of the material aspects of life. Thus it is possible to talk of the 'material culture' of a society, or 'culture' in the sense of a particular life style. The term becomes problematic when it is used in explanation, and in partic- ular when it is cited as a causal force in society. The term is often used in explanations to encompass the factors which are left over after considering the economic, the social and the political, which leaves it as an imprecise analyt- ical term. There is also a danger of reifying culture, conceiving it as an observable 'thing' which has independent existence and causal powers (a 'superorganic' view of culture). Yet clearly 'culture' does not exist in the same way as 'society' or 'the economy'.[1]

One particular view of 'culture' stresses a focus on the material develop- ment of the 'idea of culture'.[2] Culture cannot have an independent, factual existence, and yet it is often referred to by social actors to justify their actions. It is thus important to focus on 'how the very idea of culture has been devel- oped and deployed as a means of attempting to order, control and define'. The idea of culture 'is not what people are doing . . . it is the way that people make sense of what they have done. It is the way their activities are reified as culture'.[3] From this perspective, culture is socially constructed and is a process involving the creation of a set of socially held meanings and their reification as 'natural'. The important questions are how and why do social actors reify culture, making it a real force in society? Is this socially constructed culture deployed to repro- duce or legitimate power relations in society, thereby mediating contradictions within capitalist, patriarchal societies? Are cultural constructions reified to effect social closure, revealing culture as a system of power? In this way, although the investigation of culture involves the exploration of meaning or representation, it is not divorced from the material origins of these meanings or representations. Meaning is socially produced and in turn impacts upon social life.

The construction of identity in western society has been an important part of defining and maintaining social divisions (for example, gendered, class-based or racial identities). Identity is also a social construction, either created by indi- viduals for themselves within a particular societal context, or attributed to individuals. The social construction of identity is thus an element of 'culture' (as defined above), as the creation of identity often involves the reification of socially held ideas. Examples of this include racist constructions of 'black' or 'Asian' identity, and sexist constructions of masculinity and femininity. The social construction of identity is achieved in various ways. However, a common device is the use of 'positioning' metaphors where an individual is attributed a certain identity with respect to their 'proper' position in a reified construction of a 'proper' social order.[4] Socially held ideas about society and space thus play a role in engendering people. The use of symbolic distance divides women and men by constructing sexual/gender boundaries. Location with respect to these boundaries is important because the construction of gender identity is in part the result of 'a critical positioning in inhomogeneous social space'.[5] The key example discussed here is the metaphor of separate spheres, an ideal view of society which involved the creation of gendered identities through positioning individuals both socially (men were 'naturally' superior to women) and spatially (masculinity was associated with the 'public' sphere and femininity with the 'private' sphere).

How these socially held meanings (culture) interacted with the law relating to married women's property rights is the central focus of what follows. An important theme is the tension between conceptions of law as abstract or as contextual (i.e. influenced by its societal context). Within the legal profession, law is upheld as an abstract construction, representing a universal solution to disputes which is independent of context.[6] The law draws its power from its abstract nature, which allows it to overcome the heterogeneity of social life. This abstraction is achieved through the use of legal formalism, 'a means of transforming disputes from the immediate texture of a dispute to a structured discourse controlled by the judiciary'.[7] This discourse allows the legal system to deal with people and their real-life problems by reducing individuals to abstract categories.[8] The legal process recreates individuals' identities as specific 'legal subjects' which have assigned to them particular legal characteristics and rights. Law, according to this perspective, is divorced from context. Where links between legal reasoning and the form of society are considered at all, the law is constructed in relation to a conception of an ideal stable form of society.[9]

A socio-legal perspective sees law as socially constructed, drawing in complex ways on the society in which it is created.[10] Thus the importance of historical context must be taken into account in interpreting law. Legal subjects are constructed by 'positioning' individuals within the law and its metaphorical landscapes. The fixing of such notions in the law as an important social institution has the effect of helping to legitimate such views more widely in society. Legal agents make their decisions with reference to particular ideologies. Law can be used to impose the view of elites in society upon others. If the law is formed within patriarchal, capitalist society it is inextricably bound in with, and reproduces, the power relations found there. An example of this is the representation of women as having 'natural' characteristics in order to disempower them in legal situations, thereby recreating women's subordination to men in the law.[11] Legal discourse thus 'may be employed in attempts to ... maintain the desired conditions of social life'.[12]

At the same time the tensions generated by applying abstract notions to the realities of the material geography of social life can lead to demands for change in the law. Law does not reflect the view of a consensual society but instead represents an arena for competing views of the organisation of society.[13] Law can be contested and legal processes are not only shaped by legal discourse but also by how they are situated within broader processes of social change.

MARRIED WOMEN'S PROPERTY LAW IN SCOTLAND

Scottish law with regard to the ownership of property within marriage was a complex mix of common law, statute law and their intersection with other laws. Certain basic characteristics need to be understood.[14] Scottish law recognises two types of property. Heritable property (or heritage) is that passing to an heir-at-law of a deceased person, while moveable property comprises all property not classed as heritage.[15] Upon marriage, common law placed certain restrictions upon the person of the wife and her rights with reference to her property. The

Table 1 **Married women's property rights and relevant statutes**

Common law (from the 16th century) – on marriage the wife's property passed into the category of 'goods in communion', over which the husband (as guardian of his wife) had uncontrolled right of disposal.

The Conjugal Rights (Scotland) Amendment Act, 1861.

The Married Women's Property (Scotland) Act, 1877.

The Married Women's Policies of Assurance (Scotland) Act, 1880.

The Married Women's Property (Scotland) Act, 1881 – husband's jus mariti excluded from marriages contracted after this date.

The Married Women's Property (Scotland) Act, 1920 – husband's *jus administration is* abolished. Married women accorded equal legal status to single women.

---

husband became the wife's curator, and the wife's moveable property (with some exceptions) passed under his complete control. This was known as the husband's *jus mariti*. The wife could own heritable estate but she could not act with regard to this estate without her husband's consent. This was known as the husband's right of administration, or *jus administrationis*, a curatorial power. A series of statutes between 1855 and 1920 altered this position (see Table 1). The *jus mariti* was abolished in 1881 (in marriages contracted after that date), and the *jus administrationis* in 1920. Throughout this period, however, it was possible to alter the effects of common and statute law by entering into marriage contracts. By the nineteenth century these contracts had the general purpose of placing property in a trust which took it beyond the control of the marriage partners (excluding the *jus mariti* and the *jus administrationis*) and their creditors.

This body of law was of particular significance for the middle classes and intersected with the two important facets of middle-class life noted above, namely the form of gender relations and their relationship to property. The court cases considered here involved individuals who were largely members of the middle classes. There is a range of socio-economic status from small property and business owners to landed gentry. In the nineteenth century this body of law was of great concern to the middle classes. Common law failed to cope with the new forms of property which comprised their wealth and changing attitudes to relations within marriage. The vast majority of middle-class couples made use of marriage contracts to circumvent common law, and much of nineteenth-century reform was based on trying to create statute law which applied to all social classes.

'MIDDLE-CLASS' IDEOLOGY AND LAW

The history of married women's property law in England, and to a lesser extent in Scotland, has been well covered elsewhere.[16] For much of the nineteenth century, this body of law operated in such a way that it discriminated against the property rights of married women. The nineteenth century was a period of change, however. Reform of married women's property legislation was closely tied to the women's suffrage movement and to broader reform of the law generally. This reform was also associated with the important intellectual themes of the period: those of individual freedom and natural human rights which some used to attack the patriarchal ideal and reflected the changing economic and social position of women in a time of rapid transition. Changing economic conditions, such as the emergence of new forms of property and the growth of a middle class not reliant on land as a repository of wealth, meant that common law was increasingly unable to cope with economic realities.[17]

As gender roles and identities were contested in society, so the legal profession took on board changing concepts about the form of that society which impacted on the views of law lords. However, until statute law was introduced (in 1920) to abolish the concept of the husband as the guardian of married women, the law continued to treat women as having a subordinate and dependent legal status.

This body of law, and the way that it constructed gender identities, made use of a particular representation of an ideal socio-spatial order of society, that of the middle-class ideology of separate spheres. This representation incorporated notions of a masculine public sphere, with men associated with the market place, politics and so on, and a feminine private sphere, in which women were associated with the home and domesticity.[18] Scottish Enlightenment theories had given a new importance to the ideology of domesticity which continued to influence social thought throughout the nineteenth century in Scotland.[19] Separate-spheres ideology incorporated notions of both an ideal social order and a proper spatial ordering of society. The definition and gendering of public and private space represented an intertwining of social and spatial ideals.[20] Masculine and feminine identities were associated with particular geographical locations. Separate-spheres ideology is not advanced as a descriptor of social reality. Men and women in their daily practices broke through the ideal on an everyday basis.[21] Indeed, many of the cases considered here arose from the conflict between the ideal view of society embedded in the law and the realities of people's lives. However, as Breitenbach and Gordon note, 'the institutional life of Scotland has acted as a force to control and confine women within the domestic sphere'.[22]

This representation of an ideal, stable society was used by social actors to promote and defend a particular version of the law. Its encapsulation in the legal framework, and its reification through the use of 'natural' representations of identity and location, transformed it into a real and powerful force in society. Inherent within this representation of society was a distribution of power, combining patriarchal power and power over property. The use of this representation of socio-spatial relations thus became a focus for the contesting of power relations in society, which can be traced by exploring the making, interpretation and application of law.

CULTURE AND IDENTITY IN THE MAKING OF LAW

The formal construction of law was carried out by middle-class professional men and male Members of Parliament. Influenced by the women's movement, and in particular the Married Women's Property Committee, MPs attempted to move reform bills through Parliament, some of which resulted in new legislation.[23] It is possible to trace in the debates surrounding the creation of new law the use of ideal views of socio-spatial organisation and gender identity. Opponents to change in the law wished to uphold stable concepts of public and private spheres and gender identity, while those seeking reform sought to challenge some aspects of this view of society. Stereotyped, 'natural' representations of identity played an important part in these debates.

For example, 'natural' representations of men and women influenced the opinions of those giving evidence to the 1881 Select Committee on the Married Women's Property Bill. Women were seen as responsible for the household.[24] There was debate over whether a married woman should have the legal right to contract for employment without her husband's consent and control the earnings derived thereby. The question was put to Dr Kirkwood if he 'would allow [a wife] perfect freedom to contract for her services . . . Would you allow her to become an actress, to put a strong case, against her husband's will?' Dr Kirkwood answered 'yes', but considered 'there is not the slightest fear of a woman abandoning the care of her house and children for the sake of contracting for her services unless the family really needed her earnings. It will cure itself.'[25] Opponents of reform were more direct. Lord Fraser, asked whether he was aware that the Select Committee on the English reform Bill had decided women were free to contract for employment, replied 'I can only say that I should be very much astonished if that ever became law in a civilised country.'[26]

Fixed notions of roles and identities related to behaviour in the public sphere were thus important in these debates. Notions of masculine/public and feminine/private identities spilled over into considerations of property rights. The central debate over the reform of the law in the 1870s and early 1880s was whether to abolish the husband's right of administration and allow the wife perfect freedom with regard to her property. The 1881 Bill intended to end the *jus administrationis*. The retention of the curatorial right rested on arguments that 'in this way [the husband's] legitimate authority was preserved'.[27] The right of administration 'proceeded on the assumption of the inexperience and greater want of knowledge on the part of the wife, and her disposition to trust more and rely more upon other people', and its retention was 'advantageous to the good government of any family'.[28] Several witnesses to the Select Committee could see no reason for abolishing the *jus administrationis*. Lord Fraser was most outspoken about a married woman's role. Asked whether married women should not be protected from the event of their husband's losing all their property, he replied:

> it depends on whether it is the wisest thing to reserve the property to the wife, and let her get three per cent, or whether it is not wiser to enable the wife to say, 'There is my money, trade with it, and make an income, so that we may live.' I am of opinion that the latter course is the best, trusting the husband and having confidence in his judgement.

Regarding the income from property, he stated that 'to allow the wife to administer it according to her own will might be to her own prejudice', and 'why she should . . . have money in her own pocket to deal with as she thinks fit, I cannot understand'.[29]

The arguments of the opponents of change can be read more broadly as attempts to protect their ideal vision of stable socio-spatial relations in society. The Lord Advocate, commenting on why the Select Committee had reduced the scope of the Bill, considered that 'it was not possible to carry out such a complete separation of interests without serious disturbance to the social relations of the country and the state of public feeling'.[30] Opponents even stressed the negative impacts on women and marital relations of equality of property rights. One member of the Select Committee was moved to ask if:

> in an age like this, when the tendency is in the direction of the extravagance and love of money, may the provisions of a Bill of this nature, facilitating the wife's power of making money without the husband's consent, and neglecting her more immediate family obligations, not lead to a relaxation of natural obligations, and so do more harm than good?[31]

Mr Lamond echoed this sentiment when he stated 'the fact of a lady having a separate purse will tend . . . to induce her to spend rather more than she would otherwise do'.[32] There was also a defence against a perceived threat to masculinity inherent in this discourse. The Lord Advocate, commenting on the 1877 Bill, suggested that letting women own their own property 'would subvert the ordinary relations of man and wife. It would create an Empress and a slave, instead of an Emperor and a slave, as is said to exist at present.' Another commentator described the Bill as 'a measure for taking the breeks off the man and putting them on the woman'.[33]

Thus the construction of gender identity with reference to the 'proper' place of women and men in an ideal socio-spatial order was an important discourse in the creation of new law. Supporters of change challenged these stereotypical views of feminine identity. Mr George Anderson argued in support of the 1877 Bill that 'it seems anomalous that we should consider a woman because she is married incapable of administering or dealing with her property'.[34] Opponents of reform appealed to culturally acceptable notions of femininity to legitimate their opposition.

CULTURE AND IDENTITY IN THE INTERPRETATION OF LAW

In the courtroom, legal decision-making rested in part on the construction of gender identity. The law lords were all male and were drawn from the upper social classes. In interpreting the law, they drew on pre-nineteenth-century institutional writings on common law, statute law, case law and their own view of socio-spatial relations. Throughout this period the decisions of the law lords were influenced by separate-spheres ideology. The identity of married women and men as legal subjects was created by using their supposedly 'natural' characteristics to position them in particular locations within this ideal socio-spatial view of society. The law lords' language and logic, as applied in the courtroom, included an implicit socio-spatial representation, one which invoked closure and recreated the patriarchal power relations of society.

Separate-spheres ideology was expressed in the interpretation of law through the notion of the husband as guardian of his wife. Very clear views on marital roles were held by the law lords. In 1868 Lord Ardmillan held that 'it is a husband's duty to practise self-restraint, to rule his household prudently, and to guide and regulate his wife's conduct, and set her an example'.[35] The Lord Justice-Clerk in 1866 considered the wife's duty to her husband to be 'to love, honour and obey him, to live with him, and to give him the advantage and solace of her society'.[36] Curatorial powers were held to rest with the husband because 'it is the mutual intention of the parties that the husband as the natural head of the family should have these powers'.[37] A wife was seen as being dependent upon her husband's activities in the public sphere. The law held that 'there is an obligation, both natural and legal, on a husband to provide for his wife'.[38]

The association of married women with the private sphere was used in the creation of their identity as legal subjects. The case of Menzies v. Murray (1875)[39] provides a good example of the creation of married women as legal subjects. Miss Catherine Menzies, in contemplation of marriage to Captain J. H. Murray in 1845, executed an ante-nuptial contract placing her estate of around £9,000 in the hands of trustees. Later in life she attempted to terminate the contract, an act which the court would not allow as the rights secured to a wife by her contract could not be renounced while the marriage continued. The basis of this decision was that married women needed to be protected from making decisions (perhaps under duress) that could be to their own disadvantage. According to Lord Deas:

> the object and effect of the law is not to lay a restraint on the wife to her prejudice, but to throw around her a protection for her benefit ... a wise and equitable protection, not unknown in other relations of society ... for instance, in the case of persons under age, weak and facile individuals, persons who have voluntarily interdicted themselves and so on.[40]

Marriage involved a woman surrendering 'her liberty, and to some extent her will, – to merge her wishes and her interests in those of her husband, – to change her very character, and to be, in short, no longer mistress of herself'.[41] For Lord Neaves the irrevocability of the contract

> never could be effectual if the law looked upon the wife after marriage as a free person ... in such contracts the law looks upon the condition of the married woman as one requiring protection, even from her own acts ... a married woman ... should be protected as if her mind and will were in abeyance.[42]

Again, the grounding of such reasoning in a conception of a natural order of society is clear. As Lord Deas commented, 'it appears to me that it is founded in nature – that the admirable subjugation of the will of one sex to the pleasure of the other for the mutual benefit of both calls for [protection] in return on the ground of humanity'.[43]

As the Lord Justice-Clerk noted, however, this particular identity for married women existed only as long as the marriage did, as 'what she may do on the dissolution of the marriage is an entirely different matter. She is then a free agent.'[44] Divorce, desertion or widowhood transformed women as legal subjects. The law contained a series of legal subjects which were applied to women, fracturing their legal identity. Widows had a right to terce, a third or a half of the husband's moveables depending on whether there were children. During marriage this right was suspended and the husband had control of the property. However, as Lord Cowan noted, 'the moment the breath is out of his body his administration ceases, and [the wife's] proprietory right emerges, free of control'.[45] At widowhood, then, a married woman was no longer a woman needing protection, but was instantaneously transformed into an entirely different legal subject.

Gendered representations of space and the positioning of men and women within those representations were thus a central part of the construction of legal and gender identities. Married women as legal subjects were characterised as dependent, in need of protection and associated with the private sphere. These identities were used to invoke closure. By reproducing the power relations inherent in patriarchal society as 'natural' or given by constructing 'natural' identities, the law was able to justify the continued control of married women's property by their husbands. The use of these 'natural' characteristics to create abstract identities for married women legitimated their oppression within the law. The law needed such abstract identities to work, to remove judicial reasoning from the reality of people's lives.

THE MATERIAL IMPLICATIONS OF 'CULTURE' AND IDENTITY

This exploration of the relationship between middle-class culture and married women's property law has illustrated the importance of the construction of meaning and the use of metaphorical representations of society. However, the construction and deployment of such representations were rooted in material social relations, and in turn impacted on the material relations of property ownership and power relations in society.

Though the supporters of reform of married women's property rights differed in the degree of change they felt necessary, there was overwhelming support for the view that the law as it stood in the nineteenth century discriminated against women. This view was partly based on a realisation by many people that it was becoming less tenable to cling to rigid stereotypes of married women. Equally important was the widely held view that the law was unfair with regard to the life chances of married women, who could lose control of substantial amounts of property to their husbands. There was frequent reference in parliamentary debates to cases where great hardship was caused to married women when their husbands lost what had been their property in business or speculation, particularly since the laws of bankruptcy tended to favour the husband's creditors over the claim of the wife. In other cases unscrupulous husbands lost their wives' fortunes, or used them as they wished. Mr James Campbell, giving evidence to the 1881 Select Committee noted that:

> It is certainly within my own professional experience, that there are cases of very
> great hardship under the existing law; I mean cases where a wife's property . . .
> has been carried away by the husband's creditors under circumstances operat-
> ing very harshly against the wife.[46]

The decision-making employed in some court cases helps to illustrate how
the power relations of the patriarchal society were reproduced in the law and
how women were disadvantaged by legal reasoning which drew on the stereotypical notions discussed above. Again, the notion of the husband as guardian
was important here. The husband had to deal with life in the public sphere, being
responsible for financial and legal obligations on behalf of his wife. Until 1920
the husband's right of administration meant that all decisions regarding the
disposal of property required his consent (except in the case of married women's
separate estate). This can be illustrated by a case of 1886 in which two married
women signed a document accepting the provisions of their father's will in place
of their legal rights without notifying their husbands. The court held that this
document was not valid. Lord Craigiehill gave the opinion that:

> I am somewhat startled by the contention . . . that an absolute right to elect . . .
> belonged to the wife to such a degree that the husband was not entitled even to
> expect the courtesy of being consulted, and that the consent and concurrence of
> the husband was not a necessity to the validity of the transaction.

The signing of the document 'embodied a transaction . . . by which they parted
with something which was theirs by legal right. That they could not do before
1881 without their husband's consent, nor can they do so now.'[47]

A case in 1892 further illustrates the, at times, twisted logic of the law and
its material impact. After her husband had been declared bankrupt, the wife
challenged the right of the trustee realising her husband's assets to claim the
household furniture which she had bought. Since the marriage was contracted
prior to 1881 the furniture fell under the husband's *jus mariti*. Lord Young
commented that:

> As to the Married Women's Property Act, I think this is a case of entrusting
> the husband with the furniture in the house. He had a duty to keep his house
> furnished and habitable for his wife and children. He would not fulfil that duty
> by providing them with the bare walls of an unfurnished house. He ought to
> have a furnished house. The furniture was entrusted to him in order that he
> should perform this duty. That exposes it to the diligence of the husband's
> creditors.[48]

Thus in this case, despite the fact that the husband was seen as having a 'duty'
to provide furniture for his wife which made it his property, the wife was left
without any furniture as its ownership by the husband allowed his creditors to
seize it.

A case of 1889 serves as a further example. In 1881 (prior to the 1881
Act) Andrew Henderson, a blacksmith, married Isabella Bird, who had bought
an inn and farm from her previous husband. The marriage was unsuccessful and
after living apart for six years both parties raised actions for divorce. Isabella

had in the meantime maintained a livelihood from the inn and farm. Again, all this property had been transferred to the husband at marriage under his right of *jus mariti* and there was no evidence that it had been legally transferred back to Isabella. Lord Shand concluded that:

> It is proposed that we should hold the wife entitled to retain the profits of a business which was so remunerative that she could lay by a considerable sum . . . [but] nothing was said as to the subjects being or becoming the property of the wife, and she was simply left with the stock and cropping of the farm and the furniture of the inn, presumably in order that she might be enabled to earn enough wherewith to aliment herself.[49]

Thus the husband was entitled to recover this property from which Isabella had made a livelihood for six years as, legally, he had not abandoned his claim established by his *jus mariti*.

Although other court cases were more complex, and women were not always the victims of husbands or the law, examples of these kinds of cases could be repeated many times. Such decisions, legally sound but nevertheless causing considerable hardship to women, were an important factor influencing moves to reform the law. They also illustrate how this body of law and its application employed a form of legal reasoning which used stereotypical, socially held ideas to legitimate the unequal treatment of married women. In this way, socially constructed notions of cultural norms had material impacts and reproduced the patriarchal power relations inherent in society.

CONCLUSION

This essay has explored the social construction of gender identity and the role of these constructions in the legal regulation of property within marriage. The form of the law and its interpretation relied upon debates in society over questions of gender identity. While those supporting reform sought to gain more equality for women, they were defeated, until 1920, by those who sought to defend a particular view of socio-spatial relations. It was the views of the victors in these debates that became encapsulated in law. Legal professionals and politicians reified particular cultural constructions as 'natural' and unarguable. The creation of gendered legal subjects thus demonstrates how 'the category of Woman is constantly subject to differing constructions [as] each discourse brings its own Woman into being and proclaims her to be natural Woman'.[50] Legal agents performed the task of creating an abstract version of society which legitimated, even if it did not obscure, the unequal treatment of married women under the law. This is not to argue that the law lords were inventing separate-spheres ideology themselves, or that they were 'controlled' by some independently existing cultural 'structure'. They were operationalising their own understanding of society, influenced by their own social world, particular to their class, family and religious background. The law can thus be seen as a vehicle or medium for universalising the social experience of a powerful group in society, middle-class males, which maintained the patriarchal power relations inherent in that society. The process involved the fusion of spatial representations with hegemonic views of social organisation. As social closure was achieved around representations of a 'proper' socio-spatial order, so men's domination of women was recreated in the law and, in turn, in people's lived legal and social relations. The creation of separate spheres as a cultural construct is thus an example of how culture involves 'a very clear process of demarcation and interpretation' in the formation of 'a structured system of representation . . . a system of power'.[51]

NOTES

1 See the discussion in P. Jackson, *Maps of Meaning* (London, Routledge, 1989).

2 D. Mitchell, 'There's no such thing as culture: towards a reconceptualization of the idea of culture in geography', *Transactions of the Institute of British Geographers*, n.s., 20 (1995), 102–16.

3 *Ibid.*, 104, 108.

4 S. Pile and N. Thrift, 'Mapping the subject', in S. Pile and N. Thrift (eds), *Mapping the Subject: Geographies of Cultural Transformation* (London, Routledge, 1995), pp. 13–56; M. Keith and S. Pile (eds), *Place and the Politics of Identity* (London, Routledge, 1993).

5 D. Haraway, *Simians, Cyborgs and Women: The Reinvention of Nature* (London, Free Association Books, 1991); G. Rose, 'Engendering and degendering', *Progress in Human Geography*, 18 (1994), 507–15; L. McDowell, 'Space, place and gender relations: Part I. Feminist empiricism and the geography of social relations', *Progress in Human Geography*, 17 (1993), 157–79; L. McDowell, 'Space, place and gender relations: Part II. Identity, difference, feminist geometries and geographies', *Progress in Human Geography*, 17 (1993), 305–18.

6 W. W. Pue, 'Wrestling with law: (geographical) specificity vs. (legal) abstraction', *Urban Geography*, 11 (1990), 566–85.

7 G. L. Clark, 'The geography of law', in R. Peet and N. Thrift (eds), *New Models in Geography*, vol. 1 (London, Unwin Hyman, 1987), pp. 310–37.

8 D. Delaney, 'Geographies of judgement: the doctrine of changed conditions and the politics of judgement', *Annals of the Association of American Geographers*, 11 (1993), 522–41.

9 Clark, 'Geography of law', 310–37.

10 *Ibid.*; Delaney, 'Geographies of judgement'; N. K. Blomley, *Law, Space, and the Geographies of Power* (London, Guilford Press, 1994); N. K. Blomley and G. L. Clark, 'Law, theory and geography', *Urban Geography*, 11 (1990), 433–46.

11 C. Smart, 'Disruptive bodies and unruly sex: the regulation of reproduction and sexuality in the nineteenth century', in C. Smart (ed.), *Regulating Womanhood: Historical Essays on Marriage, Motherhood and Sexuality* (London, Routledge, 1992), pp. 7–31.

12 Delaney, 'Geographies of judgement', 62.

13 Blomley and Clark, 'Law, theory and geography'.

14 A. D. M. Forte, 'Some aspects of the law of marriage in Scotland: 1500–1700', in E. Craik (ed.), *Marriage and Property: Women and Marital Customs in History* (Aberdeen, Aberdeen University Press, 1984), pp. 104–18; G. C. H. Paton, 'Husband and wife: property rights and relationships', in the Stair Society (ed.), *An Introduction to Scottish Legal History* (Edinburgh, the Stair Society, 1958), pp. 99–115.

15 Law Society of Scotland, *Glossary: Scottish Legal Terms and Latin Maxims* (Edinburgh, Butterworths/Law Society of Scotland, 1992).

16 L. Holcombe, *Wives and Property: Reform of the Married Women's Property Law in Nineteenth Century England* (Oxford, Martin Robertson, 1983). For historical comparisons see A. Goransson, 'Gender and property rights: capital, kin, and owner influence in nineteenth- and twentieth-century Sweden', *Business History*, 35 (1993), 11–32; L. K. Kerber, 'Separate spheres, female worlds, woman's place: the rhetoric of women's history', *Journal of American History*, 75 (1988), 9–39; P. Lucie, 'Marriage and law

reform in nineteenth-century America', in E. Craik (ed.), *Marriage and Property: Women and Marital Customs in History* (Aberdeen, Aberdeen University Press, 1984), pp. 138–58.

17 Holcombe, *Wives and Property*.

18 J. Dwyer, *Virtuous Discourse: Sensibility and Community in Late Eighteenth Century Scotland* (Edinburgh, John Donald, 1987); L. Davidoff and C. Hall, *Family Fortunes: Men and Women of the English Middle Class, 1780–1850* (London, Hutchison, 1987).

19 L. Moore, 'Educating for the 'women's sphere': domestic training versus intellectual discipline', in E. Breitenbach and E. Gordon (eds), *Out of Bounds: Women in Scottish Society 1800–1945* (Edinburgh, Edinburgh University Press, 1992), pp. 10–41.

20 Davidoff and Hall, *Family Fortunes*.

21 Breitenbach and Gordon, *Out of Bounds*.

22 E. Breitenbach and E. Gordon, 'Introduction', in Breitenbach and Gordon, *Out of Bounds*, p. 8.

23 Holcombe, *Wives and Property*.

24 Parliamentary Papers (P.P.), 1881, *Report from the Select Committee on Married Women's Property (Scotland) Bill*, vol. 9, 661–727.

25 *Ibid.*, 11, 49

26 *Ibid.*, 28

27 *Hansard*, 1881, 3rd series, vol. 260, 1525.

28 *Ibid.*, 1880, 3rd series, vol. 252, 1552–3; *ibid.*, 1877, 3rd series, vol. 233, 1409.

29 P.P., 1881, 21–33.

30 *Hansard*, 1881, 3rd series, vol. 260, 1523.

31 P.P., 1881, 39.

32 *Ibid.*, 54.

33 *Hansard*, 1877, 3rd series, vol. 233, 1413, 1410.

34 *Ibid.*, 1405–6.

35 Chalmers v. Chalmers, 1868, 3rd series, 1867–68, vol. 6, no. 97, 547–53. The cases consulted for this paper are published in a series of volumes which underwent a number of changes of titles. All the titles begin 'Cases Decided in . . .' and then state the various courts involved. Originally the volumes were published by Thomas Clark, Edinburgh, and later by T. and T. Clark, Edinburgh. Individual details for each case are cited in the notes.

36 Smith v. Smith, 1866, 3rd series, 1865–66, vol. 4, no. 61, 279–83.

37 M'Dougall v. City of Glasgow Bank, 1879, 4th series, 1878–79, vol. 6, no. 156, 1089–96.

38 Dunlop v. Johnstone, 1867, 3rd series, 1866–67, vol. 5, no. 4, 22–27.

39 Menzies v. Murray, 1875, 4th series, 1874–75, vol. 2, no. 95, 507–20.

40 *Ibid.*, 512–13.

41 *Ibid.*, 513.

42 *Ibid.*, 517.

43 *Ibid.*, 516.

44 *Ibid.*, 511.

45 M'Intyre v. M'Intyre's Trustees, 1865, 3rd series, 1864–65, vol. 3, no. 199, 1074–5.

46 P.P., 1881, 38.

47 Miller and Co. v. Galbraith's Trustees, 1886, 4th series, 1885–86, vol. 13, no. 121, 764–8.

48 Anderson v. Anderson's Trustee, 1892, 4th series, 1891–92, vol. 19, no. 126, 684–7.

49 Henderson v. Henderson, 1889, 4th series, 1889–90, vol. 17, no. 4, 18–25.

50 Smart, 'Disruptive bodies', 7.

51 Mitchell, 'There's no such thing as culture', 111–12.

10

MRS POOTER'S PURCHASE: LOWER-MIDDLE-CLASS CONSUMERISM AND THE SALES, 1870–1914
Christopher P. Hosgood

By the late nineteenth century the rhythm of the shopping year was punctuated in dramatic style by the biannual 'sales seasons'. These 'sales' were the most talked about, and certainly the most controversial, events in the shopping calendar. While observers were divided on the question as to whether or not sales provided shoppers with real bargains, most acknowledged that the sales represented a new and potentially dangerous opportunity for social engagement. Sales introduced two distinct but often interconnected issues – gender and class – into the debate over an emerging consumer culture. While shopping was quickly identified with women in the popular imagination, sales shopping introduced a new twist in that it was associated not only with women, but also with a particular social group, the lower middle class. The specific concern of this chapter is to locate the suburban shopper – clearly identified by the press as a lower-middle-class woman – in the carnivalesque atmosphere of the summer and winter sales.

There can be little doubt that historians have been influenced greatly by the portrayal of lower-middle-class life in George and Weedon Grossmith's comic novel *The Diary of a Nobody* (1892), which introduced Charles and Carrie Pooter.[1] As J. F. C. Harrison correctly observes, the diary lays bare the petty vanities and ambitions of a group who craved, above all else, respectability.[2] However, significantly and perhaps inadvertently, the Grossmiths depict a couple whose respectability is not only determined by their assumption of a particular moral code, but also by 'keeping up appearances' through the accumulation and purchase of 'things'.[3] Unpacking the Pooters' purchase enables us to consider some important questions. How were sales represented in the press? Why were sales considered subversive by so many commentators? What does the sales shopping experience tell the historian about consumerism, and class and gender relations? Twinning a study of consumerism with a reconstruction of the lower-middle-class experience will inform our understanding of both; we will better appreciate the attempts of the lower middle class to carve out their own social niche, and we will better appreciate the pervasive impact of the consumer culture. Perhaps shopping, as it promoted consumerism, with its emphasis on solitary endeavour and individual achievement, to the detriment of co-operative action, explains more about the nature of the lower-middle-class experience than a concern for their imitative notions of respectability.

Most recent work on nineteenth-century consumer culture is grounded in the theoretical assumption that consumerism acted as a vital conservative force. It is argued by scholars such as William Leach and Thomas Richards that by fetishising items of consumption, the Victorian 'things' identified by Asa Briggs, late Victorian society came to associate success with the accumulation of goods, rather than the cultivation of, among other things, the appropriate moral baggage.[4] In other words the general tenor of academic work, as Victoria de Grazia concludes, indicates that in the late nineteenth century the commodification of culture represented the success of the 'state' in convincing society that the ability for individuals to purchase 'abundance' in a market-driven economy created and sustained the 'good' society.[5]

Yet the problem remains that despite the general conclusion that consumerism acted as a conservative force, and despite recent work by historians such as Lori Loeb and Susan Porter Benson[6] and literary critics, such as Rachel Bowlby,[7] investigating the way in which consumerism was promoted, we know very little about the mechanics of consumerism – the physical act of acquiring consumer goods, or, more simply put, shopping. The goal of this chapter is to examine the shopping experience during the sales and then consider the ideological impact of consumerism by examining a social constituency that proved particularly vulnerable to the pull of consumer culture – the lower middle class. Without questioning the overarching conclusion that consumerism did act to accommodate citizens to the late-industrial urban community, this chapter will argue that at the more humble level of daily experience shopping could, and did, act as a more subversive force; it will be seen that for the lower middle class, and particularly for lower-middle-class women, wedded to a world from which they had little hope of escaping, consumerism offered a temporary release from economic constraints and social conventions.

It is now over twenty years since Geoffrey Crossick first exhorted historians to investigate the English lower middle class. On that occasion he suggested that small business interests and white-collar employees be designated the two wings of a residual lower middle class; its members bound together either by their marginality to the social, cultural and economic world of the middle class or by their pathetic attempts to ape the gentility of their superiors.[8] Such an analysis confirmed once again the unheroic nature of the lower-middle-class *mentalité*, and explains Crossick's eventual conclusion that as a group they 'claimed no vital social role'.[9] Crossick's more recent work, in collaboration with Heinz-Gerhard Haupt, offers a re-evaluation of this earlier position and concludes that white-collar and small business interests should not be considered in tandem. Crossick and Haupt's work is significant because they make it clear that they now credit the petite bourgeoisie (small business families) in Europe with a greater spirit of independence than they had earlier acknowledged. They argue convincingly that the petite bourgeoisie created their own social and cultural world, centred on the inter-relationship between enterprise and family life, which enabled them to react more purposefully to outside social forces and agencies.[10]

By hiving off these small business interests from the old lower middle class, we are left with a rump of white-collar workers who collectively formed a lower middle class which presumably shared many common experiences, and hence which is attractive to historians as a potentially more cohesive social body. The problem is that a distinct lower-middle-class *mentalité* has proved elusive. The most lasting image of lower-middle-class behaviour and attitude in the late-nineteenth century is often centred on the appearance and character of Mr Charles Pooter, hero of the Grossmith brothers' comic novel *The Diary of a Nobody*. So powerful is the Pooter legacy that it reconfirms the validity of the more general representation of clerks as shallow, deferential, obsequious imitators of middle-class manners. The middle class sought to distance itself from the lower middle class through stock fictional accounts in which individuals and their families were represented as unimaginative, contemptible cyphers who clung to a rigid interpretation of respectability so as to hide their lack of status. Thus novelists and journalists seemingly saw it as their duty to reinforce their middle-class audience's sense of superiority over a class they despised by advertising the lower-middle-class' veneer of shabby gentility.[11] At its most vicious, in work by writers such as T. W. H. Crosland, this treatment depicted a lower-middle-class suburban world of clerks characterised as 'pitiful people!'[12] and 'a low and inferior species'.[13] The men were all 'calculated to make gods and little fishes laugh'[14] and were 'hen-pecked, shrew-driven, neglected, heartsick', while the women were identified principally as sales-goers. Thus, 'tawdriness, glassiness, imitation, and meretriciousness are the only wear for Suburbia'.[15] More dispassionate and subtle, but ultimately equally as damning of lower-middle-class behaviour, *The Diary of a Nobody* reinforced this perception of a lower middle class living a life in imitation of its social superiors. But what of lower-middle-class behaviour in the real world? How did they act and what does this tell us about their social expectations?

The evolving consumer culture may have become associated with a land of plenty in which ever expanding opportunities of consumption served to reinforce an assumption of financial security and social position. Advertising promoted a world view that enticed consumers into believing that their social experiences and circumstances could be altered by consumer decisions. Advertisements hinted at what you would be once you had purchased an item – spending money was an act of faith confirming your legitimate claim to belong to the right set. The message was clear: to buy, rather than to live by a particular moral code, was the stuff of life. Of course there were dangers; overspending could lead to financial embarrassment and social disaster. The reality was that bills had to be paid and extravagances covered by often insufficient incomes. Nonetheless, by the late nineteenth century lower-middle-class claims to gentility were based increasingly on a theatre of behaviour modelled after the superficial world view of consumer culture rather than the moral code stressing traditional middle-class values. Buy what was fashionable so that you could confirm your rank as a gentleman, a lady or as a respectable family.

There is little doubt that historians can legitimately argue that the consequence of this tyranny of fashion was that consumer culture imposed a powerful control over the lower middle class. By associating fashion with conformity, the lower middle class could not afford to be identified as either bohemian or plebeian. To depart from the reigning code of fashion risked compromising rank and position. Consequently the lower middle class was always following and never leading. To misjudge public opinion, as a perceptive writer to *The Englishwoman* noted, was to invite ostracism: to be labelled 'dowdy', or 'unwomanly' or 'unsexed'.[16] Consumerism provided the lower middle class with the fiction that they belonged in the middle-class world; consumerism ironically and cruelly reinforced the subordination of the lower middle class and potentially provided the middle class with a flattering sense of their own cultural superiority. And yet, despite this nicely packaged image of the lower middle class as sycophants, there is little evidence to suggest that the middle class was flattered by such imitation. There is ample evidence to suggest that the middle class masked their fear of this potentially subversive and growing horde of lower-middle-class suburban consumers behind a rhetoric of contempt. Why? *Fin-de-siècle* social critics recognised that shopping, a vital social force, was distinct and independent of the economic force, consumerism, which encouraged the purchase of consumer items. While intimately connected, consumerism and shopping existed independently of each other; shopping provided an important opportunity to disrupt accepted conventions of social behaviour.

Where, in all of this, do the Pooters appear? Of course, we must pause at this point to acknowledge that *The Diary of a Nobody* must be used as a source only with some caution. It can be argued that the novel tells us a great deal more about middle-class attitudes about the lower middle class than it can about the lower middle class itself. However, with this in mind, and despite concerns about the 'linguistic turn', *The Diary of a Nobody* is an important text which illustrates the fundamental tension which informed the lower-middle-class cultural experience of 'keeping up appearances'. The opening paragraph of *The Diary of a Nobody* introduces the central dilemma: how to display and maintain membership in the consumer society while balancing the very real need to watch every penny of a limited, and inadequate, at least for the purposes of maintaining a household modelled on middle-class standards, income. At the outset, then, we find the Pooters claiming an early (if Pyrrhic) victory as Charles negotiates a £2 rent reduction by bringing the landlord's attention to the noise caused by the trains roaring by at the bottom of the garden. Then we find that this financial success is immediately offset by his purchase of a 'cottage' piano 'manufactured by W. Bilkson (in small letters), from Collard and Collard (in very large letters)' on the three-year hire-purchase system.[17] This theme is returned to on a number of occasions, such as when the Pooters discover the expense of buying Christmas cards and conclude that 'the great disadvantage of going out in Society and increasing the number of our friends was, that we should have to send out nearly two dozen cards this year'.[18] Significantly, the Grossmiths' pinpoint, perhaps inadvertently, another important element of tension in the Pooter household. Their struggle to keep up appearances illustrates two quite different perspectives on the nature of the lower-middle-class identity. Charles Pooter's stoic attempt to adopt the (assumed) moral code of his employer can be contrasted to Carrie Pooter's consumerism, reflected in her shopping expeditions and attempts to be fashionable.

The Pooters may be fictional but their dilemma was very real to lower-middle-class families. The title of one self-help manual for women is fairly suggestive: *How to live on a Hundred a Year, make a Good Appearance and Save Money.* The key to happiness, and a successful family life, was to be able to remain a 'lady' and live in such a way that your acquaintances did not know the true nature of your finances.[19] One example of the agony of poor clerks can be found in the diaries of Sydney Moseley; he wanted desperately 'to get on' and so saved as best he could, but then broke down and bought a bike. 'Am sorry I bought bike. To keep one's head up, keep out of debt. Hate to be in debt. Loss of dignity.'[20] The Grossmiths locate in Mr Pooter's daily struggle to live a decent life the lower-middle-class dilemma which I have identified all too briefly above. Despite his attempts to live by a moral code which he assumes to be borrowed from his social superiors, the reality is that many of his attempts at gentility are based on the acquisition and display of consumer items. Significantly the Grossmiths have Pooter celebrating his salary raise by buying Carrie the little costume she 'saw at Peter Robinson's so cheap'.[21] Perhaps Pooter learned his most valuable lesson when he attempted to return his recent purchase of a new and fashionable stylographic pen which never worked and, to his horror, got him into trouble at work. In refusing the return the shopman reminded Mr Pooter that 'buying and selling were two different things'.[22]

I

From humble origins in the middle of the nineteenth century, the sales had become by the end of the century the most eagerly anticipated events of the shopping year. In July, following the end of the 'Season', and January, following the Christmas rush, shops and department stores in London and the provinces prepared for the arrival of the bargain hunter. An examination of the rituals of sales shopping, and the way in which the sales experience was reported in the trade and popular press, confirms that shopping space was hotly contested both as gendered and as class space and, not surprisingly, this layering of conflict complicates any reading of the evidence. Quite rightly, most of the recent work on shopping has placed gender at the heart of the debate as the most influential determinant of consumer behaviour;[23] however, class also played an important role. Indeed, in fundamental ways the two cannot be entirely disentangled. While this chapter is most concerned with lower-middle-class consumerism, it must be remembered that gender was always the central feature of representations of shopping. Consequently, the press's persistent campaign to ridicule the behaviour of sales shoppers was all the more insidious because frequently it represented an attack on the participants because they were women and lower-middle-class.

Late-century sales had their origins in three specific traditions. First, in the practice of drapers selling off fabric remnants, particularly at the end of the spring/summer and autumn/winter fashion seasons. Secondly, in the attempts of retailers to stimulate business, particularly if the Christmas trade was sluggish. Illustrative of many such attempts were sales initiated in mid-December 1857 by Marshall and Snelgrove and then, in response, Swann and Edgar, two of London's leading drapers; each placed their 'fancy goods', including silk, on sale because of the 'universal depression in trade'.[24] Thirdly, in the popularisation of the sale as a gimmick adopted by the so-called 'pushing shops' of the 1870s. These shops aimed for a quick turnover of popular, cheap articles promoted through aggressive advertising. By the 1880s the sale had been adopted by even the most superior of London and provincial shops as a legitimate business strategy. It was at this point that the sales became firmly rooted in January, following the Christmas season, and July, following the Season. Indeed, as an American guide for tourists visiting London explained, the sales should not be considered 'bargain' sales but part of the regular routine of the year.[25]

Shops throughout the country, from the West End and suburban high streets of London to provincial high streets, participated in a ritual which seemed to gain momentum with each passing year. Indeed, it was the participation of the very best shops – Marshall and Snelgrove, Jay's, Peter Robinson's, Dickins and Jones, Swan and Edgar's, Woollands, Harvey Nichols, and Derry and Tom's to name a few – that gave the sales their tremendous appeal. Whereas in the early years shopkeepers attempted to keep the sales within a week-long period, they were gradually extended, into early February and mid-August, and occasionally beyond. While some shopkeepers, such as Lewis's of Manchester and Liverpool or suburban London drapers, attempted to maintain the sales momentum throughout the year, often by strategically advertising particular articles for sale on specific days or weeks, the so-called 'great' establishments or houses of the West End concentrated their efforts on the traditional sale months. Shopkeepers realised that the success of the sales depended in large part in creating a sense of excitement, which was the more impressive if contained within a short period. As the best bargains disappeared, the choice before shopkeepers was either to end their sales, and leave customers anticipating their next opportunity for a bargain, or to try and whip up a new level of excitement by resorting to ever more hyperbolic levels of advertising – relatively calm advertisements of 'Great Stocktaking Sales' or 'The Great Event of the Season' or 'Great Midsummer Sale',[26] were replaced by announcements of a 'Monster Sale' and 'The Greatest Sale of the Year'.[27] While some retailers resorted to gimmicks in order to maintain interest in their sales, most took advantage of the sales to sell outdated, less than popular or slightly shop-worn articles. So popular did sales become that retailers of every imaginable product participated. While drapers and dealers in ladies apparel featured most prominently in the early sales, clothiers, jewellers, furniture dealers and indeed almost every retailer of non-perishable items came to participate in these biannual traditions.

By the 1890s the press had developed a stereotype of sales activity which featured three common elements. First, sales were invariably represented as chaotic affairs. Secondly, they were wholly identified with women. These two features are clearly present in a sale-scene cartoon which appeared in 1890 and illustrated the disorder around the shop counter. Prominent among the customers are some of the stock characters of shopping jokes: lost and hopeless men, husbands struggling to carry their wives' purchases, mothers with nannies and babies in tow and, most prominently, respectably dressed women acting outrageously. In one small vignette within the larger illustration a woman customer, fed up with the lack of service, attracts the attention of a shop assistant, frozen in horror by the bedlam around him, by hooking his collar with her umbrella handle.[28] The third feature of sale representations, less visible and infrequently voiced openly but vital nonetheless, was their association with the lower-middle-class consumer. Occasionally we catch a direct glimpse of the contemptuous middle-class voice. T. W. H. Crosland caustically commented to lower-middle-class sales-goers that the sales 'are designed and invented simply to tickle your suburban maw, and we laugh in our sleeves [sic] while we flourish them in front of you'.[29] Writing in *Hearth and Home* in 1909 Mrs C. S. Peel, while sympathetic to the experience of the woman shopper, denounced the 'fetish of "keeping up appearances", which really embitters the life of hundreds of Englishwomen whose means are not equal to their position,' most notably the 'harassed and careworn' wives of the lower middle class.[30] More frequently the press referred euphemistically to the poorer suburban woman with a reduced dress allowance or a fixed income – in other words to the lower-middle-class inhabitants of 'villadom', home of the 'great Clerk-class'.[31] Journalistic convention consistently represented the sales as disorderly scrums of lower-middle-class suburban women. 'The bargain hunters: a tragicomedy of suburban life', which appeared in *Punch* in 1902, is a fine example of this convention. The shoppers are women, the action is furious, and the drama involves two suburban women, shopping for an upcoming evening party which they are both attending, contesting the same blouse.[32]

Typically sales-shoppers were designated as social climbers who took advantage of the sales in a pathetic attempt to accumulate current fashions in order to emulate the dress of their social superiors. These attempts, so it was argued by critics of the sales, were doomed to failure because the clothing consigned to the sale tables was, almost by definition, out of fashion or, most cruel of all, had never been fashionable in the first place because it was not legitimate remnant stock. The editor of a 'Feminine Affairs' column was contemptuous of women 'with pretensions to good taste' who shopped at the 'cheap sales': 'There are thousand [sic] of women walking about at this moment in cheap "skirt and coat" congratulating themselves on being fashionably attired at very small expense. If they could only see themselves at the back! How they would loathe their "bargains" . . . Do you see the stupidity of it?'[33] Sales stock was also roundly criticised by feminists as mostly damaged or dirty, ugly or a cheap imitation of a dying fashion; they lamented the success with which advertisers persuaded 'almost poor' sales-goers to spend more than they could afford on things that would not last – 'ephemeral finery' (figure 9).[34]

Critics argued that at best the sales reflected women's love for a bargain. Yet even shopping for bargains was turned against women because there was a common suggestion that any savings were illusory. Jokes in the comic papers consistently lampooned women's weakness for a sale. '*Single Man*: A woman dearly loves a bargain. *Married Man*: Yes, she loves it too *dearly*; she generally pays about twice the value of the "bargain".'[35] Similarly: '*Customer*: 'what is the price of this material? *Assistant*: That is two shillings a yard, madam. *Customer*: Oh, that is much to dear. *Assistant*: But it is reduced from three shillings. *Customer*: Is that so? I'll take ten yards.'[36] Significantly such assumptions often were echoed in women's illustrated journals. In an editorial titled 'A-Saling We Will Go', the

SELLING OFF WINTER STOCK.—THE ANNUAL GAME OF "FOX AND GEESE."   *Judge.*

Fig. 9 This cartoon exemplifies the comic press's representation of women as credulous shoppers.

Lady's Pictorial suggested that during the January sales 'temptation is placed in our way, and every woman is fired to possess bargains'. The article concluded: 'every woman is at heart a bargain-hunter, even if she buys what she does not want, it is a joy to her to feel that she has bought it cheap.'[37] Other women noted that 'we are not able to stand against the overwhelming temptations to buy which besiege us at every turn. What is shopping these days but an unsuccessful struggle against overwhelming temptations?'[38] Such commentary served only to reinforce the misogynistic rhetoric of writers such as T. W. H. Crosland who feared that the world was becoming a 'whirling Peter Robinson's'.[39] Crosland argued that the modern woman should shop less, but 'woman is the daughter of the horse-leech, and screams give, give, give, till she dies'.[40]

Indeed, it became a common assumption that women were by instinct 'bargain hunters' and it was this desire which spread at sales time like a 'fever'. Edith Guest identified this susceptibility in a detailed account of the sales which appeared in *Hearth and Home* in 1902; 'sale fever' led women 'to the fierce contests of the bargain counter. Contests too [sic] by no means without bitterness, and by no means pleasant things for the timid woman.'[41] In July 1902 *Punch* featured an illustration of the bacilli responsible for 'summer sale fever', a 'complaint very prevalent just now among the weaker sex'.[42] A magnified cross-section of a cell, the cartoon contained likenesses of such items as parasols, scarves, boas and frocks, all with 'bargain' or 'reduced' or 'sale price' tags' (figure

BACILLI OF SUMMER SALE FEVER.

A COMPLAINT VERY PREVALENT JUST NOW AMONG THE WEAKER SEX.

Fig. 10 *Punch's* **medical breakthrough identifying the source of women shoppers' credulity.**

10). The outcome of this journalistic construction of a 'sale fever', seen in yet another *Punch* cartoon, was to ridicule suburban women; they were represented as getting up early so as to travel into the West End where they literally fought with other suburban women over scraps of material in 'the battle of the remnants' sales.[43] Sales became associated with scrums of suburban women, suffering from a temporary loss of reason, in violent search for a bargain. Mrs Belloc-Lowndes noted that it was common for large crowds of women to gather outside shops half an hour before opening: 'and the scene, when the magic hour of nine has struck, recalls nothing so much . . . as that of a town being taken by assault'.[44] These images were reinforced by women writers such as Mrs E. T. Cook:

> Sale days are truly terrible experiences to the uninitiated. If you happened, unwittingly, to go to some familiar shop on one of these yearly occasions, the mass of crowded, struggling, gasping humanity, nearly all pushing, and nearly all fat, would lead you to imagine that life and death, at least, were intimately concerned in the tussle, instead of merely the question of securing the 'first choice' of 'remnants'.[45]

Women were commonly designated as frivolous, compulsive shoppers who participated in the sales in order to sate their desires rather than to acquire the necessities of life. Or, as one writer summarised, the modern woman was depicted 'as a vicious, self-indulgent, brainless kind of person, who is either a victim of vanity or possessed by the passion for amusement'.[46] Moreover, women were transformed, if popular press accounts are to be believed, from angels into viragos, as their 'voices lost their chirrupiness, and accrued a stinging accent of sarcasm'.[47]

Sales, and the crowds that they created, were roundly condemned by authors in journals such as *Vanity Fair*, which enjoyed a wealthy readership. The tone of these articles usually denounced the disruption to orderly life caused by the excitement of 'sale fever'. Clarence Rook complained that women in the shopping districts made it difficult for men to move about comfortably on the pavements. 'I have been shoved off the pavement by rabid ladies in High St. Kensington; and I have seen the bargain sales in Chicago. The women of the world are struggling to get a remnant at cost-price.'[48] Raymond Pierpoint lamented the crowded streets of 'people who seemed to have no settled convictions, except a desire to jostle any and everybody who happened to come in the way'.[49] There was an anxiety about the promiscuousness attendant on the bustle of the sales crowd which was captured in a piece by W. R. Titterton:

> The whole street reeks with desire. You shudder. The current is seizing you, enticing. Women's bodies innumerable around you sway and bend . . . The feet of the crowd move to a dance-step. The smell of the perfumes is stifling. Warm bodies crush around you. The lights reel . . . Thank God! A side street. Into which you turn and watch hell passing by.[50]

While there is a fantastical sense to this description, it nonetheless captures the genuine discomfort some felt with the 'saturnalia' of sales shopping which caused shoppers to 'lash' themselves into a state of 'frantic excitement and bewilderment'.[51]

II

Thus far this chapter has considered the ways in which the sales were represented. The press took advantage of the sales phenomenon to construct a stereotype of the typical shopper, in large part characterised as a lower-middle-class suburban woman, so as to further ridicule and undermine the social pretensions of a social group despised by the middle class. Lower-middle-class shoppers were in no position to defend themselves publicly, and so the result was the general and widespread acceptance of the shopping image constructed by the late-nineteenth-century press. Yet, while we can appreciate this middle-class contempt, we need to ask why the sales, and the bargain-hunters who participated, so disconcerted the middle class? The answer lies partly in the sales experience itself. Sales shopping did upset traditional and accepted patterns of economic activity and social engagement, and thus within the realm of respectable society did indeed represent a potentially subversive influence. For the lower-middle-class shopper, however, the sales quickly became extremely important economic and social events.

While commentators, frequently but not exclusively male, argued that women shopped because they had a 'rampant mania for possessing things'[52] the reality was that many women, and particularly those of the lower middle class, had to clothe their families and furnish their homes on inadequate incomes. The reality was that for many families on the margins of the lower middle class, living in 'genteel poverty', life was a constant struggle. 'Only by screwing and scraping, by much deprivation and self-sacrifice, can the man who has never received more than £80 per annum, and who has kept up appearances and provided himself with food and shelter, put by sufficient to furnish a "humble home".'[53] For these families the sales became an acknowledged godsend which enabled them to purchase the necessities of respectable life. Penny journals, such as *Woman's Life*, which often published tips on how to find a good bargain, designated the sales as vital for young women working in offices and shops and housewives who were struggling to dress respectably or maintain a family on small incomes. For example, Helen Erecson-Smith advised readers who wished to dress smartly on a limited annual budget to buy remnant material at the winter sales which could be transformed into the most fashionable summer dresses.[54] Indeed, as the first serious shopping analysts, principally commentators in women's journals, observed, the sales were indispensable to those who shopped rationally.

In one of the first comprehensive shopping guides to London, 'Olivia' spoke of an emerging 'shopping code' and argued that shops should be critically assessed, like pictures or plays.[55] Sales featured prominently in the discussion and 'Olivia' admitted that women were of two minds about sales: 'The magic word that stocks our wardrobes, deletes our purse, disorganizes our routine, fascinates us, repels us, delights us, disappoints us twice a year regularly in London – for how much is it not answerable?'[56] Nonetheless, the trick of successful sales shopping was to shop at the 'very finest houses' which were usually too expensive where the clever shopper was much more likely to find a better deal.[57] Others agreed that for those with good judgement sales at quality shops like Peter Robinson's were 'a real opportunity'.[58] In other words, commentators believed that the modern shopper was a better consumer, and hence more discriminating. Housekeeping manuals began to urge women to learn to shop: 'Well and properly carried out, it becomes almost a science.'[59] Consequently, one observer noted that whereas in the early days sales had been little more than a trap to catch the unwary, the more sophisticated shopper who did not take advantage of them was 'scarcely sensible'.[60] Or again, 'profitable purchasing at the sales depends upon a combination of study and instinct'.[61]

Significantly, while many in the press portrayed women as indecisive shoppers, arbitrarily purchasing articles which caught their fancy, some journalists in the women's press began to describe a quite different shopper. It must be admitted that the women's press was not consistent in its depiction of women, and indeed sent conflicting messages to its readers. Nonetheless, their successful shoppers, particularly during the sales, increasingly were possessed of an almost military single-mindedness and ruthlessness characterised by the expression, which gained common currency in the late nineteenth century, of 'doing the shops'.[62] By the 1890s, as a service to its readers, women's journals were publishing comprehensive lists of the various West End houses, which included reviews of the specific goods on sale, so that judicious shoppers could simplify their shopping trips.[63] By the early 1900s the *Lady's Pictorial* included a seven-page annual feature, 'The Season of Sales'. Importantly, the tenor of articles and letters in women's journals counteracts the popular comic press stereotype of women sales-shoppers as experiencing a 'sale fever'. As the American writers Scott and Nellie Nearing observed, the bargain-hunter should in no way be ridiculed for she was the agent of progress. 'She is knowing, alert, and she gets what she wants. She is a radical in a new movement for the efficient spending of income. Let no one despise the bargain hunter.'[64] The sales threatened existing social conventions because they provided opportunities not only for more rational, independent, suburban women shoppers, but also, and this was particularly the case in London, opportunities for these women to escape suburbia and legitimately invade, and temporarily control, the West End

There is convincing evidence to suggest that the sales were also important to the lower-middle-class consumer because they provided a carnivalesque experience which allowed them a freedom of action and territory not normally open to them. It is clear from the anecdotal evidence that the sales were considered most subversive by some observers because they temporarily suspended normal experience and behaviour. While it can be argued that this temporary inversion was not spontaneous, and became increasingly stage-managed by the large stores, the sales retained a vibrancy and vitality which was never quite tamed by shop authorities. As we have seen, many writers decried the rough and tumble of the sales; however, other observers' feelings were more ambiguous as they relished the opportunity to 'let go'. It must be emphasised that for the lower-middle-class shopper the sales were clearly not just, as one observer concluded, 'the pure spirit of sport'.[65] Conversely, there is no doubting the exhilaration that many experienced at the sales. Everyone participating was party to a contest that was in clear opposition to the usual norms of shopping conduct. Critics of the sales may have over-dramatised much of the violence and disorder, but it is also apparent that the sales rituals did involve a good degree of physicality. Journal articles suggested that shopping at the sales could be exhausting and demanding, but the underlying message was that it could also be invigorating. For many women the sales represented their 'happy hunting ground'.[66] Enjoyment of the sales reflected 'a love of adventure, mixed with the love of contest, and perhaps just a little of the spirit of gambling thrown in'.[67] Sales were akin to sporting affairs, a form of gambling; everyone knew that some of the stock was a bargain, and some was rubbish, all of which gave the sales an extra 'piquancy'.[68]

Furthermore, and this is very important, despite the popular representation of sales-goers as lower-middle-class, the reality was that sales shoppers came from all ranks, from the very wealthy to the respectable working class. Sales were advertised throughout the range of family and women's magazines; from penny journals such as *Woman's Life*, to threepenny weeklies such as *House and Home* and *Lady's Pictorial*, to sixpenny journals such as *Vanity Fair* and the *Illustrated London News*. By the turn of the century the last acknowledged that even wealthy shoppers had succumbed to the lure of the sales.[69] Further, the mix of shoppers was even more inclusive by the 1900s as shops such as Harrod's began to charter trains, offering excursion fares, so that thousands of provincial women could participate in the London sales experience.[70] Significantly, the sales were not just occasions for behavioural inversion, they also represented an opportunity for territorial inversion. Sales offered the suburban lower-middle-class shopper an opportunity to contest their marginal position by storming the new bastions of middle-class culture – the shops of the West End and their kind elsewhere. In other words the sales provided an unrivalled opportunity for social mingling; the egalitarian nature of shopping represented a modern-day world turned upside down. Potentially successful bargain hunting was a consequence of skill and energy rather than rank or birth.

At this time it should be said that commentators generally agreed that shopping in England was more formal than the American or continental experience. In his recent study of department stores Bill Lancaster confirms that Britain had failed to develop the 'walk-about' shop. He suggests that shopping actually became more formal and a fear of shopping in department stores developed in the early Edwardian years.[71] Editorials in women's journals confirm the distinctiveness of the English experience; whereas in America and Paris customers were allowed to examine and handle goods without attracting attention, 'here a shopwalker instantly bears down on a customer'.[72] Under such circumstances, when even experienced and monied shoppers quailed under the shopwalker's gaze, what chance had the timid lower-middle-class shopper who needed to count every penny before concluding a purchase? On a tour through the West End with R. D. Blumenfeld in 1900 Andrew Carnegie was reported to have observed that by making people who shopped, but did not buy, uncomfortable 'shop people drive away more people than they attract'.[73] Others recalled visiting the West End and not having 'the courage to face the aristocrat behind the counter'.[74] The haughtiness of shop assistants in the most exclusive shops was legendary. *Punch* lampooned their aristocratic affectations on a number of occasions by playing up 'mistaken identity' jokes. In one cartoon Captain Bulsize marches into a shop and addresses a presumed assistant who is languidly standing by the counter: 'Here! I want a hat, please! *Sir James*: So do I.'[75] Still others recalled that on their day trips 'Up West' they 'never dared even consider a purchase'.[76]

H. Gordon Selfridge was well aware of this problem and it was partly in reaction to it that he planned his Oxford Street store to help the 'common people': he wanted them to 'think on higher planes, to strive after a finer quality of living' as well as make them 'happier, broader minded, more self-respecting and more dignified'.[77] While Selfridge's musings must be read carefully, there can be no doubt that he was steeped in an American retail tradition quite different from that prevalent in London, he did represent the ultimate extension of the new shopping experience. By promoting customer service to such a remarkable degree it is appropriate that his shop be singled out by his biographer 'as a spectacle of the new century, a shopping palace, a glimpse of Aladdin's Cave'.[78] Ordinary folk agreed, commenting that although it was not awe inspiring, like Dickins and Jones, it was cheerful and practical and 'nobody pestered you to buy'.[79] While Selfridges remained unusual among the West End and superior high-street shops, it must be said that autobiographical evidence suggests that suburban and provincial shops and department stores were becoming less formal. For example, Eileen Elias's mother shopped at Jones and Higgins in Peckham, where all the shopwalkers and assistants knew the family and took a personal interest in seeing that they got what they wanted.

> You got novelty and excitement; you got friendliness from the shop assistants; you got a glimpse into a dream-world where a suburban house could be furnished from top to bottom with Turkey carpets and aspidistra-pots and kitchen labour-saving devices; you got a picture of yourself as you would be.[80]

Meanwhile, the large drapers and department stores continued to cultivate a shopping experience which pampered those lucky enough to possess the poise and assurance of those born into rank and privilege. Shop assistants, dispersed throughout the store, all dressed in suits and dresses akin to shop livery, were at the ready to serve the legitimate customer. The palatial trappings of new stores were designed to develop a sumptuous public space which would flatter customers. Rich furnishings, draperies and carpets, exotic fixtures, grand sweeping staircases faced with marble and featuring bronze balustrading, theatrical salons, were all part of the contrived ambiance.[81] Schoolbred's, of Tottenham Court Road, reflected this concern for atmosphere in its advertisement for its new 'refreshment room' in 1892. Visitors wanting 'luxurious shopping' could relax in the 'large, handsome, well-proportioned room . . . decorated in excellent taste', with 'stained glass windows', 'soft, rich carpet' and 'charming pictures'.[82]

Consequently, the extent to which decorum was abandoned at the sales was all the more extraordinary. Initially some trade representatives were dismayed; one draper asked: 'is the end and intention of a sale to call in and supply a class of customers who never come at any other time?'[83] Apparently so! Social commentators might decry the disorder of the sales, but even the most exclusive houses came to adopt them as a legitimate business tactic. Indeed, to a large extent the excitement and disorder of the sales was artificially engineered by shop managers and owners; commonly they employed techniques such as keeping customers waiting at a number of doors which were then opened simultaneously to allow several streams of shopper to rush towards their bargains. Remnant tables were set up so that customers, usually required to engage the help of a shop assistant, could handle the goods themselves. While this provided an opportunity for conflict with other shoppers over a particularly appealing bargain, it also provided shoppers with the freedom to examine goods more independently. In particular the bustle of the sale freed shoppers from the usual restraint imposed by the shopwalker. *Punch*, always ready to support someone down on their luck, disingenuously crowned the shopwalker, usually a 'King of Men' with 'princely strut and stiffened spine', as the suffering 'hero of the summer sale':

> On Remnant Days – from morn till night,
> When blows fall fast, and words run high,
> When frenzied females fiercely fight
> For bargains that they long to buy –
> From hot attack he does not flinch,
> But stands his ground with visage pale,
> And all the time looks every inch,
> The Hero of that Summer Sale![84]

During the sales shoppers quite literally had the run of the shop. *Punch* pinpointed the novelty of this extraordinary opportunity in a cartoon which played upon advertisements that supposedly appeared in some London shops during the sales; placards invited shoppers to walk through the shop with the same freedom as in the British Museum. *Punch* could not resist the chance to compare the relative calm of the British Museum with the absolute mayhem of the shop – but the important point here is that the sales offered an opportunity of freedom, both in behaviour and access. 'Lady Jeune' remarked on this freedom in the *Fortnightly Review*. The greatest seduction offered by ingenious shopkeepers were the twice-yearly sales which allowed the shopper to walk about unmolested, feeling no pressure to purchase.[85] The excitement was also generated by the shoppers who appear to have relished the opportunity to act out of character and participate in a carnivalesque world.

At a functional level the sales served the needs of both retailer and consumer. The stores and shops were able to sell off stale stock and/or make a profit on 'sale' goods brought in to supplement existing stock. Careful shoppers were able to buy goods which they would not normally have been able to obtain. At a more elemental level, however, the sales worked to challenge existing economic and social patterns. Suburban lower-middle-class shoppers took the opportunity for release offered by the sales. Women escaped the domestic, neighbourhood routines which governed their daily lives by participating in a competitive, energetic ritual. Part of the excitement of bargain hunting was the opportunity to abandon conventions of propriety associated with the regular, daily shopping experience. There was a temporary behavioural inversion as shoppers either invaded territory which they did not normally inhabit or disregarded ingrained rules such as queuing or waiting patiently for service. It was this behaviour which so worried middle-class observers because it was such a visible reminder that the lower middle class, which connected them so directly with the vast array of inferior social grades, was not always as pliable and conventional as they liked to believe. Reminded of the precariousness of their own rank, commentators responded in part by ridiculing and lampooning, often quite viciously, the Pooters of suburbia for their forays into department stores and shops for the biannual sales. True, once the sales had ended, normal patterns were restored and lower-middle-class shoppers once again assumed their deferential character – but they still had their bargains, their paraphernalia of gentility, and the next sale was already just months away.

While the sales experience provoked tension and conflict, it can also be argued that by participating in this sales ritual, the consumer was seduced into a shopping experience which confirmed their participation and membership in a culture which was wedded to the acquisition of goods. After all, one function of the 'sale' was to enable a broader group access to consumer items. While the sales offered a temporary sense of authority for the shopper, the reality was that in the long term the consumer was being manipulated into participating in a cycle of seasonal activities over which they had little control. This chapter has argued that consumer culture acted in contrary ways – while consumerism may have imposed a steadying social influence, shopping clearly represented a locus of social tension. Late Victorian and Edwardian shop space was contested space. The sales shopping experience suggests that members of the suburban lower middle class were not always the cautious and timid individuals of the middle-class imagination. Sales shopping suggests that women shoppers' experience of a public life which challenged accepted codes of respectable behaviour was determined both by their gender and by their class.

NOTES

1 George and Weedon Grossmith, *The Diary of a Nobody* ([1892,] Oxford, Oxford University Press, 1995).

2 J. F. C. Harrison, *Late Victorian Britain, 1875–1901* (London, Routledge, 1991), pp. 62–3.

3 Asa Briggs, *Victorian Things* (London, Batsford, 1988).

4 William Leach, *Land of Desire: Merchants, Power, and the Rise of a New American Culture* (New York, Vintage Books, 1993); Thomas Richards, *The Commodity Culture of Victorian England: Advertising and Spectacle, 1851–1914* (London, Verso, 1991).

5 Victoria de Grazia and Ellen Furlough (eds), *The Sex of Things: Gender and Consumption in Historical Perspective* (Berkeley, University of California Press, 1996), p. 9.

6 Lori Loeb, *Consuming Angels: Advertising and Victorian Women* (Oxford, Oxford University Press, 1994); Susan Porter Benson, *Counter Cultures: Saleswomen, Managers, and Customers in American Department Stores, 1890–1940* (Urbana, University of Illinois Press, 1986).

7 Rachel Bowlby, *Just Looking: Consumer Culture in Dreiser, Gissing and Zola* (New York, Methuen, 1985).

8 Geoffrey Crossick (ed.), *The Lower Middle Class in Britain: 1870–1914* (London, Croom Helm, 1977), p. 12. See also the recent appraisals of the period by F. M. L. Thompson, *The Rise of Respectable Society: A Social History of Victorian Britain, 1830–1900* (London, Fontana Press, 1988), and Harrison, *Late Victorian Britain*.

9 Geoffrey Crossick, 'Shopkeepers and the state in Britain, 1870–1914', in Geoffrey Crossick and Heinz-Gerhard Haupt (eds), *Shopkeepers and Master Artisans in Nineteenth-Century Europe* (London, Methuen, 1984), p. 247.

10 Geoffrey Crossick and Heinz-Gerhard Haupt, *The Petit Bourgeoisie in Europe, 1780–1914* (London, Routledge, 1995).

11 See Arlene Young, 'Virtue domesticated: Dickens and the lower middle class', *Victorian Studies*, 39 (Summer 1996), 485.

12 T. W. H. Crosland, *The Suburbans* (London, John Long, 1905), p. 24.

13 *Ibid.*, p. 10.

14 *Ibid.*, p. 37.

15 *Ibid.*, p. 131.
16 *The Englishwoman*, February 1913, 131.
17 Grossmith, *The Diary of a Nobody*, p. 3.
18 *Ibid.*, p. 77.
19 *How to live on a Hundred a Year, make a Good Appearance and Save Money* (London, 1874), pp. 48–9.
20 Sydney Moseley, *The Private Diaries of Sydney Moseley* (London, Max Parrish, 1960), p. 16.
21 Grossmith, *The Diary of a Nobody*, p. 85.
22 *Ibid.*, p. 100.
23 Judith Walkowitz, *City of Dreadful Delight: Narratives of Sexual Danger in Late-Victorian London* (Chicago, University of Chicago Press, 1992); Erica Rappaport, 'The halls of temptation: gender, politics, and the construction of the department store in late Victorian London', *Journal of British Studies*, 35 (1996), 58–83; Bill Lancaster, *The Department Store: A Social History* (Leicester, Leicester University Press, 1995).
24 *Morning Chronicle*, 16 December, 17 December 1857.
25 Mary Cadwalader Jones, *European Travel For Women: Notes and Suggestion* (New York, Macmillan, 1890), p. 117.
26 *Manchester Evening News*, 1 July, 25 July, 2 December, 1890.
27 *South Manchester Chronicle and Suburban News*, 3 January 1890, 1.
28 *Snap Shots*, 27 December 1890, 12
29 T. W. H. Crosland, *Lovely Woman* (London, Grant Richards, 1903), p. 134.
30 *Hearth and Home*, 4 March 1909, 754.
31 E. J. Larby, *'Villadom': or Lower-Middle-Class Snobs by 'One of Them': A Plea For A Middle-Class Trade Union* (London, E. J. Larby, 1923), p. 3.
32 *Punch*, 22 January 1902, 67–8.
33 *To-Day: A Weekly Magazine-Journal*, 28 July 1894, 364.
34 *The Englishwoman*, February 1913, 129–30.
35 *Fun*, 28 February 1898, 67.
36 *Tit-Bits*, 27 July 1895, 289.
37 *Lady's Pictorial*, 29 December 1906, 1100.
38 *Fortnightly Review*, vol. 57, New Series, 1895, 124.
39 Crosland, *Lovely Woman*, 13.
40 *Ibid.*, p. 101.
41 *Hearth and Home*, 16 January 1902, 466.
42 *Punch*, 16 July 1902, 36.
43 *Ibid.*, 11 January 1911, 27.
44 Mrs Belloc-Lowndes, 'London's drapers', in George Sims, *Living London*, vol. 2 (London, Cassell, 1902), p. 212.
45 Mrs E. T. Cook, *Highways and Byways in London* (London, Macmillan, 1902), p. 311.
46 *Lady's Pictorial*, 24 October 1903, 808.
47 *The Draper*, 12 July 1902, 973.
48 *The Reader*, 12 January 1907, 308.
49 *Vanity Fair*, 11 August 1909, 182.
50 *Ibid.*, 23 December 1909, 776.
51 *Lady's Pictorial*, 23 December 1899, 1012.
52 Crosland, *Lovely Woman*, p. 21.
53 Anon., *The Life of the Railway Clerk* (London, Railway Clerks' Association, 1911), p. 17.
54 *Woman's Life*, 5 June 1909, 966.
55 Anon., *Olivia's Shopping and How She does It: A Prejudiced Guide to the London Shops* (London, Gay and Bird, 1906), p. 7.
56 *Ibid.*, p. 62.
57 *Ibid.*, p. 65.
58 *Illustrated London News*, 28 December 1901, 1018.
59 Mrs Alfred Praga, *Starting Housekeeping* (London, Chapman and Hall, 1899), p. 10.
60 *Hearth and Home*, 28 December 1898, 298.
61 *Illustrated London News*, 13 January 1906, p. 60.

62 *Lady's Pictorial*, 20 December 1890, 1042.
63 For example *Hearth and Home* and *Lady's Pictorial* included regular columns on the sales.
64 Scott and Nellie Nearing, *Woman and Social Progress* (New York, Macmillan, 1912), p. 173.
65 *The Reader*, 5 January 1907, 289.
66 *Illustrated London News*, 29 December 1906, 990.
67 *Ibid.*
68 *The Reader*, 5 January 1907, 289.
69 *Illustrated London News*, 13 January 1906, 60.
70 *Hearth and Home*, 14 January 1909, 481.
71 Lancaster, *The Department Store*, p. 69.
72 *Illustrated London News*, 18 August 1906, 246.
73 R. D. Blumenfeld, *R.D.B.'s Diary, 1887–1914* (London, William Heinemann, 1930), p. 119.
74 W. N. P. Barbellion, *The Journal of a Disappointed Man* ([1919,] London, Hogarth, 1984), p. 108.
75 *Punch*, 20 March 1886, 143. This social confusion was pushed to the extreme in *The Man from Blackley's,* a play developed out of a short piece which originally appeared in *Punch*; a customer treats the shop assistant as a commodity, hiring him to make up the numbers for a dinner party.
76 Eileen Elias, *Straw hats and Serge Bloomers* (London, W. H. Allen, 1979), p. 183.
77 H. Gordon Selfridge, *The Romance of Commerce* (London, John Lane, 1918), p. 384.
78 Reginald Pound, *Selfridge – A Biography* (London, Heinemann, 1960), p. 50.
79 Elias, *Straw Hats and Serge Bloomers*, p. 184.
80 Eileen Elias, *On Sundays We Wore White* (London, W. H. Allen, 1978), p. 72.
81 See, for example, the description of the new Debenham and Freebody building (1907) which was featured in *The Builder*, 20 March 1909.
82 *Lady's Pictorial*, 31 December 1892, 1033.
83 *The Draper,* 21 August 1880, 535.
84 *Punch*, 30 January 1892, 60.
85 *Fortnightly Review*, n.s., vol. 57 (1895), 127.

11

THE ENGLISH WEAKNESS? GENDER, SATIRE AND 'MORAL MANLINESS' IN THE LOWER MIDDLE CLASS, 1870–1920
A. James Hammerton

In recent years historians have made up for earlier neglect of the lower middle class in some illuminating studies of class formation, occupational profiles and religious affiliations.[1] But compared to those at work on the upper, middle and working classes, historians of the 'lower middle' have been slow to probe the gendered dimensions, masculine identities and domestic lives of such groups as clerks, commercial travellers and shopkeepers.[2] This is surprising when one considers the fact that late Victorian and Edwardian commentators in Britain based so much of their mockery of 'black-coated workers' more on their domestic experience and gender relations than on their workplace identity, a hint of the extent to which gender issues informed contemporary thinking about the lower middle class. Their masculine identity might have originated in the workplace, but in popular satirical commentary it was expressed overwhelmingly in the private world of domesticity, and in family relations, which is the element we know least about. This chapter will therefore focus on the gendered dimensions of those satirical constructions as a first step towards wider understanding of lower-middle-class masculinity.

The importance of lower-middle-class masculinity and its representation extends well beyond late Victorian and Edwardian preoccupations because of its direct relationship to larger patterns in the transition to modernity. It is a paradox that the domesticated suburbanism of the group that satirists and novelists parodied so mercilessly before the First World War had by the mid-twentieth century become the norm which mostly defined the modern condition. By the 1920s the suburban, virtually servantless, existence, which previously invited so much scorn of the pretentious 'clerkly class', had become widely diffused across the middle-class structure especially, so that satirical portrayals of domesticated men became less class-specific. Recent work which has placed women's new consumerism at the centre of arguments about modernity, illustrating, in Nava's words, 'a major narrative of twentieth century life', chart a process in which erstwhile lower-middle-class characteristics were subsumed in the identity of a much wider suburban population.[3] The new awareness was quickly taken up in ubiquitous cartoon representations of men as hapless victims of their wives' shopping habits, a stock-in-trade metaphor for emasculated manhood across class lines. The private world of the suburban middle class, increasingly differentiated internally, was becoming a more universal aspiration for men as well as women between the wars. Understanding of pre-war mockery of the similarly domesticated world of lower-middle-class men may therefore illuminate these later developments.

This reading suggests that the late Victorian and Edwardian period was a unique moment in the formation of a stereotyped and deeply gendered lower-middle-class masculine identity, albeit one constructed only to be treated with contempt. It has been easy to ignore because its celebration of separate spheres recalls precisely the 'normative' domesticated manliness we have come to associate with the early Victorian professional and entrepreneurial middle class, for whom male cultivation of domestic virtues could flourish within a context of the independence and authority claimed by public men of affairs.[4] Satire therefore took the essence of lower-middle-class difference, lack of independence and authority, extending to implied powerlessness, as its starting point, but, as I will try to show, it drew on gender relations and elements of men's relationship to domesticity to highlight the essence of lower-middle-class weakness, which became linked to wider criticism of national character.

Viewing lower-middle-class masculinity through the lens of satire provides some clues to explain both its scholarly neglect and the wider difficulty of conceptualising difference within 'normative', heterosexual masculinities, especially those in marriage. Conventional sociological wisdom maintains that basic assumptions of hegemonic masculinity are maintained as the norm to which men are held accountable, even when individuals reject those assumptions for themselves.[5] R. W. Connell postulates the notion of the 'patriarchal dividend, the advantage men in general gain from the overall subjection of women', even when they fail to meet all the standards of hegemonic masculinity.[6] But he adds that for men whose class situation and practice are marginal, the patriarchal dividend can often be lost.[7] It follows, to state the obvious, that the extent of the patriarchal dividend commanded by men can be highly variable, in both public and private contexts, and regardless of the normative assumptions to which they might subscribe. Lower-middle-class marriage was emblematic of the much prescribed sanctuary of domesticity within a framework of separate spheres, which men were simultaneously expected to enjoy and to command.[8] Yet satire represented lower-middle-class husbands as dependent weaklings who had surrendered their mastery to women and lost the patriarchal dividend. Other sources might give a different impression, but satire at least directs our attention to ways in which the presumed 'normative' heterosexual masculinity of private life can obscure our understanding of subtle differences and historical change.

Satirical portrayals contrast sharply with those to be found in other lower-middle-class sources. In autobiographical self-representation one finds little consciousness of popular mockery, but rather an emphasis on the same moral and cultural development found in working-class autobiography and in prescriptive texts.[9] This should not be surprising, since many of the autobiographers had themselves emerged from working-class families, often from the upwardly mobile labour aristocracy, and in such families one child might pursue a white-collar career and another a blue-collar career.[10] The dominant theme here is that of 'moral manliness', a definition of masculine identity seemingly taken directly from religious prescription, which exhorted puritan self-denial, devotion to duty, self-improvement, and above all moral propriety and consideration of wives and children within a context of separate spheres and paternalistic protection.[11] But satirists mostly equated moral manliness with effeminacy and weakness.

In symbolic representation, at least, the central figure at issue here is the suburban clerk, who embodied a diverse spectrum of related white-collar workers like commercial travellers and shop assistants, and more problematically the 'classic' petite bourgeoisie of small businessmen and shopkeepers, all occupying, according to Szreter, an 'inherently contentious' border area.[12] This catalogue barely hints at the diversity of the lower middle class in occupational function, residence, and family and cultural background, which is central to variations in masculine identities.[13] The reductive tendencies of satire happily obscured these complexities, offering up a relatively one-dimensional masculine stereotype which simplified tensions arising from contested authority in marriage, struggles over income distribution, sexual relationships and child-rearing, to name just a few. Because the satirical images framed popular perceptions and still pervade our understanding of lower-middle-class masculinity, they deserve more critical scrutiny.

For over a century the most common source for popular representation of this group has been George and Weedon Grossmith's *Diary of a Nobody*, which immortalised the ineffectual and pretentious Mr Charles Pooter in *Punch* in 1888; it has remained central to the dominant discourse around lower-middle-class men ever since. Pooter's character captured the prevailing tone of the elite's patronising scorn of the marginal and insecure lower middle: blindly loyal to his employer at the bank but most comfortable in his suburban home; thoroughly domesticated but with a pompous belief in his household mastery; and routinely deflated by the contempt of tradesmen, friends, servants, worldly men, spiritualist women, his rebellious son and, most cutting of all, his wife, Carrie. The *Diary* traced the ultimate deflation of the suburban clerk, reproducing his meagre authority at work in the domestic scene, where his attempts to ape his betters and to play the benevolent patriarch are invariably undermined. Crucially, though, Pooter's was not a relentlessly hostile image; it was also an affectionate and nuanced one, in tune with much commentary of the 1880s. The *Diary* thus concludes with financial and domestic triumph for Charles Pooter, and endorsement from many of those who had scorned him.[14]

The restrained satire of the 1880s contrasts both with what preceded and followed it. Much literature of the 1830s and 1840s had taunted the pretensions to respectability of male clerks and shop assistants in cutting satires of 'gents', or degraded 'dandies'.[15] The dominant targets were young, single, callow and underfed, though overdressed, youths, and the focus was on their pathetic and upstart attempts to emulate real gentlemen; this was the customary motivation of hostile caricature. It also embodied a markedly different lower-middle-class image, that of rebellious and disorderly youth, contemptuous of respectable norms and a sexually predatory threat to women on the streets. Its later manifestation is palpable in Charles Pooter's unfilial son, Lupin. But the early portrayals lack a full-blown satire of the married middle-class man to match that of the later Pooter. For its equivalent we have to turn to Dickens and his circle, initially in Dickens's *Pickwick Papers* of 1837, but most elaborately in his friend, Douglas Jerrold's 1845 series in *Punch*, 'Mrs Caudle's Curtain Lectures'. Here the privacy of lower-middle-class marriage, rather than the public performance of the single gent, is offered to our gaze, and the dominant target is the nagging pretentiousness of Mrs Caudle, who commits the full range of snobbish sins that later become the province of Pooter. By contrast, Mr Caudle, significantly not a clerk but a more independent petit-bourgeois 'toyman and doll merchant', displays all the feckless resistance to domestic duty, and to conjugality, associated with earlier masculine models, the very antithesis of moral manliness. He prefers his drinking companions and his masonic lodge to the fireside company of Mrs Caudle, and he resists, mostly unsuccessfully, her projects to move to a more salubrious dwelling in Clapham, the 'turtle dovery', to have her mother live with them and to control Job's spending.[16]

By the 1880s, then, satirical representation had largely transposed the lower middle-class trophy of social emulation and pretentious respectability from women to men, as the raffish gadabout, Job Caudle, was tamed into the domesticated Charles Pooter, who came to signify the feminisation of the lower-middle-class husband. But the nuances in Grossmith's portrayal of Pooter were important; while cutting in its relentless depiction of his life of trivialities, it remained affectionate in its ambivalent vindication of the work ethic and domestic order, which no doubt explained the esteem it enjoyed among an enthusiastic and socially diverse readership. Contemporary non-fictional discussion conveyed a similar ambivalence. By the turn of the century, however, the criticism had begun to take on a harsher edge, without the affectionate indulgence, and this can be linked to wider anxieties about masculine identity and the direction of modern urban society.

The new emphasis is best illustrated by a direct descendant of *The Diary of a Nobody*, Barry Pain's series, *The Eliza Books*, which flourished, in five successive volumes, during the Edwardian years.[17] This series was an obvious and successful attempt to capitalise on the success of the *Diary*; it reproduced all the familiar exaggerations of Charles Pooter's pompous self-importance, snobbish social emulation and bungling domestic interference, but it introduced a more strident note of combative struggle between Eliza and her husband, the unnamed narrator. It also played more explicitly on themes of suburban mediocrity and cultural narrowness. In each of their marital squabbles it is Eliza's husband, the self-conscious commercial clerk, whose petty obsessions with domestic detail and outward appearances, contrasted to Eliza's down-to-earth concerns with practical economies. Like Pooter, his ineffectual assertions that he is 'master in his own house' end in humiliating reversals which reveal Eliza's superior management and wisdom; their origin in his preoccupation with control of domestic detail also imply his diminished masculinity. Even his symbolic last stand, a determination to 'decline to wheel the perambulator', is confounded when he resorts to pushing it in the back garden with one hand, while reading a copy of *Home Hints*, held in the other, only to crash into the wall.[18] Eliza is brought to confess her anxieties about his compromised manliness when he aspires to take up an offer to join a London club, which turns out to be a swindle. After initial doubts, she urges him to join, despite the expense:

but, after all, it works out about a bob a week. And if it mixes you up with men a bit, it may do you good. You see, you don't do any of the things that other men do, and you don't seem to know any of the things that they know.

When he rejoins that, on the other hand, 'I know some things that they do not', she presses the point:

> Of course . . . And it's been getting worse lately. Only the other day you were showing that girl the right way to clean knives, and that's not a thing I like to see. I don't say you should take to drinking and gambling, but you might keep out of the kitchen and act more like an ordinary man.

Neither Eliza nor the reader is likely to be convinced by his defensive admission that 'Well, I am not an ordinary man. I admit it. And I am far from being ashamed of it.'[19]

In Pain's final volume, *Eliza's Son*, the result of this emasculated manliness and social pretension is elaborated in the character of their offspring, Ernest. Eliza's pride and joy turns out to be the quintessence of suburbanism, displaying a selective inheritance of his father's aspirations to social superiority and his mother's to shrewd practical economy. Rebellious, and contemptuous of his father's transparent affectation, he nevertheless develops to a fine art his talent for knowing the price of everything and the value of nothing. Unlike Pooter's socially rebellious son, Lupin, Ernest concentrates his defiance on an exclusive obsession with money. From the age of six he develops a balance sheet even for Christmas presents ('It prevents one's generous impulses from running into extravagance') and has no time for playmates, sport, holidays or music, all of which interfere with good business. Even more than his parents, Ernest signifies the narrow philistinism of limited lower-middle-class suburban existence, which other social critics were already beginning to elaborate more fully.[20] If *The Eliza Books* failed to successfuly replicate the nuances and enduring humour of Mr Pooter, their detailed onslaught on lower-middle-class narrowness and diminished manhood more accurately reflected trends in the social critique of suburbia.

To date, the most persuasive explanation for this shift to a more strident critique of feminised masculinity around the turn of the century has been the influence of late nineteenth-century imperialism, associated with a masculine 'flight from domesticity'. In this reading late Victorian men, predominantly from the professional upper middle class, consciously rejected the more domesticated manliness of their fathers, which had more easily accommodated a masculine identity traversing both public and private spheres.[21] The expansive impulse of the 'new imperialism' tempted middle-class sons with visions of adventure and exploration, which were viewed as antithetical to domesticity, to marriage and to women.[22] The increasingly popular genre of adventure stories for boys ensured that these elite aspirations would, at least in the imagination, be shared by boys of mixed backgrounds.[23]

While the varying extent of the power of imperialism and this late Victorian and Edwardian flight from domesticity in different sections of the middle class remains uncertain, their influence was indeed ubiquitous. Texts like *The Diary of a Nobody* were unlikely to represent domestic life without some exploration, mostly based on class, of the tensions resulting from the clash between domesticated manliness and a male flight from domesticity.[24] The origins were firmly anchored among elites, but the impact was much more pervasive.[25] Still, it is unclear whether imperialism accounts for the harsher critique directed at feminised lower-middle-class men around the turn of the century, and it is mostly absent from the mainstream satirical texts. There are other causal candidates which only tenuously relate to the popularisation of imperial models of manhood. During the 1890s eugenic concerns about cultural and physical degeneration reached their peak.[26] Moral panics about homosexuality dating from the Oscar Wilde trial added to suspicions about any masculine identity which betrayed hints of effeminacy. But other reasons for the new hostility, closely related to the pace of urban development, bear closer scrutiny.

By the Edwardian years the long-established trend for social exploration of the structural and cultural lives of the poor had extended to the lower middle class, whose lives were intensively surveyed, categorised, diagnosed and criticised. Journalists seized on the evidence of neglect and hardship to link the expanding lower middle with a larger national malaise. They linked the plight of young single male clerks, impecunious and adrift in London, directly to the trials of discordant marriage, as immature youths were driven to 'seek relief in matrimony, only to find that their last state is worse than their first' as they struggled with their wives to reconcile gentility with poverty.[27] This provided the cue for sombre advice on the disastrous temptation for clerks of early marriage, which had been recognised as a more general middle-class problem since the early nineteenth century.

The pinched and haggard state of the struggling single clerk was thus connected directly to the hardships and tensions of lower-middle-class marriage. A flood of prescriptive advice attempted to circumvent the material problems faced by lower-middle-class couples struggling to maintain a respectable front on incomes often below those of skilled manual workers. The prudent outer-suburban wife was urged to control her husband's smoking and drinking and to insist that he shop for her at the cheaper central London stores; on £150 a year there was no room for false pride, and no considerate husband could afford to be 'too proud to carry the fish basket or parcel of tea home with him'.[28] No prescriptive analysis of lower-middle-class living standards could delve far into the practicalities without, in this way, raising acute questions of husband–wife relations, the division of labour and the exercise of authority, in ways disturbing for the stability of separate spheres and domestic ideology. As early as the 1850s sympathetic commentators admitted that marriage required far too many clerks to domesticate themselves to an unsavoury degree, prompting them to avoid marriage altogether.[29]

In literary and journalistic commentary more generally the approach was radically different, and borrowed both from the earlier mockery of the 'gent' and from contemporary social investigation. It is best understood in the context of the more general critique of modern urban society and rejection of Victorian values at the end of the nineteenth century. Titles such as *The Blight of Respectability*, *The Suburbans* and 'Philistia' were vehicles for an outpouring of elite resentment against suburban pretension and mediocrity.[30] These works scapegoated the suburban lower middle for the much larger malaise detected in urban life, now focused on the same alienating suburbs which had been created only a generation earlier to resolve the similarly sensationalised problem of inner-urban decay; they foreshadowed the wider critique of suburban values, of American influences and of the feminised consumerism, recently described by Sally Alexander, which developed after both world wars.[31] Indeed, the Edwardian critique of Pooterism was a crucial early stage of the shift in focus from an explicit class preoccupation with the lower middle to the more general attack on suburban values. Such criticism was an integral part of more general responses to elements of modernity, which focused on the more visible and destabilising disturbances of traditional values in urban life. Recent work has drawn attention to the crucial role of the woman shopper and the rise of the department store in this process, but the anxieties prompted by female consumerism were inseparable from wider concerns about national cultural degeneration, in which a breakdown of the gender order and diminished manliness in suburbia were central.[32]

One of the most serious of these critics, C. F. G. Masterman, was certain that the degraded values and 'absence of vision' he detected in suburban life were intrinsic to hastening national decline. Energies liberated by the escape from poverty had been misdirected into 'random and meaningless sociabilities', disputes over garden fences, frivolous entertainment and 'criticism of manners and fashion, dress and deportment'. All of this for Masterman betrayed symptoms of unchecked English individualism in pursuit of unworthy goals, a population preoccupied with guessing competitions, spectator sport and sensational divorce cases, and encouraged by an irresponsible yellow press, 'mean and tawdry and debased, representing a tawdry and dusty world'. But the crowning sin of suburbia was to be in the vanguard of responsibility for race suicide: 'the headlong collapse in the birth-rate of this country in the past twenty years – a fall greater than in any other nation in Europe'. 'Suburban populations' had responded to their inability to reconcile their desired standard of comfort with limited incomes by postponing marriage or practising birth control. Masterman echoed the familiar complaints of Edwardian eugenicists by heralding national decline, as the country's 'better stocks' produced smaller or childless families. But he linked this to wider socio-political aspirations since smaller families enabled the standard of comfort to be 'reduced to the level of income, and the clerk and professional classes can be identified with the prevailing order, instead of becoming centres of social upheaval'. Suburban narrowness was thus at the centre of the degradation of English civilisation.[33]

We have already seen how popular satirical works like *The Eliza Books* exploited the critical preoccupation with suburbia in their mockery of the lower middle class. In routine replications of Grossmith's text, Pooterism seemingly fed on itself, as the 'dreary and dismal solitude' of suburban life became inseparable from comical stock-in-trade descriptions of black-coated workers at home, where they were exposed as incompetent buffoons by their wives and servants.[34] Even more explicit was a genre of journalistic commentary which used humour to popularise the more serious criticisms, from the likes of Masterman, of lower-middle-class suburbia, masculinity and modernity. Together with similar fictional stereotypes these works helped to speed up the discursive process of rendering suburban man an emasculated and ridiculous victim of a more intelligent but selfish and consumerist wife. In books, magazines and newspaper articles these satirical texts articulated the familiar characteristics of the same suburban oaf who remained a staple of the cartoon industry long after the Great War. In the process they subjected the most minute aspects of lower-middle-class life to microscopic, though bitterly satirical, scrutiny.

Recent historians of the lower middle class have drawn on this relentlessly stereotyping material mainly to confirm the widespread incidence of snobbish condescension among elites towards the lower middle, which is ironic in view of the fact that the most regular contemporary charge against suburbans themselves was also an unwarranted snobbishness.[35] One of the most frequently cited anti-suburban commentators in this tradition is the prolific journalist, Thomas Crosland, in his book of 1905, *The Suburbans*.[36] His own background was Yorkshire nonconformist and lower-middle-class, his reputation among journalists that of the cantankerous, cynical but compassionate individualist; one is tempted to find parallels in present-day journalistic types like Auberon Waugh. Crosland's satirical barbs, though, betrayed some wider contemporary resentments over signs of change in the gender order. Any departure of men from a traditional model of masculine identity, and of women from domesticated subordination, was fair game for his savage pen.

Crosland's perverse and sarcastic voice was well suited to easy targets like suburban clerks. In a single text he blamed suburban vulgarity for the catastrophic decline in every aspect of English civilisation. Tawdry consumer goods, benighted architecture, a declining theatre, deteriorating art and literature, a shabby, secularised nonconformity in religion and a decline in standards of marriage were all laid at the door of penny-pinching and pretentious suburbans, with their 'snobbish insistence on appearances'.[37] Professionals such as architects had sold out to the commercial spirit by truckling to the paltry tastes of vulgar suburbans. Writers and dramatists like Jerome K. Jerome and H. G. Wells catered to the lowest common denominator of literary taste. Moreover, while many suburbs were mixed in class composition, in fact they were all, including 'tone setting' professionals, 'sons of generations of impecunious snobbery', infected by the clerk's mentality, 'a mere projection of their own unholy, ill-paid, hungry, subservient, but nevertheless silk-hatted and frock-coated clerical assistants'.[38] Clerks, in effect, defined the essential spirit of a more socially diverse suburbia.

This was only the more colourful and typical of the Edwardian outpouring of ridicule aimed at suburbans. However, we need to look beyond the catchiest phrases and one-liners, which are trademarks of the entire genre, to the deeper resentments which motivated criticism of Pooterism. Crosland's *Suburbans* was actually an expansion of a single chapter from a book published two years earlier entitled *The Egregious English*. That text was only one of a succession of seemingly light-hearted, opinionated books by Crosland which appeared in rapid succession between 1902 and 1905. These were organised around categories of ethnicity and gender: *The Unspeakable Scot*, *The Egregious*

English, The Wild Irishman, Lovely Woman and *The Lord of Creation*, together with *The Suburbans* and, in 1912, *Taffy was a Welshman*, all targeted Crosland's favourite enemies and ruthlessly pursued his pet racial and gender stereotypes. They sold well, some being first serialised in magazines like *The Gentlewoman*, and they inspired equally satirical responses, laced with mock outrage, especially in reply to his attacks on women.[39] They deserve attention less for their popularity and controversial reception than for their relentless attack on what Crosland saw as the two groups responsible for the decline in English civilisation: first, lower-middle-class men and, secondly, women generally. While at times his comments were frivolous, they also drew on deeply serious and bitter resentments against social and political change which were widely shared.

At first glance this may seem to be far removed from Crosland's other pet hate, homosexuality, for which he reserved his greatest journalistic venom. In fact his contempt for homosexual and suburban men was closely linked. He was quiet at the time of the Wilde trial in 1895, but in 1912 when the complete version of Wilde's *De profundis* was published, with verses critical of Lord Alfred Douglas, Wilde's lover of the 1890s, Crosland undertook the ghost-writing of Douglas's vicious attack on Wilde, which misrepresented their relationship and attacked Wilde's writing for its immorality. Like many of his contemporaries, Crosland's ideal of manliness was affronted by Wilde's behaviour, as it was by the weakness he saw as being inherent in suburban men; the common denominator was a degree of effeminacy which offended more robust masculine standards.[40]

Crosland laid an exhaustive catalogue of sins at the feet of the lower middle class. Shabby gentility and pretension, vulgar tastes, avarice and shameful deference, all these compromised English civilisation and standards of manliness. The familiar resentment against genteel pretensions from men whose work was the antithesis of manly independence informs most of his writing. Also the stress on the pettiness of commercial values echoes much of the critical discourse in English social commentary associated with Matthew Arnold's earlier attack on materialism and philistinism, and Crosland had ample company in depicting the degradation of citizenship by commercial and material ethics.[41] But marriage and the suburban home were the key sites where suburban ills were played out and revealed most fully, and it is here that he came closest to giving a coherent picture of his view of lower-middle-class masculinity. There was little to be found here that smacked of 'moral manliness'.

Crosland's critique of suburbia turned domestic ideology, with its idealisation of the 'angel in the house', on its head by attributing its meanness, its petty materialism and men's weakness to women's domestic dominance and control. Men's faults, in effect, were what women made them. They controlled their sons' education and shaped them into materialistic replicas of their small-minded fathers.[42] Men's absence at work gave women unchallenged ascendancy over the domestic sphere and enabled them to define its values.

Crosland's parody of the moment of the husband's return from work after suffering the trials of a petty office and overcrowded public transport typified his gendered resentments. The hour of the worker's homecoming had been used through much of the nineteenth century as a signifier to define

Fig. 11 Jane Maria Bowkett, *Preparing Tea* (1861) reproduced in Christopher Wood, *Victorian Panorama: Paintings of Victorian Life*, from a photograph from the late Mrs Charlotte Frank (picture now destroyed, signed, with monograph).

domestic ideology across social classes.[43] It fired the imagination of artists who idealised the return of the absent male to the cosy domestic hearth. Joseph Clarke used it in *The Labourer's Welcome* (1865) to romanticise conjugal domesticity among the rural poor. In Jane Bowkett's *Preparing Tea* (1861) the portrayal was also idealised, but nuanced, as the preoccupied waiting wife gazes wistfully, we might guess with mixed emotions, out at her husband's approaching train (figure 11).[44] In Crosland's hands such subtleties are abandoned. Lamenting the 'absence of responsible male population throughout the day' as a 'more serious matter than appears at first sight', rendering 'what is already suburban more suburban still', and surrendering the household to the unquestioned rule of women, Crosland insisted that for suburban housewives 'the daily round, the common task, does not really begin until within an hour or so of the blessed moment when "he" – that is how Mrs Subub invariably speaks of her better half – is expected to return'. Then, with 'master expected any minute', the 'bustle and excitement' conveyed in Bowkett's painting, began:

> The Canterbury Lamb is hustled into the oven without ceremony. Little Johnny is despatched to the corner shop for packets of dessicated soup and a penny egg for custard. The dining-room is dusted swiftly with a tea-cloth, and the children's faces rendered free from marmalade with the help of mamma's apron. The parlour fire is persuaded to glow by dint of liberal applications of sugar and paraffin-oil. Papa's slippers are put to warm in the fender. Best of all, the next-door neighbour goes home to her own affairs.

However, upon arrival the conjugal ideal, and with it domestic ideology, is further compromised, for instead of a considerate, affectionate and forbearing husband and father, the homecoming brought an irritable and demanding presence quite inconsistent with the preparations. Already aggrieved about his trying day, he might grumble further about the loss of his week's lunch money on a horse, then terrorise the family about the whereabouts and, later, the inedibility of the 'damned dinner', the lack of beer and other 'little comforts'. 'Is he a mere money-making machine, or what? The *Daily Telegraph* may well say that marriage is a failure.'

With characteristic perversity Crosland pronounced all this tetchiness to be good household discipline, improving its 'tone and nerve and efficiency', one of the rare occasions where he canvassed the possibility that suburban husbands might retain some trappings of household mastery. But it was not enough to give the substance of real power:

> The fatal flaw in the system is in the man's whole-day absence from his own domain. When the underground and the bulgy buses have swallowed up their husbands, suburban wives take in deep breaths of freedom and content. By ten o'clock a.m. they are shaking dusters out of windows and exchanging gossip, or renewing feuds over garden walls. Lunch in such houses is a Barmecide feast of cut-and-come-again from the ham-and-beef-shop. Master is not at home and consequently nothing matters. In the afternoon we slumber, or go to see our aunt, or our mother, or our newly married sister, there to drink tea to repletion and to discuss 'him' and 'yours' to our feminine hearts' content. A strange country verily, and a pitiful people! Of its dead-level of dulness and weariness and meanness and hard-upness who shall relieve it?[45]

Oblivious to the glaring contradictions, Crosland insisted that the bad-tempered domestic tyrant he depicted was nevertheless a 'hen-pecked, shrew-driven, neglected, heart-sick man'.[46] His pet contrast was that between, on the one hand, an ideal of domesticity located among the well-to-do early nineteenth-century bourgeois, for whom an Englishman's house could truly be 'his castle', where the domestic virtues could flourish, and, on the other, living conditions among modern suburbans, where women's passion for appearances resulted in vulgarity, dense overcrowding, poky buildings and, worst of all, dual occupancy through subletting to a second family, all 'subversive of the best interests of domesticity'.[47]

To anticipate his critics, Crosland included a chapter in his book on men, *The Lord of Creation*, entitled 'The Misogynist', where he attacked 'clever, contemptuous single men or unhappy married men', whose hypocrisy in their scorn of women was betrayed in their upholding of the very system of female domestic rule, learnt from their mothers, which continued to allow women to manipulate them. Crosland excluded himself from this misogynist company through a sleight of hand which insisted that the only socially responsible course was not to hate women, but to 'hate women's vices'.[48] His listing of these was voluminous and, like much of his writing, was a prose elaboration of the domestic cartoon caricatures which were common to journals like *Punch*. But at least two of these vices were deadly serious.

The first was aimed at women as consumers, the precise agency which enabled them to bring everything Crosland judged to be cheap and tawdry into the suburban home. He echoed an anxiety which had been developing for more than a generation, as women's consumer role became more public with increasing commercialisation, the rise of the department store and high-street shopping. Perhaps we see here some of the concrete responses to the ways in which women had been challenging men's domination of city streets, rendering them, in Walkowitz's words, 'contested social terrain'. In the 1880s Karl Pearson had angered the female members of the earnest 'Men and women's club' with his sneers against women 'shopping dolls'.[49] Similar resentments were voiced against the 'butterfly shopping class', aimed at lower-middle-class women who preferred to ride in buses rather than trams.[50] Crosland's criticism was linked more to his view of suburban vulgarity, for which women as shoppers were directly to blame; their consumerism also distorted the power balance in marriage, since their irresponsible spending further enslaved their husbands. The wife's determination to be 'in fashion', for example, invariably meant that expense was 'no object':

> providing she can get the money. She has no notion of thrift; she is perennially in arrears with the milk and the insurance-man; and when money gets very tight indeed, she lectures her husband on his wicked inability to make more than he is getting.[51]

For Crosland, then, women's consumerism was central both to suburban vulgarity and pretentiousness, and to the palpable fact that 'marriage was a failure', a phrase from the well-known 1888 marriage debate in the *Daily Telegraph* which reverberated through Crosland's pages and still informed wider discussion about lower-middle-class marriage.[52]

Even this was light-hearted alongside Crosland's attack on middle-class women's propensity for birth control, the 'most frightful and most prevalent of feminine weaknesses', which, significantly, he assumed to be entirely a woman's initiative. Her reluctance to tolerate more than two children, so that 'the British family shows a decided tendency to shrinkage', convinced Crosland that 'one's contempt for the modern woman is based on very sure grounds'. The modern woman gloried in a 'sin' which would have shamed her grandmother, as she 'brought her contempt for mankind and the order of things to the pitch of being at perpetual war with the prime duty of womanhood'.[53] Left unstated here was the implication of this for Crosland's view of men, but since his catalogue of women's crimes had been couched in terms of their responsibility for men's weaknesses, his readers, possibly conscious of the below-average family size of the lower middle, could easily infer that on top of all his other unmanly qualities, the lower-middle-class wage-slave was sexually emasculated, for which women also bore responsibility.[54]

Crosland brought these attacks together in his critique of the English national character, in which, again, the vices of women and the weaknesses of lower-middle-class men were presented as the quintessence of a fallen and feminised English identity. What had once been a nation of male adventurers and entrepreneurs had become a nation of employees: servile, deferential to employers and slaves to women's vanity. This spirit infected the entire nation, but it took its cues from the long catalogue of suburban values which Crosland, echoing more serious critics like Masterman, deplored in all his books. Suburbanism had come to constitute the new national character; it was peculiarly English, and resulted in a degraded form of citizenship, in which petty selfishness and pretension had made a mockery of civic duty. Suburban men thus no more deserved the vote than the suffragettes, whose call for independence, he insisted, had itself originated in suburbia.[55]

Crosland's was only the most prolific and repetitive of this catalogue of lower-middle-class defects. It drew on some older traditions which associated male and female weakness, especially in the feminisation of the clerk; it linked suburbanisation to widespread anxieties about physical and cultural degeneration; and it gave detailed elaboration to a discourse which was embedded in contemporary literature, drama and familiar satire in the press and cartoon industry. The same discourse informed much pro-imperialist writing, like that of Rider Haggard, which celebrated the virtues of rural England. Such writers rejected the urban commercial values of English civilisation and promoted imperialism as a way of reviving the old rural strengths which had suffered a century of degeneration at the hands of urban culture and, more recently, the suburban spirit.[56]

Absent from this discourse was any acknowledgement of the extent to which 'moral manliness' defined the identity of lower-middle-class men. The modicum of domestication which was entailed in moral manliness was judged in this reading to be a product of female domination rather than a beneficent and paternalistic gesture of support given to weaker subordinates. And there could be nothing manly in all the hints of sexual emasculation implied in the relentless picture of the hen-pecked suburban wage-slave. Among Edwardian novelists from lower-middle-class backgrounds, like H. G. Wells and Arnold Bennett, the cutting satire could be more nuanced, especially in the representation of courtship and marital relations. But while struggling clerks might in some novels achieve a degree of domestic and marital fulfilment, the stultifying effects and limitations of pettiness and dependence in the workplace made it difficult even for sympathetic authors to present these diminutive men as heroes except within comic conventions.[57] In most portrayals, as with Denry Machin in Bennett's *The Card*, lower-middle-class manliness constituted an ability to escape from stultifying class limitations, and particularly from the occupation of the clerk.[58]

Diminished men continued to parade their emasculation through the pages of late Victorian and Edwardian novels, projecting a demeaning image of which lower-middle-class readers could hardly be unaware.[59] Only with difficulty might they turn to literature for self-affirmation rather than humiliation. The popular novel of 1907 by Shan Bullock, *Robert Thorne: The Story of a London Clerk*, for example, gave a sympathetic portrait of a London civil-service clerk. While conditions of work in the tax office were presented as typically narrow, the possibility of masculine salvation, at least, could be envisaged through companionate marriage and domesticity. At four o'clock Robert found his other self, flung off his office coat and 'strode manfully out'. While reading classics from George Eliot, Matthew Arnold, Carlyle and Darwin with his young wife, Nell, Robert reflects that:

> We really do have minds, we black-coated slaves, and souls of a kind, and we strive and crave. And sometimes into our little homes comes a sense of the mystery of things, and then we ask questions, and maybe send up feeble cries for light.

Nell greets his anxiety that through their work he and his colleagues would 'lose our manhood' with the reminder that manhood was not simply played out in the workplace. 'You're not clerks always . . . You have homes and children and wives and plenty of interests . . . You can be men as well as clerks.' Robert enters fully into Nell's ideal of domesticated manhood, as he shares kitchen tasks with her and joins other fathers on Sunday mornings wheeling the pram – with none of the resentful self-consciousness registered by Eliza's husband. His respect for Nell follows the prescriptions of moral manliness to the letter, although when her brother seems to be going astray he notices that her standard of sexual morality is 'more severe' than his, which he interprets as the penalty of women 'being sisters and mothers and wives of men'. But ultimately both Nell and Robert acknowledge the impossibility of fulfilment in England, where urban degeneration had taken its toll on both sexes, by emigrating to a land which would allow them to become 'real men and women', and they live happily ever after in New Zealand.[60]

If self-affirmation was reflected only ambivalently in fiction, more direct sources suggest a different story. The critical-satirical discourse contrasts markedly with the narratives of self-improvement, celebrations of struggle and religious progress which dominate lower-middle-class men's autobiographical writings. Despite the extreme reluctance of lower-middle-class writers to expose their private lives to public gaze, most texts do betray more complex aspects of family life and masculine identity than in the simplifications of satire.[61] These range from celebration of the 'hugger-mugger' intimacies of family togetherness to bitter denunciations of repressive imprisonment of family members within stifling and inflexible codes of behaviour patrolled by fathers, and from co-operative practices of marital partnership to turbulent struggles of parents divided over child-care practices.[62]

These impressions are confirmed in other recent work which deals with lower-middle-class courtship and marriage. For example, press controversies focusing upon lower-middle-class marriage practices, which engaged wide-spread reader participation, show the determination of these men to redefine respectability in their own terms, in contrast to the fawning Pooterish deference detested by Crosland.[63] Similarly, as jurors in breach of promise cases, lower-middle-class men believed themselves to be upholding standards of chivalric manliness when they routinely awarded generous compensation payments to women abandoned by their fiancés.[64] These men still benefited from the patri-archal dividend, even if their share of it was increasingly contested. The contrast with the critical discourse could hardly be greater, and yet it pervaded literary production across the spectrum. Why, then, were writers like Crosland so bitter in contrasting a normative, idealised masculinity with that of the lower middle?

The answer may lie in the ways in which satire consciously dissected a relentless process of suburbanisation, rapidly establishing itself as the modern norm, in which redefinitions of masculinity were central but contested. Benefit of hindsight enables us to see the heavily lampooned masculinity of the lower middle class as an early manifestation of modernity in domestic life and rela-tionships. But the inward, domesticated and private values which could still be so easily mocked before the Great War soon afterwards became central to a fundamental re-evaluation of national character. Alison Light argues that between 1920 and 1940 the reaction against the romantic language of national pride and heroic masculinity 'produced a realignment of sexual identities which was part of a redefinition of "Englishness"' leading to a new social and political conservatism.[65] Those Mr Pooters who occupied their time at home with 'a tin tack here, a venetian blind to put straight' and playing dominoes with their wives moved a little closer to the centre of idealised masculine identity after 1918.[66] The hour of the lower middle had by then truly arrived, when their domesti-cated manliness might more accurately be described as normative, although its satirical representation tells only part of the story. But anxieties expressed in the pre-war critical discourse illustrate the tensions and differences between appar-ently similar normative masculine identities, based very largely on a one-sided view of marital relationships. By contrast with satire, autobiographical repre-sentations of private life confront us with a more complex picture of domesticity, which is the site where some of the least understood dynamics of masculine identity still remain to be traced.

NOTES

An earlier version of this chapter appeared in *Meridian: The La Trobe University English Review*, 15 (1996), 187–206.

1 For example G. Crossick (ed.), *The Lower Middle-Class in Britain, 1870–1914* (London, Croom Helm, 1977); G. Crossick and H. Gerhard-Haupt (eds.), *Shopkeepers and Master*

Artisans in Nineteenth-Century Europe (London, Methuen, 1984); for the best work exploring the cultural and social world of selected lower-middle-class occupational groupings see C. Hosgood, 'The "pigmies of commerce" and the working-class community: small shopkeepers in England, 1870–1914', *Journal of Social History*, 22 (1989), 439–60; C. Hosgood, 'The "knights of the road": commercial travellers and the culture of the commercial room in late-Victorian and Edwardian England', *Victorian Studies*, 37 (1994); G. Anderson, *Victorian Clerks* (Manchester, Manchester University Press, 1976); for a useful general synthesis see J. F. C. Harrison, *Late Victorian Britain, 1875–1901* (London, Fontana, 1990), pp. 58–66.

2 The following works make fruitful studies of engagements between the public and private divide, masculinity and domesticity: J. Tosh, 'Domesticity and manliness in the Victorian middle-class: the family of Edward White Benson', in M. Roper and J. Tosh (eds.), *Manful Assertions: Masculinities in Britain Since 1800* (London, Routledge, 1991), pp. 44–73; J. Tosh, 'What should historians do with masculinity?: reflections on nineteenth-century Britain', *History Workshop*, 38 (1994), 179–202; A. Clark, *The Struggle for the Breeches: Gender and the Making of the British Working-Class* (London, Rivers Oram, 1995); L. Davidoff and C. Hall, *Family Fortunes: Men and Women of the English Middle-Class, 1780–1850* (London, Hutchinson, 1987); G. Dawson, *Soldier Heroes: British Adventure, Empire and the Imagining of Masculinities* (London, Routledge, 1994).

3 M. Nava, 'Modernity's disavowal: women, the city and the department store', in M. Nava and A. O'Shea (eds.), *Modern Times: Reflections on a Century of English Modernity* (London, Routledge, 1996), p. 38.

4 Davidoff and Hall, *Family Fortunes*, pp. 13–18, 108–13.

5 S. R. Bird, '"Welcome to the men's club": homosociality and the maintenance of hegemonic masculinity', *Gender and Society*, 10:2 (1996), 120–32.

6 R. W. Connell, *Masculinities* (St Leonards, Allen and Unwin, 1995), p. 79.

7 *Ibid.*, p. 116.

8 On marital prescription directed at middle-class men see A. J. Hammerton, *Cruelty and Companionship: Conflict in Nineteenth Century Married Life* (London, Routledge, 1992), pp. 73–82, 149–53.

9 D. Vincent, *Bread, Knowledge and Freedom: A Study of Nineteenth-Century Working-Class Autobiography* (London, Methuen, 1982), pp. 109–95.

10 For discussion of this crucial issue, which is rarely acknowledged, see D. M. Copelman, *London's Women Teachers: Gender, Class and Feminism, 1870–1930* (London, Routledge, 1996), pp. 34–5.

11 My current study of lower-middle-class marriage and masculinity is based in part on a survey of over one hundred lower-middle-class autobiographies and oral-history transcripts. For examples of 'moral manliness' see F. T. Bullen, *Confessions of a Tradesman* (London, Hodder and Stoughton, 1908), p. 78; Mr and Mrs F. H. Crittall, *Fifty Years of Work and Play* (London, Constable, 1934); Essex family life and work experience survey (Qualidata, University of Essex), no. 47; for prescriptive elaboration see T. D. Talmage, *The Marriage Tie: Thirteen Discourses on Marriage and Family Life* (London, Nicholson, 1890), pp. 38–9.

12 G. Crossick, 'The emergence of the lower middle-class in Britain: a discussion', in Crossick (ed.) *The Lower Middle-Class*, p. 12; Simon Szreter, *Fertility, Class and Gender in Britain, 1860–1940* (Cambridge, Cambridge University Press, 1996), p. 464.

13 I recognise that these material categories do not exhaust the complex forces that contribute to the formation of different masculinities. John Tosh stresses the need to distinguish different expressions of masculinity by scrutinising the 'balance struck' between 'home, work and all-male associations', as well as the most neglected and difficult to recover component, the subjective identity; Tosh, 'What should historians do with masculinity?'.

14 The entire 1888 *Punch* serial, with some additions, was reproduced in G. and W. Grossmith, *The Diary of a Nobody* ([1892,] London, Penguin, 1965).

15 For a comprehensive discussion of these early Victorian literary types see A. D. Young, 'Class, domesticity, and the English novel', unpublished Ph.D. thesis, Cornell University, 1994, pp. 138–52, 198–207.

16 D. Jerrold, 'Mrs Caudle's curtain lectures', *Punch*, vols 8 and 9 (1845).
17 The separately published volumes were B. Pain, *Eliza* (London, S. H. Housfield, 1900); B. Pain, *Eliza's Husband* (London, Chatto & Windus, 1903); B. Pain, *Eliza Getting On* (London, Cassell, 1911); B. Pain, *Exit Eliza*, (London, Cassell, 1912); B. Pain, *Eliza's Son* (London, Cassell, 1913); subsequent editions included additional material. All references are taken from the following collected edition: B. Pain, *The Eliza Books* (London, T. Werner Laurie, 1931). Like Grossmith, Pain was closely involved with a theatrical and literary circle which included Jerome K. Jerome, J. M. Barrie and Robert Barr, in the 1890s all regular contributors to Jerome's increasingly titillating periodical, *The Idler*. The potential for mock inversion of gender roles and the inherent gender ambiguities in Pooterism made it an easy target for such groups, as it was on the stage generally. On Grossmith's prominence on the stage in Gilbert and Sullivan's comic operas and his career as a solo piano entertainer see T. Joseph, *George Grossmith: Biography of a Savoyard* (Bristol, T. Joseph, 1982).
18 Pain, *Exit Eliza*, pp. 195–200.
19 *Ibid.*, pp. 160–6.
20 Pain, *Eliza's Son*, pp. 295–308.
21 The development of this early and mid-Victorian model of masculinity is described in Davidoff and Hall, *Family Fortunes*, pp. 13–18, 107–48, 229–40, 302–8, 321–35.
22 Tosh, 'Domesticity and manliness', pp. 65–8; for further exploration of the relationship between imperialism, domesticity and masculinity see Dawson, *Soldier Heroes*. R. N. Price, 'Society, status and jingoism: the social roots of lower middle-class patriotism, 1870–1900', in Crossick (ed.), *The Lower Middle-Class*, pp. 89–112, makes an explicit connection between jingoist patriotism and lower-middle-class status anxieties.
23 For elaboration of the interwar consumption of these stories see K. Boyd, 'Knowing your place: the tensions of manliness in boys' story papers, 1918–39', in Roper and Tosh (eds), *Manful Assertions*, pp. 145–67.
24 See, for example, the humiliating meeting between the robust American, Hardfur Huttle, and Charles Pooter in Grossmith, *Diary*, pp. 195–200.
25 For stereotypical comic constructions of husbands' urges to escape from their wives and domestic responsibilities to homosocial recreations see J. K. Jerome, *Three Men on the Bummel* ([1900,] Harmondsworth, Penguin, 1983); the setting was among a higher class but Jerome's work was popular among lower-middle-class readers.
26 Texts like M. Nordau's *Degeneration* (New York, Howard Fertig, 1968), translated from the German in 1895, had a powerful influence on *fin-de-siècle* ideas of physical decline.
27 R. White, 'Wanted: a Rowton House for clerks', *Nineteenth Century* (1897), 596.
28 G. S. Layard, 'Family budgets, II, a lower middle-class budget', *Cornhill*, 10 (1901), 656–66.
29 J. S. Harrison, *The Social Position and Claims of Clerks and Bookkeepers* (London, Hamilton Adams, 1852), pp. 4–6.
30 W. Gallichan, *The Blight of Respectability: An Anatomy of the Disease and a Theory of Curative Treatment* (London, University Press, 1897); T. W. H. Crosland, *The Suburbans* (London, John Lang, 1905); R. G. White, *England Without and Within* (London, Sampson, Low, Morton, Searle and Rivington, 1881); see also C. F. G. Masterman, *The Condition of England* (London, Methuen, 1909), pp. 80–94.
31 S. Alexander, 'Becoming a woman in London in the 1920s and 1930s', in D. Feldman and G. Stedman Jones (eds.), *Metropolis London: Histories and Representations since 1800* (London, Routledge, 1989), pp. 244–5.
32 Nava, 'Modernity's disavowal', pp. 38–76.
33 Masterman, *The Condition of England*, pp. 80–94.
34 R. Andom, *Martha and I: Being Scenes from our Suburban Life* (London, Jarrold and Sons, 1898), p. 236; this lengthy text was a further play on the Pooter theme, claiming to be an autobiographical account of the domestic side of the author's life in South Woodford, but it was less successful than either the Grossmiths' or Pain's.
35 Crossick, 'The emergence of the lower middle-class', p. 32; W. S. Brown, *The Life and Genius of Thomas William Hodgson Crosland* (London, Cecil Palmer, 1928), p. 172.

36 Crossick, 'The emergence of the lower middle-class', p. 32; Price, 'Society, status and jingoism', pp. 93, 101; Young, 'Class, domesticity, and the English novel', pp. 189–90.
37 Crosland, *The Suburbans*, p. 139, passim.
38 *Ibid.*, pp. 44–5.
39 T. W. H. Crosland, *The Unspeakable Scot* (London, Grant Richards, 1902); T. W. H. Crosland, *The Egregious English*, (London, Grant Richards, 1903); T. W. H. Crosland, *Lovely Woman* (London, Grant Richards, 1903); T. W. H. Crosland, *The Lord of Creation* (London, Grant Richards, 1904); T. W. H. Crosland, *The Wild Irishman* (London, Grant Richards, 1905); T. W. H. Crosland, *Taffy was a Welshman* (London, Ewart, Seymour, 1912). For a satirical response to Crosland's *Lovely Woman* see G. E. Farrow, *Lovely Man* (London, Skiffington, 1904).
40 Brown, *Crosland*, pp. 258, 311, 320 ff; M. Fido, *Oscar Wilde* (London, Hamlyn, 1984), pp. 139–41.
41 Crosland, *The Egregious English*, pp. 12–13.
42 Crosland, *The Suburbans*, pp. 51–5.
43 On threshold rituals generally see J. R. Gillis, *A World of Their Own Making: Myth, Ritual and the Quest for Family Values* (New York, Basic Books, 1996), pp. 193–5.
44 J. Clarke, *The Labourer's Welcome* (1865); J. M. Bowkett, *Preparing Tea* (1861) both reproduced in Christopher Wood, *Victorian Panorama: Paintings of Victorian Life* (London, Faber and Faber, 1976), p. 60.
45 Crosland, *The Suburbans*, pp. 21–4.
46 *Ibid.*, p. 50.
47 *Ibid.*, pp. 138–9.
48 Crosland, *Lord of Creation*, pp. 90–100.
49 Quoted in J. Walkowitz, *City of Dreadful Delight: Narratives of Sexual Danger in Late-Victorian London* (Chicago, University of Chicago Press, 1992), pp. 149–50.
50 John Burns, quoted in J. Winter, *London's Teeming Streets, 1830–1914* (London, Routledge, 1993), p. 202.
51 Crosland, *The Egregious English*, pp. 129–30; Crosland, *The Suburbans*, pp. 129–35; for similar postwar criticism see E. Wilson, *The Sphinx in the City: Urban Life, the Control of Disorder and Women* (London, Virago, 1991), p. 106.
52 Crosland, *The Suburbans*, pp. 69–70.
53 Crosland, *Lovely Woman*, p. 126.
54 On the low fertility of clerical workers see Szreter, *Fertility, Class and Gender*, p. 478.
55 Crosland, *The Egregious English*, pp. 42–61; Crosland, *The Suburbans*, pp. 55, 69.
56 Alun Howkins, 'Rider Haggard and rural England: an essay in literature and history', in C. Shaw and M. Chase (eds.), *The Imagined Past: History and Nostalgia* (Manchester, Manchester University Press, 1989), pp. 81–94.
57 Young, 'Class, domesticity, and the English novel', pp. 182–90.
58 A. Bennett, *The Card* ([1911,] London, Penguin, 1975).
59 See, for example, H. G. Wells, *The History of Mr Polly* ([1910,] London, J. M. Dent, 1993); H. G. Wells, *The Wheels of Chance* ([1896,] London, J. M. Dent, 1935); H. G. Wells, *Love and Mr Lewisham: The Story of a Very Young Couple* ([1900,] London, J. M. Dent, 1993); E. M. Forster, *Howard's End* ([1910,] London, Edward Arnold, 1932). For an autobiographical example of resentment of the literary stereotype, which singled out Wells for misrepresentation and celebrated the talent and dignity of white-collar husbands, see Bullen, *Confessions*, p. 78.
60 S. Bullock, *Robert Thorne: The Story of a London Clerk* (London, T. Werner Laurie, 1907), pp. 181, 186–7, 210, 275–6, 278, 288–91.
61 For examples of themes summarised here see A. E. Coppard, *It's Me O Lord! An Abstract and Brief Chronicle of Some of the Life with Some of the Opinions of A. E. Coppard* (London, Methuen, 1957); R. Church, *Over the Bridge: An Essay in Autobiography* (London, Heinemann, 1955); V. S. Pritchett, *A Cab at the Door, An Autobiography: Early Years* (Harmondsworth, Penguin, 1974); A. F. Goffin, *The Story of a Grey Life: Being the Autobiography of Arthur Frederick Goffin, 1879–1964* (Brunel University MS collection no. 271).
62 See, for example, Church, *Over the Bridge*; Goffin, *The Story of a Grey Life*; Bullen,

Confessions; L. P. Jacks, *The Confessions of an Octogenarian* (London, Allen and Unwin, 1942), pp. 86–94.

63 J. M. Robson, *Marriage or Celibacy? The Daily Telegraph on a Victorian Dilemma* (Toronto, University of Toronto Press, 1995).

64 G. S. Frost, *Promises Broken: Courtship, Class and Gender in Victorian England* (Charlottesville, University Press of Virginia, 1995).

65 A. Light, *Forever England: Femininity, Literature and Conservatism between the Wars* (London, Routledge, 1991), p. 8.

66 Grossmith, *Diary*, p. 19.

12

GENDER, CONSUMER CULTURE AND THE MIDDLE-CLASS MALE, 1918–39
Jill Greenfield, Sean O'Connell and Chris Reid

An increasing body of work has highlighted the part rendered by women's magazines in the rising tide of twentieth-century consumerism.[1] However, with the exception of Frank Mort's recent work on masculinity in post-1945 Britain, magazines aimed at a masculine readership have received scant attention.[2] This chapter examines the relationship between consumer culture and middle-class male identity in interwar Britain, focusing upon magazines and their role in the commercial orchestration of the middle-class male consumer. More exactly, it concentrates on *Men Only* – Britain's first recognisable 'modern' lifestyle magazine for men – exploring its portrayal of masculinity and appropriate forms of male consumption. This is supported by evidence drawn from contemporary motoring magazines, relating how these specialist periodicals employed gendered representations of consumption in much the same way as *Men Only*. In the process, the primary aim of this chapter is to acknowledge the important role of the middle-class male, and masculinity, within the so-called 'new consumerism' of the 1920s and 1930s. Existing accounts have tended to focus entirely on the role of women and femininity in this phenomenon.[3]

Two principal themes are explored. First, attempts made by the producers of consumer magazines and goods to inspire and influence male consumers are investigated. It is argued that this was achieved by manipulating many of the concerns and desires that also motivated the female consumer, while accommodating men's anxiety regarding the perceived links between consumption and femininity. Surpassing these difficulties often involved stereotyping female consumers who, it was argued, endangered the rational basis of masculine consumption. Moreover, many of those deploying these stereotypes clearly believed them, preferring not to recognise 'feminine' traits in the male consumer. Thus, the commercial targeting of the male consumer in interwar Britain was heavily dependent on gender relations.

Secondly, this connection between consumption and gender relations between the wars is probed. This was a difficult period for gender relations, the interpretation of which has proved problematic for historians. Heroic models of masculinity so beloved of the pre-1914 middle classes had been greatly undermined by the realities of emasculating trench warfare. However, as Graham Dawson's account of the popularity of T. E. Lawrence has shown, reconfigurations of this form of masculinity were still attractive to the post-1918 generation.[4] Other accounts have tended to portray interwar gender relations as primarily characterised by a male backlash against the real and imagined advances of women during and following the war.[5] While convincing in some respects, this explanation is unsatisfactory in a great many others. Although some of the material represented herein might conceivably support 'backlash' explanations, its relevance is more readily appreciated when informed by a fuller understanding of the interwar socio-economic environment. It will then become clear that new forms of middle-class masculinity were evolving in these years. These new forms, while drawing upon some aspects of pre-1914 masculinity, were also markedly modern. They were modern in the sense that masculinity was increasingly shaped by the demands and desires generated by consumer society.

The cultural, economic and social impact of the interwar decades upon all social classes was significant. For many middle-class families these upheavals were most tangibly experienced through greater geographical and social mobility. Increasing real income allowed many aspiring middle-class families to purchase one of the 2,800,000 private homes built between the wars.[6] At the same time the decreasing attractiveness of domestic service, largely due to competing and more attractive employment opportunities for single women, meant that housework was undertaken, in some cases for the first time, by middle-class wives. New suburban housing developments, characterised by their generous gardens, ensured that the external fabric of the house was on display, necessitating a continual flow of additional work to maintain the standards adopted by the aspiring middle classes.

Of course, there were marked and keenly felt distinctions within and between middle-class groups. The entry of new groups to the middle classes and the downgrading of others – the 'new rich' and 'new poor' – exacerbated status anxieties.[7] A plethora of etiquette books were published to enable the middle classes to navigate a variety of social situations, from the organisation of garden parties to correct conduct on public transport.[8] Within this environment, the world of goods inevitably contributed to the expression of status and identity for both middle-class men and middle-class women.

Thus, the new forms of domesticity fostered by suburbanisation provided nascent markets for domestic and leisure products. This, in turn, brought fresh opportunities for the advertising and publishing industries. Advertising expenditure almost doubled between 1920 and 1938 from £31 million to £59 million, with the print media receiving some 87 per cent of the latter total.[9] Much of this represented advertising revenue for the large publishing conglomerates, flowing from sales of a proliferation of lifestyle magazines.[10] The annual *Newspaper Press Directory* provides valuable, if brief, details on the profusion of new publications catering for various hobbies, leisure activities and consumer interests.[11] Its pages also reveal the publishing industry's increasing use of market-research data to devise publications that secured readers and advertising revenue.[12] Magazine publishers were seeking greater profitability by providing products that were attractive to readers with diverse leisure interests. However, they were also aiming to win large contracts from advertisers by offering them space in magazines which were read by large numbers of identifiable consumer groups.

The role performed by women's magazines in 'manipulating desire as against satisfying already existing needs' has been acknowledged.[13] While they had a long history, women's magazines registered significant increases in both number and sales during the first decades of the twentieth century.[14] By the late 1930s there were over fifty magazines aimed at women readers, several of which had attained readership figures in the hundreds of thousands.[15] There is less awareness of the relationship between male consumers, magazines and advertisers. Without a clear recognition of the latter, there is a danger that the historiography of this period will inevitably replicate the gender dichotomies accepted during the 1920s and 1930s. In effect, without an investigation of the intricacies of male consumption, there is a risk that consumerism in interwar Britain will be regarded as having been largely about women and femininity. Thus the argument here supports Christopher Breward's critique of Thomas Richards's assertion that 'consumption became something that women undertook on behalf of men'.[16] Men were also pleasurably involved in the world of goods. With respect to middle-class men, gratification was often derived from acquisitions that expressed their success in the masculine world of commerce. Furthermore, men like women – and masculinities like femininities – were knowingly and unknowingly agents of commerce.

Two different types of magazine which illuminate various aspects of the relationship between middle-class men, advertisers and consumer magazines will be examined. The first, *Men Only*, represented an explicit, ambitious and potentially risky attempt to influence male consumption. It was a precarious publishing venture because its espousal of male consumption, in particular of fashion goods, had many obvious parallels with the women's magazines that were often the object of male scorn. In addressing fashion issues, *Men Only* appealed to narcissistic aspects of masculine identity that were often taboo. The second example, that of motoring magazines, provides a different perspective on middle-class male consumption. By the 1930s, the car had become a signifier of the affluent middle classes, there being approximately one car for every five families by 1939. As the car was strongly identified with masculinity, it was possible for motoring magazines unashamedly to promote its consumption. However, this was often conducted via a discourse that identified male interest in the car with practicality and utilitarianism rather than aesthetic considerations. In this way, motoring magazines succoured the continuation of traditional notions of middle-class masculinity through their denial of what many contemporaries would have considered 'feminine' preoccupations. Both types of magazine allowed male consumers to pay fetishistic attention to the details of consumption, whether of that season's new cars or suits.

MEN ONLY

Men Only, which first appeared in December 1935, was Britain's first men's lifestyle magazine. Published monthly by C. Arthur Pearson Ltd, which also published many successful women's periodicals, it was priced at 1 shilling and was clearly aimed at comfortably-off middle-class males. It rapidly established itself, claiming 50,000 readers by May 1937, although given its pocket-sized format and risqué cartoons, accompanied by a monthly 'artistic' female nude photograph from May 1937 onwards, it is likely that readership figures were much higher.[17]

Men Only was clearly modelled on the successful American magazine *Esquire*, which first appeared in 1933. Kenon Breazeale has indicated how that magazine was a product of the contemporary American marketing industry's concept of 'consumer engineering'.[18] Just as factory management turned to psychology to improve production techniques, consumer engineers attempted to employ psychological theory to make consumers more active and efficient, to stimulate their desires and overcome inertia.

In attempting to produce men's lifestyle magazines as vehicles for the commercial orchestration of masculinity, both *Esquire* and *Men Only* were classic examples of consumer engineering. *Men Only*'s first editorial made clear that it saw itself as a radical departure in publishing history:

> A MAGAZINE for men only. Here is a novelty and no mistake. Until to-day, every magazine published in this country has been produced with at least one eye on the woman reader. We on the other hand are not interested in women readers. We don't want women readers. We won't have women readers. There is no single magazine or newspaper dealing fairly and squarely with masculine interests . . . Obviously it is time we men had our own magazine – and here it is . . . We shall deal with matters of interest to men.[19]

Matters of interest covered in early issues included hunting, golf, horse racing, the countryside, the army and navy, finance, food and drink, men's health and fashion. The latter was described as a 'very special feature' of the magazine. It is this area of *Men Only*'s content that will form the primary focus of this discussion. Offering extensive coverage of men's fashion was *Men Only*'s greatest risk. It was on its fashion pages, with their attractive and colourful photographs of new fashions, that *Men Only* most clearly resembled a women's magazine. It was also, of course, on the fashion pages that *Men Only* and its advertisers most obviously sought to orchestrate male consumption. However, in order to achieve its commercial aims, *Men Only* had to deny the similarities it bore to women's magazines. It also had to offer its readers a vision of masculine identity that was similarly disassociated from feminine interests and tastes. Thus, although *Men Only* was notably modern, like women's magazines, in acknowledging and exploiting the male interest in 'new consumerism', it nevertheless framed its depiction of gender identities within recognisably traditional models of masculinity and femininity.

Those who have promoted men's fashion have often been 'policed' by strong ideologies of heterosexual, conformist masculinity. At the turn of the twentieth century, for example, following the Oscar Wilde scandal, there was a strong association between the 'homosexual' or other forms of 'perversion', and sartorial indulgence.[20] *Men Only*'s editors, therefore, encroached upon potentially dangerous territory in offering in-depth coverage of the latest men's fashions. Their treatment of the subject utilised strategies that drew upon and exploited a combination of male anxieties and desires. Thus, *Men Only* offered its readership a robust reassertion of traditional, that is pre-1914, discourses on gender. Masculine virtues and all-male association were celebrated, while the 'plague of feminism' that had allegedly afflicted Britain since 1918 was roundly denounced.[21]

Frequent articles on subjects such as outdoor sports and hobbies, experiences at public school, travel and life at sea facilitated the solemnisation of male camaraderie. Juxtaposed with these were constant sniping articles and references to the damage done to the modern male by the socio-economic advances achieved by his female contemporaries. In the process, *Men Only* served up an extraordinary expression of masculine anxiety and weakness. The tone was set in the first issue by an article entitled 'The Gate-Crashing Sex', written by a judge insufficiently confident to reveal his identity, bemoaning the corroding influence of young women in universities and the professions. He argued that these young women could 'disabuse their minds that they are a refining influence. They are merely an emasculating one'.[22] However, women were not only believed to be eroding masculine vigour by entering the workplace. Other articles also implicated the feminised middle-class home in this process. For example, a 1936 editorial described how women had 'swathed the world in cotton wool'. Men were virtually powerless to prevent this occurrence because:

> wanting an ordered world in moments of alarm, they [women] pat a cushion, place it comfortably against our backs, and beg us to relax. And because there is a lazy streak in all of us, we succumb . . . We are mesmerised into inertia.[23]

Another article, frankly entitled 'Forty and Fat', dealt with the problems of 'successful men' too busy to exercise. Their portly physiques, it was argued, arose through no fault of their own. Rather, it was the fault of wives who dished up overly generous portions of steak-and-kidney pudding and jam rolls which, the author suggested, 'we gobble up for the sake of domestic peace'.[24] The use of the fraternal 'we' spoke of a shared dilemma, while appeals to the rational man's natural diplomacy provided a convenient excuse for the professional man to shift the blame for his expanding girth on to his spouse. Women's magazines allowed no such latitude. Their articles on the feminine physique repeatedly warned housewives that they were in danger of losing their husbands if they did not maintain their appearance.[25]

So, irrespective of whether they stayed at home or went out to work, middle-class women could not do right as far as *Men Only* was concerned. For the middle-class man uncertain or troubled about the changing socio-economic and gender relations of the time, *Men Only* had a great deal to offer. Whether expressing concerns regarding changing work patterns or domesticity, *Men Only* consistently depicted a rise in female independence and influence as at the heart of the problem. Even the fear of another war with Germany was expressed in this manner. A 1936 article by Lt.-Col. T. A. Lowe suggested the future of the nation lay in the mass emigration of eligible young women, who were competing with men on the job market, to the colonies where they would find eugenically acceptable marriage partners among the lonely administrators and enforcers of empire. Such a move would, he maintained, preserve 'our sex and race' and counter the financial incentives being offered, as part of the Nazi's pro-natalist policies, to German women to marry and bear children.[26] Whilst offering a lightning-conductor for male anxieties, the magazine also provided space for

the articulation of masculine desire. If articles on masculine endeavour represented one such expression, and the monthly female nude another of a different
kind, then so too did *Men Only*'s fashion pages. Fashion coverage emphasised a
very particular model of masculinity, one that was very 'English', undoubtedly
metropolitan and clearly middle-class. However, this did not exclude readers in
the provinces or the Empire who were, through this and other aspects of the
magazine, invited to take a share in this privileged form of masculine identity.
The aggressive promotion of an associational but assertively heterosexual
masculine culture throughout the magazine facilitated *Men Only*'s monthly
fashion features. Once again feminine influence was deprecated. Stereotypical
female consumers were depicted as faddish, gullible and irrational. Somewhat
ironically, women's magazines were offered as the prime example of the feminine enslavement to irrational consumption.

It is a mark of C. Arthur Pearson Ltd's market appreciation that it could
engage in the publication of several successful women's periodicals while simultaneously producing *Men Only*, which disparaged its stablemates as 'queer'
inventions and 'gaily-covered futilities', offering the reader nothing more than a
'new shade of lipstick and a pattern for her spring frock'.[27] In fact, *Men Only*
followed an almost identical format to that employed by women's periodicals in
seeking to guide the consumer choices of its readers. In attempting to offer a
distinction between itself and women's magazines, and between men and
women, *Men Only* depicted the middle-class male as interested in fashionable
clothing not for vanity or through gullibility but for reasons of utility or practicality. Thus, the opening salvo in the regular 'The Well-Dressed Man' column
declared:

> The day has gone when a man rather prided himself on wearing 'any old thing.'
> Consider the really successful men of your own profession. They are not
> stupidly 'dressy', but they do know what to wear and they can mix easily in
> any circles.[28]

Men who allowed female relatives to purchase clothes on their behalf gambled
with their masculine credibility. Matching tie and silk handkerchief sets were
witheringly condemned as a 'shade effeminate'; 'practically all' of these offend-
ing items were apparently 'originally acquired by a man as a present from a
woman'.[29] The menswear trade, readers were later informed, looked scornfully
upon men who allowed women to buy their socks, ties and so on, labelling them
'squaw men'. However, it was also made clear that this derogatory phrase was
of American origin and the claim was made that the 'squaw man' was becoming far less common in Britain.[30]

In promoting men's fashion, *Men Only* offered a comfortingly traditional
image of the English gentleman's relationship with his tailor. November 1937's
'The Well-Dressed Man' column bemoaned the increasing 'fordism in tailoring',
as suits were produced for new mass markets. It argued that having a suit made
should be a 'pleasant and leisurely rite' with direct and personal contact between
maker and wearer.[31] London's Saville Row was idealised as the centre of this
masculine ritual and it was maintained that the world gave more regard to men's
clothes from London than to women's clothes from Paris.[32] By promoting men's

fashion and encouraging readers to identify with and ascribe to a metropolitan style in menswear, *Men Only* appealed to a narcissistic side of masculine identity rarely acknowledged by middle-class men. It thereby enabled aspiring or already affluent middle-class readers to amass the cultural capital that would enable them to make investments in clothing that expressed their taste and status. In April 1939, for example, coverage of trends in sports-suit design acknowledged the important role that dress had in the complex world of middle-class distinction:

> Admitted, there are many men who think that an old tweed jacket and flannel trousers make an ideal kind of informal dress. But there are lots of others who, while liking the style in itself, consider that it has become a great deal too popular; that it is almost an off-duty 'uniform'; and that it has lost a lot of its appeal, so far as they are concerned, by getting too far down the social scale. Perhaps you feel the same way about it. It isn't a question of snobbery. Call it 'discrimination'.[33]

Men Only's fashion experts also provided a reference guide for men anxious about dress etiquette, inviting letters from readers on what was a delicate subject for some feeling their way in middle-class society. The letters, never printed in full and referred to cryptically, dealt with issues such as the advisability of wearing the official tie of a regiment in which one had not served. The answer to that particular question was a rather frosty 'Must you?'[34]

However, *Men Only* did not simply offer advice. It was also a willing participant in the commercial orchestration of the middle-class male consumer. As noted earlier, despite its ridicule of women's magazines, it owed its successful existence to the same commercial forces that motivated them. Thus, *Men Only* contained a great deal of material that would not have been out of place in the most commercially orientated women's magazine. For example, *Men Only* ran a regular feature called 'A Look Round the Shops' which promised to inform readers about 'useful and really ingenious gadgets of the sort that make you wonder why, in the name of necessity, someone hasn't thought of them before'. The first essential item identified was the 'new seven in one golf club' with an adjustable club head which meant it could also convert to a putter.[35] Among later bargains was the 'splendid chemical cleaner' recommended as good for chapped hands, as an antiseptic, an improved shaving lather, an 'excellent' shampoo for a man or his dog, a tonic for tired feet and a cleanser for dentures – all for 1*s* 3*d* a tube![36] Details of this product and many others were available by writing to *Men Only*. In this respect, *Men Only* imitated the advertorial tradition of women's periodicals. The advertorial represented a blurring of advertisement and advice column.[37] Its use in *Men Only*, however, clearly caused its editors some embarrassment. On several occasions the editorials defended the magazine's advertising policy. Thus, *Men Only* stressed the service it provided in bringing 'the shops' to 'soldiers, sailors, country gentlemen, civil servants abroad' and 'professional men in the provinces', thereby helping 'to carry the best goods into the best homes'.[38]

Advertorials were also evident in *Men Only*'s fashion coverage which promoted as much as it reported sartorial change. In doing so, *Men Only* had to overcome suspicion about male interest in clothing, a hurdle surmounted by constructing a clearly heterosexual magazine. *Men Only* also capitalised on the long-established, but often unacknowledged, male interest in clothes. For middle-class men in particular, clothing had long been an outlet through which masculinity, status and taste could be expressed.[39] Thus, ultimately, *Men Only* was correct to describe its coverage of fashion as an 'absorbing topic' for men. However, it refused to recognise the association between men's interest in clothes and that of women, preferring instead to construct an artificial distinction between the consumption of men and women. Thus, in 1937, it argued that 'men did not want to be bothered with trivial chatter about things they could see in shop windows. They wanted to know the shape of clothes to come.'[40] This was despite the presence of regular columns like 'A Look Round the Shops'. *Men Only* went on to claim that men treated clothes as they did cars; they wanted to read about the new models weeks before they appeared. Accordingly, male consumption, whether of cars or clothes, was planned and rational. Promotional material was read for evidence of quality and utility before purchasing decisions were made. In contrast, women's purchasing was depicted as unplanned and based on impulse.

Men Only represented a clear attempt to orchestrate the consumption habits of middle-class men in much the same way as women's magazines aimed to manipulate those of their female readers. *Men Only* manipulated status anxieties and images of masculinity – sometimes skilfully, often crudely – to influence men's consumption choices. Although it had no direct competitors during the 1930s, it was not unique either in targeting male consumers or playing upon their anxieties. In the following section we shall see that similar distinctions between male and female consumption were clearly represented in motoring magazines of the period. Beneath the veneer of utilitarianism, the consumption of the car was also influenced by factors identified as feminine by many contemporary commentators.

MOTORING MAGAZINES

The 1920s and 1930s was Britain's first era of mass motoring with car-ownership soaring amongst middle-class families. In 1919 there were 100,000 cars on Britain's roads, rising to two million by 1939.[41] Motoring magazines such as *Autocar* and *Motor* offered established and aspiring motorists news on such matters as new models. By the early 1920s they had a substantial readership, *Autocar*'s motor show editions achieving a circulation of almost 100,000 by 1922.[42] As was the case with *Men Only* and the women's magazines of the period, motoring magazines were also heavily involved in the promotion of consumption. Their publishers took substantial revenue from motor manufacturers' advertisements and, not surprisingly, the magazines rarely engaged in criticism of either manufacturers' policies or individual models. Significantly, the one grumble that did appear in the motoring magazines was the possible dangers implicit in manufacturers designing cars with the female consumer in mind.

The private car market in the interwar years can be divided into two periods. From the immediate postwar years to the late 1920s, rivalry between manufacturers was conducted via price competition. However, from the late 1920s onwards price competition diminished significantly as model differentiation became increasingly important.[43] Accordingly, car manufacturers emphasised comfort, design and styling, while striving for the flexibility required to exploit market niches. This negated the risks inherent in single model production whilst enabling manufacturers to cultivate what a Political and Economic Planning (PEP) survey described as 'technical, aesthetic or snobbish appeal'. PEP also offered a summary of the interwar motorist's requirements from their car:

> Unlike most other engineering products, cars have been at once capital goods and fashion goods. Many motorists wanted not the best value in cheapness and efficiency but in [sic] these qualities combined with imposing appearance; others were attracted by distinctiveness and the opportunity to display real or fancied discrimination.[44]

If the car was increasingly central to the middle-class family's status and identity, this was particularly true for the men of such families. In 1938 the Society of Motor Manufacturers and Traders estimated that an annual salary of £250 was needed by anyone hoping to meet both the initial and running costs of a new car.[45] Such a salary was beyond the means of most single, middle-class women, and certainly those of the majority of working women.[46] It is clear, therefore, that most women drivers had access to the wheel via a family car. It was also the case that in the majority of car-owning families the driving seat was a masculine domain. In 1933, the only year for which information is available, women held only 12 per cent of driving licences.[47] Moreover, there is also evidence to indicate that women were marginalised in the car-buying process until the late 1960s.[48]

Women were at the margins of the developing car culture for three reasons. First, as has already been indicated, their socio-economic position prevented all but a small minority of women becoming independent car-buyers. Second, the car was associated with masculine endeavour; tales of resourceful inventors, engineers and heroic racing drivers aiding the process. Many men, both car-owners and those involved in the motor industry itself, were strongly attracted to the car's association with rugged masculinity. Accordingly, the car was immersed in a technological language and culture that was familiar to many men but very few women.[49] Third, the association of the car with masculinity was also expedited by the broader gender ideology of the 1920s and 1930s. In ideology, if not always in reality, the middle-class woman remained at home to create a domestic idyll which her husband worked to finance. An article in a 1929 issue of *Morris Owner*, entitled 'Women's Work in the Garage', offered a vision of separate-spheres ideology translated to the car. Its author, Mrs Victor Bruce, maintained that a woman ought not to be 'urged to learn [to drive] against her will', but advocated that she be responsible for ensuring the garage was 'spick and span' when her husband returned from 'a hard day at business and a long drive home in the traffic stream'.[50]

However, the car's identification with masculinity was far from absolute, and there remained considerable debate regarding women's influence on the car and its design. Accordingly, manufacturers, market researchers, motor dealers and many motorists offered their views on the alleged feminisation of the car. Interwar motor manufacturers and dealers employed relatively crude market-research techniques and, lacking accurate information on female consumers, often erected stereotypical models of feminine behaviour.[51] Thus, the thinking of those involved in marketing the car often resembled that of *Men Only*.

Although uncorroborated by evidence, women were credited with the deciding vote in selecting the family car. In 1919 the Scottish motor manufacturers Arrol-Johnston sought agents for their vehicle in the trade magazine *Motor Trader* by explicitly citing their reasons for advertising in women's magazines:

> The 'Lady of the house' usually has a good deal to say in the choice of a car. And, having the gift of extempore eloquence and the time to think up reasons why, she often wheedles or bullies her poor old husband into buying the car SHE wants. Everybody knows that. The firm of Arrol-Johnston Ltd., recognises the power of woman in this matter. They advertise the A.J. in several ladies' journals (between blushful frilly announcements and pictures of pearl pendants) and they never let up on telling the ornamental sex why they ought to have a tame vehicle from Dumfries concealed about the buildings.[52]

Employing the same logic, one marketing textbook, published in 1931, advised motor manufacturers targeting women to ensure that their product was 'stylish and different from the cars owned by her neighbours'. Moreover, if her husband could be convinced that the car's running costs were reasonable, the 'choice of the car would ... be left largely to the woman'.[53]

Such crude portraits of the middle-class family economy presented an image of a nation of men powerless to resist their wives' feminine wiles. A similar sense of male impotence arose when the discussion turned towards women's influence on car design. Different aspects of the car were associated with femininity or masculinity. Men, it was believed, used cars for utilitarian and business purposes and were therefore attracted by cost, economy, ruggedness and reliability. Less 'masculine' features, such as colour, comfort or styling, were regularly associated with a growing feminine interest in the car. In 1929 Miles Thomas, sales manager of Morris Motors, offered readers of *Autocar* his opinion that 'the fashion element' of the car had assumed an 'extreme importance' because there were 'so many women buyers and enthusiasts'.[54] Of course, manufacturers welcomed the increasing importance of the 'fashion element' as it created new demands and desires amongst the motoring public. Furthermore, they did their best to stimulate new demand by introducing regular stylistic and design changes to their products. In this sense production engineering complemented consumer engineering.

However, some male motorists were resentful of the manufacturer's perceived capitulation to female consumers. Thus, in 1936 V. G. Townsend of Croydon wrote to *Autocar* to censure manufacturers for their 'tendency to pander to the feminine motorist' which he felt was 'only too noticeable in modern design'. As a result, 'the needs of experienced male motorists' were 'being ignored by manufacturers'. His letter concluded with the rather pathetic appeal: 'please, Mr Manufacturer, do not assume that every car is driven and owned by a woman or a nitwit'.[55] More surprisingly, alarmed voices were raised within the motor trade regarding the dangers that female taste could visit upon the car's future. In 1925, for example, *Motor Trader* urged chassis designers not to cater to 'the new influence' of women 'by spoiling good engineering by some fashionable fad'. Furthermore, a 'few notoriety seeking women' should not be allowed to encourage '[f]reakish designs in bodywork'.[56]

Unlike *Men Only*, motoring magazines did not discourage female readers, nor did they prohibit articles written by women. They included occasional offerings from women motorists that served up a different perspective on the female view of the car. Articles by women writers in *Autocar* and *Motor* were most often published in the special editions printed to coincide with the annual motor show, and were commissioned to offer a female perspective on that event. Their appearance itself implied the existence of separate male and female responses to the car. The women employed to fulfil this task were obviously experienced motorists who wrote with great clarity and interest about technical as well as aesthetic developments in car design. However, they often included deprecating remarks about their own technical knowledge. As such, they were party to the reproduction of the gendered assumptions that surrounded the car. Their contributions usually effected this in two ways. First, any new technical developments that facilitated more comfortable or easier motoring were identified with the influence of the female driver. Secondly, they repeated jokes and stories that endorsed stereotypical images of female consumers. One such article by Mrs Victor Bruce in 1927 embodied both these traits. Bruce retold an anecdote she had heard at the motor show, and evidently believed, concerning the Rover motor company's receipt of a woman's jumper together with her request that they supply a 'Rover car to match the jumper'. Earlier in the article, Bruce had explained how the new free-wheel clutch was

> a mechanical feature of peculiar interest to women, as not only are valuable advantages secured in economy and similar important matters, but the last difficulty is removed from gear changing – a process [sic] which I do not think members of my sex are very fond![57]

In reality of course, such an improvement was far more beneficial to men, as they made up the vast majority of drivers. However, in an article two years later, Bruce acknowledged and dismissed this point of view:

> The fact that an ideal car for a woman is, generally speaking, equally ideal for a man is neither here nor there; it is the influence of women which has emphasised the necessity for the most trouble free upkeep, complete weather protection, lightness of control and so on, and has given all you motorists of both sexes the almost self-maintaining car of today.[58]

Such thinking led to virtually every advance in automotive design and comfort being attributed to feminine concerns, conceits and vanity, with women being adjudged to possess a far greater influence on the car's development than their socio-economic position appeared to merit. Any element of the buying and operation of a car not corresponding to a notion of rugged masculinity was more often than not attributed to a feminine influence seen as outside male control. Yet it was men who designed cars and who formed the great majority of buyers. Consequently, the introduction of electric starters and synchromesh gears were far more significant for men than for women, although both were interpreted as evidence of an increasing feminine influence. Notions of femininity enabled car owners and manufacturers to excuse their annual model changes by attributing them to fashion-conscious and influential female motorists and motorists' wives. For the male consumer, such a policy effectively allowed them to preserve their sense of masculinity by allowing them to deny the existence of 'feminine' traits in their own consumer behaviour.

CONCLUSION

The central concern of this essay has been to offer an appreciation of the role of men and the agency of gender in interwar consumerism. Consumption amongst the interwar middle classes can be too readily depicted as the sole province of women. Equally, the commercial exploitation of middle-class consumerism can be too readily viewed as the promotion of a new type of femininity predicated upon the consumption of new products and services. But this is to miss a vital part of the equation, for the middle-class male was every bit as involved in consumerism as the female. In fulfilling his breadwinner role he had potentially more social contacts with those above or below him in the heavily stratified social hierarchy. As such, he had cause to take precise care over his consumption decisions.

The difficulty historians face in identifying the role of men and masculinity in consumption is in locating revealing sources. In this case we have employed an analysis of two different types of magazine with predominantly male readerships, not simply for the sake of telling an untold story, but because they offer compelling evidence of how anxieties about changing class and gender relations were reflected in consumer culture. Furthermore, they illustrate how advertisers and publishers exploited ideas about the female consumer in their attempt to orchestrate the male consumer. A 'straw-woman consumer' was sketched, the deprecation of whom allowed for the construction of an 'ideal' male consumer. At times it is difficult to establish whether this policy was conducted 'knowingly' or not. In the case of the motoring magazines, it appears that there was a genuine belief that women were responsible for many changes in car design. However, it has been demonstrated that such a conviction was based on preconceived gendered notions rather than evidence.

It was exactly such notions that the publishers of *Men Only* exploited in their promotion of male consumption. In this case, it is clear that the use of the 'straw-woman consumer' was an example of carefully planned and executed consumer engineering. *Men Only*'s strategy was to manipulate the male consumer along principles that had already been well developed for the female consumer. Women's magazines promoted particular forms of feminine identity through the consumption of selected products; *Men Only* did the same for masculine identity. *Men Only*'s existence provides evidence of the ability of advertisers to exploit male desires and uncertainties. Desire was exploited by addressing a narcissistic side of masculine identity that was rarely acknowledged. Uncertainty was exploited through *Men Only*'s attacks on changing gender relations. These attacks could be read as evidence for the 'backlash' theory of interwar gender relations. However, the evidence presented here suggests a more complex interpretation.

Middle-class men, targeted by the magazines examined, were living in a society experiencing significant change. Increasing suburbanisation and the resulting transformations in domestic and leisure patterns, along with the escalation in consumer durables, presented a new era of consumption which was at once exciting and bewildering. The world of goods increasingly came to underpin status and identity amongst the burgeoning middle classes. Within this status-bound section of society, two of the most important signifiers of identity were cars and housing: goods most likely to fall within the constraints of the middle-class male budget. That the car was clearly perceived as a masculine technology has been demonstrated above. Clearly the status-conscious would need other accoutrements such as the 'right' clothing and identity to fit the middle-class lifestyle. It is therefore important that historians search for evidence of the involvement of men in the 'new consumerism' in terms of their own identity, not simply as economic providers for the consumption of their wives and families. 'New consumerism' was important in the creation of identity for middle-class men, as well as women, in a period where social relations were in flux. As such, it is vital to our understanding of the interwar years.

NOTES

1 For example: R. Ballaster *et al.* (eds), *Women's Worlds Ideology: Femininity and the Woman's Magazine* (Basingstoke, Macmillan, 1991); M. Beetham, *A Magazine of her Own? Domesticity and Desire in the Woman's Magazine 1800–1914* (London, Routledge, 1996); J. Benson, *The Rise of Consumer Society in Britain 1880–1980* (Harlow, Longman, 1994); M. Pugh, *Women and the Women's Movement in Britain 1914–1959* (Basingstoke, Macmillan, 1992); C. White, *Women's Magazines 1693–1968* (London, Michael Joseph, 1970); J. Winship, *Inside Women's Magazines* (London, Pandora, 1987).

2 F. Mort, *Cultures of Consumption: Masculinities and Social Space in Late Twentieth-Century Britain* (London, Routledge, 1995).

3 See, for example, S. Bowden, 'The new consumerism', in P. Johnson (ed.), *Twentieth Century Britain: Economic, Social and Cultural Change* (London, Longman, 1994).

4 G. Dawson, 'The blond Bedouin: Lawrence of Arabia, imperial adventure and the imagining of English-British masculinity', in M. Roper and J. Tosh (eds), *Manful Assertions: Masculinities in Britain since 1800* (London, Routledge, 1991).

5 S. M. Gilbert, 'Soldier's heart: literary men, literary women, and the Great War', in M. R. Higonnet *et al.* (eds), *Behind the Lines: Gender and the Two World Wars* (New Haven, Conn., Yale University Press, 1987).

6 J. Burnett, *A Social History of Housing 1815–1970* (London, Methuen, 1983).

7 For full discussion of this question see A. A. Jackson, *The Middle Classes 1900–1950* (Nairn, David St John Thomas, 1991).

8 D. L. North, 'Middle class suburban lifestyles and culture in England 1919–1939', unpublished D.Phil. thesis, University of Oxford, pp. 346–9.

9 T. R. Nevett, *Advertising in Britain* (London, Heinemann, 1982), p. 146.

10 The major companies involved in this area included Amalgamated Press, C. Arthur Pearson Ltd, Odhams Press, D. C. Thomson, the National Magazine Company, and George Newnes Ltd.

11 Charles Mitchell and Co. Ltd, *Newspaper Press Directory* (London, annual).

12 For more on the evolution of market research see Nevett, *Advertising in Britain*.

13 Beetham, *A Magazine of Her Own?*, p. 146.

14 J. Barrell and B. Braithwaite *The Business of Women's Magazines* (London, Kogan Page, 1988).

15 *Newspaper Press Directory 1939*.

16 T. Richards, *The Commodity Culture of Victorian England: Advertising and Spectacle 1851–1914* (London, Verso, 1991), p. 206; C. Breward, *The Culture of Fashion: A New History of Fashionable Dress* (Manchester, Manchester University Press, 1995), p. 171.

17 *Men Only*, May 1937.

18 K. Breazeale, 'In spite of women: *Esquire* magazine and the construction of the male consumer', *Signs: Journal of Women in Culture and Society*, 20 (1994), 1–34.

19 *Men Only*, December 1935.

20 Breward, *The Culture of Fashion*, p.169.

21 *Men Only*, June 1936.

22 *Men Only*, December 1935. The author's profession was revealed in the March 1936 editorial.

23 *Men Only*, August 1936.

24 *Men Only*, December 1935.

25 Pugh, *Women and the Women's Movement*, p. 213.

26 *Men Only*, September 1936.

27 *Men Only*, December 1936.

28 *Men Only*, December 1935.

29 *Men Only*, April 1936.

30 *Men Only*, September 1937.

31 *Men Only*, November 1937.

32 *Men Only*, May 1937.

33 *Men Only*, April 1939.

34 *Men Only*, August 1936.

35 *Men Only*, July 1936.

36 *Men Only*, September 1936.

37 Beetham, *A Magazine of Her Own?*, p. 199.

38 *Men Only*, May 1938.

39 Breward, *The Culture of Fashion*, p. 170 ff.

40 *Men Only*, October 1937.

41 Society of Motor Manufacturers and Traders, *The Motor Industry of Great Britain* (London, annual).

42 *Advertiser's Weekly*, 3 August 1924.

43 S. M. Bowden, 'Demand and supply constraints in the inter-war UK car industry: did the manufacturers get it right?', *Business History*, 33 (1991), 241–67.

44 Political and Economic Planning, *Motor Vehicles* (London, 1950), p. 130.

45 Bowden, 'Demand and supply constraints', 256.

46 R. Strachey, *Careers and Openings for Women* (London, Faber and Faber, 1937), p. 69.

47 Ministry of Transport, *Report on Fatal Road Accidents which occurred during the Year 1933* (London, HMSO, 1934), p. 7.

48 R. Scott, *The Female Consumer* (Chichester, Associated Business Programmes, 1976), p. 139.

49 On the subject of gender and the culture of technology see J. Wajcman, *Feminism Confronts Technology* (Cambridge, Polity Press, 1991).

50 *Morris Owner*, June 1929.

51 Gail Reekie has demonstrated how the female consumer was constructed as 'other' in retailing discourse in this period. G. Reekie, 'Impulsive women, predictable men: psychological constructions of sexual difference in sales literature to 1930', *Australian Historical Studies*, 24 (1991), 359–377.

52 *Motor Trader*, 5 May 1920.
53 P. Redmayne and H. Weeks, *Market Research* (London, Butterworth, 1931), pp. 151–2.
54 *Autocar*, 1 November 1929.
55 *Autocar*, 8 May 1936.
56 *Motor Trader*, 26 September 1925.
57 *Autocar*, 21 October 1927.
58 *Autocar*, 25 October 1929.

13

AN OUTBREAK OF ALLODOXIA? OPERATIC AMATEURS AND MIDDLE-CLASS MUSICAL TASTE BETWEEN THE WARS
John Lowerson

Although it sounds like a disease, allodoxia is not; rather it is more a state of mind, or a cultural form. Strictly speaking, the composite Greek word allodoxia means 'alternative teachings' and first appears in early Patristic writings as a condemnation of heresy; St Athanasius, the champion of Christian Orthodoxy, used it in his attacks on the fourth-century Arians.[1] In subsequent common usage it has tended to give way to the more familiar 'heterodoxy' but it has been revived relatively recently by the French cultural sociologist Pierre Bourdieu, who uses it in his analyses of petit-bourgeois taste. For him it represents cultural, predominantly leisure, pursuits whose following is both limited and, paradoxically, authorised by the dominant forms of high, i.e. aristocratic and haut-bourgeois, art by whose standards they form inadequate, even illegitimate, alternatives. His characterisation of this *culture moyenne* has been rendered most easily into English as 'middlebrow', a twentieth-century ascription which does not convey as fully as it might Bourdieu's sense of the derogatory.[2] However defined, it allows its followers to occupy a cultural space which is their own, almost defensible territory. There are inevitably some problems in a direct transfer of the word from French to British middle-class pursuits because of national variations in leisure patterns and there is as yet insufficient comparative material for the scholar to rest too easily with assumed universals.

The idea of a distinctive alternative middle-class culture enjoys a great deal of unspoken approbation in many descriptions of the process of modernisation, not least in the hoary celebrations of 'respectability' and its offshoots. As such, it has seemed to many historians, not least F. M. L. Thompson in his *Rise of Respectable Society,* to have provided a useful tool for taming both an unruly aristocracy and a dangerous working class by the beginning of the twentieth century.[3] However valuable such a broad approach might be, its frequent over-simple application neglects the subtleties of differentiation within the middle classes themselves, assuming instead a canon of behaviour and taste which radiated outwards from some readily identifiable class-located centre. In many instances, not least music, such an approach seems increasingly unreliable. It clashes particularly with another major twentieth-century classification of socio-cultural divisions, that between 'high' and 'low', or 'elite' and 'mass'.[4] The latter concept in particular has proved a persistent tool in analysing 'popular' cultural change between the two world wars, with the overlapping assumptions that deeply rooted and localised forms have been eroded by the commercial and the

near-universal. Occasionally, the period of this displacement has been transferred by commentators to the 1960s, particularly where 'mass' has also been
seen as conveniently coterminous with 'American' when arguments over cultural
hegemony have assumed nationalistic as well as class dimensions. When 'pop'
became an acceptable, even celebratory, alternative description to the derogatory 'mass' , 'respectability' was virtually thrown out of the window.[5]

Difficulties emerge, however, when such an approach is taken towards the
bulk of the British middle classes, many of whom developed or adopted forms
which were both class-specific and yet sufficiently amorphous to spread outside
tightly drawn social boundaries in limited circumstances which owed much to
local community make-up. For this process the use of the two oppositional
cultural categories alone is inadequate. We need to investigate the middle ground
not just in class-definable terms but in looser cultural ones. It is here that the idea
of the 'middlebrow' is useful. Whilst it provides a shaky alternative to the notions
of high or low, it also has a value because of its emergence as an ascription at a key
point in British social change. Its first known use occurs in *Punch* in 1925 and it
has popped up intermittently since.[6] A hangover from late Victorian and
Edwardian popular phrenology ('highbrow' first appeared in the 1880s,
'lowbrow' before 1910), it is frequently derogatory, especially when used from *de
haut en bas*, but it has also been used quite readily by those who want comprehen-
sible explanations of the complex. For instance, listeners asking for an
explanation of musical terms used in early BBC classical music broadcasts put
themselves apologetically in this category: ' There must be many, like myself,
middle-brows or low-brows, who would like to understand "good music".'[7]
Where cultural historians have engaged with the middlebrow, and that but rarely,
their interest has been limited largely to literary production, in particular to
romantic novels, especially in the United States.[8] Musicology and the social
history of music have largely avoided it, preferring to concentrate solely on
productions for the elite or on the oppositional duality already mentioned. Yet,
there are good reasons for assuming that middlebrow music developed not only as
a series of 'illegitimate' alternatives to high culture, as in Bourdieu's usage, but
also created within itself a set of canons which are predominantly self-legitimating
and which identify their own categories of the barely acceptable in order to maintain standards. The risk, of course, is that it just becomes another loose way of
saying 'middle class', in which case we are back to the reign of 'respectability'

One fertile ground for investigating the middlebrow is to be found in the
amateur operatic tradition, paradoxically, in view of its size and sound, a major
part of what the sociologist Ruth Finnegan has called the world of the 'hidden
musicians' of modern social history.[9] Although it has some roots in eighteenth-
and nineteenth-century Italy, and appears in other international settings the role
of amateurs in performance is very largely dominated by a British middle-class
response to modern leisure opportunities and values.[10] There had been amateur
performances in various country houses and garrison towns in the late eighteenth century but these seem to have declined by the 1830s. There is some
uncertainty about which was the first operatic society as such, not least because
many societies overlapped with, or grew out of, ones concerned initially with
spoken drama, particularly in the early years. The oldest joint society has been

claimed as the St Joseph's Amateur Operatic and Dramatic Society of Leigh, Lancashire, founded in 1837. In the middle decades of the nineteenth century, however, there were very strong inhibitions about almost any form of amateur involvement in musical drama and there seem to have been very few amateur operas. The Manchester Athenaeum, patronised by the younger members of the affluent middle classes, allowed a Dramatic Society to form in 1847, but its early years were devoted to private play-readings and its first opera was only put on in 1885.[11] Subsequent claims that Manchester hosted one of the oldest operatic societies in Britain probably owed more to a continued desire to reinforce the city's claims for mid-Victorian hegemony than to hard evidence. The movement as a whole took off in the 1870s. Inevitably it coincided with the popularity of Gilbert and Sullivan's Savoy Operas after 1875 but their overall domination has been rather exaggerated. Among the earliest groups devoted to musical drama was IBIS, organised for the central staff of the Prudential Assurance Society. It began in 1875 as the Evening Meetings Society and changed its name in 1880. IBIS's first shows were in the European operetta tradition, with Offenbach and others, and it was 1890 before it performed Gilbert and Sullivan, beginning with *The Mikado*.[12]

The period before 1914 saw a scattered growth throughout Britain but the greatest period of consolidation came between the two world wars. One enthusiastic estimate claimed some 3,000 societies with 140,000 members by 1928. It would probably be safer to opt for somewhere around half that number, but the scale of provision is still impressive enough. The umbrella organisation NODA (National Operatic and Dramatic Association) recorded 427 affiliated societies in 1923, 925 in 1930, 1,029 in 1934 and a slight fall as another war loomed to 962 in 1939; the association's officials always reckoned that there were as many freestanding societies outside as within its membership.[13] NODA itself was founded by northerners in 1899 to deal with such matters as performance rights and an information exchange but its focus soon shifted south to London, paralleling the metropolis's hegemony in professional music-making. It was not long before this 'movement' acquired the organisational trappings and language of so many parallel secular Protestant associations, such as the Workers' Educational Association, with which it has had an occasional symbiosis. What it has done in its century of sometimes uneasy existence has been to be both 'useful' in a literal sense and to provide a powerful regional and national bonding through such devices as long-service medals for local members, a succession of magazines and regional and national conferences, backed up by training schools for singers and producers in particular.[14]

By the late 1930s, the network of societies was so extensive that only people in the remotest rural areas were without access to their offerings. Operatic societies became a major agency for musical diffusion, even when set alongside the growth of radio broadcasting. It would be too easy to stereotype these societies as 'suburban', in style if not necessarily in location, just another prop of an insecure middle-class exclusiveness. Whilst the history of many societies in their local areas could be fitted quite comfortably into that ascription, there were some noticeable exceptions. One of these was the number of societies which grew up in the South Yorkshire coalfields in the 1930s, of which several still survive, including that in Dinnington near Sheffield. Whilst much of the rest of British mining suffered greatly during the Slump, new deep pits had opened there with 'model' villages laid out as miniature garden cities. Made up of regional migrants, particularly from the depressed pits of the South Welsh valleys and County Durham, their populations gradually acquired a series of thriving recreational associations. Whilst these frequently owed their birth to the initiatives of the small, resident middle class of clergy, doctors, teachers and tradesmen, they acquired a considerable working-class membership, both as singers and as back-stage members in the case of the operatic societies. Shows were staged in welfare halls provided by the coal companies and shifts were arranged, just as for brass bands, to fit rehearsals and performances. My parents met in one such, Rossington near Doncaster: my mother was the piano accompanist, my father, unable to read music, sang with enthusiasm but no great tunefulness in the chorus, a 'Gentleman of Japan' in *The Mikado*. As with so many sporting societies, the group photographs published in programmes and displayed proudly at home offered icons of their subjects' respectability.[15] The Rossington society, unlike some of its neighbours, did not survive to the end of the 1950s; so much was dependent on the strength of musical roots in each village concerned.

Elsewhere, paternalistic employers such as Pilkington's, the St Helens glass manufacturers, encouraged growth by supporting societies as part of a works-based recreational package. New industries, such as Boots The Chemists outside Nottingham or Aspro and Horlicks in Slough, found societies an additional attraction for recruiting new workers, even to the extent of building theatres for them. A Horlicks' 1937 production of *Monsieur Beaucaire* (1919), it was claimed, 'shewed that their staff, at any rate, do not suffer from "night starvation"', the sleeplessness the drink was supposed to cure.[16] The London headquarters of the trading banks, the City Exchanges and several railway companies acted similarly to provide work-focused societies, albeit for a more distinctly white-collar membership. In Sheffield the local schoolteachers founded one in 1900, which has outlived most others in this category. Others grew out of the churches' competition with each other and with a world of increasingly non-religious leisure activities; in Lancashire in particular there were often strict denominational lines which could be crossed when it became difficult to find enough principal singers. Catholic operatic societies, singing non-Catholic operas, competed and collaborated with those from Anglican and nonconformist churches. The spread amongst the latter, such as Bolton's Methodists, or Huddersfield's Baptists, and Congregationalists including Lewes Road Church in Brighton, indicated a remarkable shift in attitudes towards the respectability of the theatre; but it also acted as a force for filtering what would be acceptable in the works being staged. Church organists and choirmasters were often key figures in founding and sustaining many societies, and their musical directorships added to a portfolio of incomes common amongst musical professionals and semi-professionals. The growth in amateur operatics before and just after the First World War coincided with a slow decline in the oratorio tradition and allowed for a greater integration of the staged dramatic with the choral.[17] They also had the recruiting advantage over the choral tradition in that they offered opportunities for deploying a much wider range of members' skills – in stage management, set design and construction, and lighting.

The implications inherent in women being allowed to indulge publicly in the simulated lovemaking implicit in light operatic forms were considerable and marked a significant step, if not in actual emancipation, at least in the extension of boundaries of a controlled freedom. It took the male members of the Manchester Athenaeum's mid-Victorian dramatic society some thirty years to move from play readings to actual performances of Shakespeare and another decade before middle-class women could appear as freely on the stage. The early growth coincided with what Dina Mira Copelman has characterised as the growing 'responsibility, pride, independence and, in many respects, freedom from some of the constraints of middle-class notions of female respectability' which she found in her study of London elementary-school teachers at the end of the nineteenth century.[18] Her subjects seem to have enjoyed the greater freedom in meeting men which dramatic and other associations offered – but it remained one of the constant features of amateur operatics that societies almost invariably found it easier to recruit women than men. Despite this fact, many societies' honorary officers and committee members were drawn entirely from men until well into the 1930s. Whether the membership of these early societies came more from such newer middle-class groups than from established ones is difficult to determine from the surviving records; certainly they often recruited the younger generations of established urban power groups and their patronage lists reveal a very close dependence on approval by their senior figures and the municipal and ecclesiastical oligarchies. Few programmes for performances were complete without a listing, often with photographs, of the aldermen, businessmen and clergy who made up the lists of honorary vice-presidents and patrons. This presumably represented approval of the new directions in musical entertainments and a certain guarantee of the respectability of the performances, particularly where translated foreign works were concerned.

This degree of approval raises a series of additional questions which can be dealt with only briefly here – the relationship of these new groups to existing theatrical provision and to activities defined by the respectability of the shows and the audience. It would be convenient but probably misleading to set them up simply in opposition to the appeal of the late Victorian music hall, with its frequently ascribed raffishness and its substantial working-class audience, although there might be a strong justification for doing so.[19] Difficulties emerge, however, when the social range of alternative music halls in larger towns, including some which would be acceptable to many middle-class audiences, is considered. This is not the place to consider the possibility of a distinctly non-respectable tradition within the middle classes but there was always the risk of naughtiness within the amateur operatic tradition itself. More than one author, of fiction as well as non-fiction, has claimed that the societies have provided trysting grounds for sexual predators and the unhappily married; in one rather extreme statement, ' this was the only environment favourable to extra-marital diversions in otherwise "respectable" communities'.[20] Such claims can rarely be validated, least of all by interviews, but they allow for lively plots and character stereotyping by some writers. The continuing strength of these accusations was reinforced by one of the most successful playwrights of recent decades, Alan Ayckbourn, who set his middle-class comedy, *A Chorus of Disapproval,* in a provincial amateur operatic society ridden with adultery and corrupt property deals: an example of middlebrow entertainment's feeding on itself.[21]

More positively, amateur operatics have enjoyed a close and necessary symbiosis with the professional theatre throughout their existence. They have usually performed works first aired by professionals and have often used the same theatres and suppliers of costumes. The important role of the Edwardian theatre in providing middlebrow cultural offerings with a touch of the risqué has been emphasised recently by Peter Bailey. The societies became a major element in their wider diffusion.[22] One major factor separating the two theatrical worlds might have come from the amateurs' audiences but the range of 'respectability' has always proved notoriously difficult to contain within convenient class delineations. There is little to suggest that many in the audiences would not also have attended professional theatre performances as well. Even in the church-based groups, such outings were often increasingly encouraged, particularly during the interwar period. Societies also visited each other's performances on a regular basis, providing an additional element for the diffusion of new material.

Societies sang but rarely for themselves or for the music's own sake, however pleasing that might be. Instead they provided local, regional and national networks of respectable entertainment which often overlapped with and drew from, rather than being opposed to, existing amateur and commercial provision, or to new public agencies of the 1920s such as the BBC. Audiences, sometimes of several thousands, depended on a core of relatives and friends of the performers but involved increasingly wider local publics. Old theatres and new cinemas offered performing venues as did church and school halls, and most towns of any size acquired a musical season in which the local operatic societies carefully divided up the available time and space with touring opera companies such as the Carl Rosa, the D'Oyly Carte and other theatre users. Much more than most previous amateur musical organisations, they were heavily dependent on box-office money. The costs of even a small production lasting a couple of days ran into hundreds of pounds between the wars, with hiring and performance charges and the need for professional help. Amateur operatics rarely experienced the professional/amateur divide which caused so much agonising and petty snobbery in sport. Occasionally there were minor difficulties where societies became involved in local musical competitions, but the application of operatic 'Henley Rules' across the board would have made a nonsense of any claims to performing qualities.[23] Instead, the two groups were seen as part of a necessary continuum in which professionals normally set the highest standards but amateur productions tried to emulate them. Apart from professional producers, musical directors and orchestral players, who found a new source of employment in servicing amateur performances, there were many semi-professionals who only occasionally fell foul of the sort of distaste for the 'shamateur' found in middle-class sports. It was quite common to find some leading singers performing in a whole range of shows within quite wide local areas; they claimed it kept their voices up to standard and was part of the mutuality the societies encouraged. They were, however, rather less than open about the level of their 'expenses'.

The societies extended the market place for new productions, reinforcing the canons of 'light' entertainment. Generally the offerings had to be romantic and tuneful, avoiding tragedy almost altogether. But the societies were always dependent on their audiences' readiness to accept new works and there were sharp variations in this. It was often the patronage of local elites which made up the budget deficits or guaranteed an overdraft when a production proved unpopular. Most societies sold both the existing and the innovatory in the performance repertoire on the back of systematic giving of all profits to local charities – it was also the only way in which they could avoid the Entertainment Tax introduced as part of the First World War's emergency fiscal measures and kept for decades afterwards.[24] Many a bed in local hospitals was paid for by the annual proceeds of the local operatic society; for instance, in Preston in 1936, 'a resolution was unanimously passed naming a bed in the New Maternity Hospital "The Preston and District Amateur Operatic Society Bed" and a plaque will be fixed over that Bed in perpetuity'.[25]

There were several sources for the interwar musical offerings of the operatic societies and these represented a broadening of middlebrow taste but also contained some themes spanning apparently divergent models. The least popular was opera itself; although parts of it were fed through broadcasting and vocal recitals to provide an icing of elite taste for the middlebrow cake, often deliberately separated out by being described as 'grand'. One convenient, but never quite universal typing of it, was its lack of spoken dialogue. The very scale of the greater works and their demands on principal singers made them ill-suited for the restricted stages of most provincial theatres, church halls and so on, as well as for the vocal power of most amateur leads. There were some exceptions: Croydon had had a Grand Opera Society, singing Wagner before 1914, and the Bristol Opera School, founded in 1923, still exists, perhaps because it has tailored its repertoire to the more manageable parts of the tradition and sung in English. An attempt to found an Opera Society in Rotherham at the same time failed after two seasons – nobody seemed to want it.[26] In Birmingham, the Grand Opera Society of the 1920s was followed in the 1930s by the Midland Music Makers who grew out of an Adult School Movement musical group, a long way from the Movement's early aim of providing basic literacy. After starting with Gilbert and Sullivan accompanied by a piano, they moved by 1938 to developing a repertoire 'of operas that are only rarely performed', a pattern taken up eventually by a number of other similar bodies.[27] The Midland Music Makers are still going strong. Glasgow also acquired a thriving Grand Opera Society during the period.

On the whole, however, the full opera tradition remained a professional preserve of the haute bourgeoisie, a pattern clearly reinforced by the founding of Glyndebourne in Sussex in 1934, with its careful re-creation of the older tradition of house-party performances in the grander country houses.[28] Generally, the emphasis of opera *per se* on tragedy and grander designs, and the fact that it had only a negligible English-bred component, made it too 'heavy' for the average provincial audience which preferred lighter pieces. It is no accident that nearly all the amateurs at the former end of the spectrum referred to themselves as 'opera' rather than 'operatic' societies, the latter being the ascription of the more popular. It is a distinction which is still carefully maintained by the growing but relatively small number of societies (just over a hundred) which follow the grand tradition. The sharp upturn in their fortunes had to wait until the 1970s and most only achieved it by a careful mix of singers, with amateurs forming the choruses and young aspirants to professional careers extending their vocal range as soloists. The widely respected Welsh National Opera and Scottish Opera grew from just such a base after the Second World War.[29]

It was 'illegitimate' offerings, with their own internal canon, that dominated the operatic movement. Essentially these were self-defining rather than offering a pale imitation of the mainstream operatic form. English amateurs had long imported and performed, in English, works from the European light operatic tradition, especially from French and Viennese composers. Works such as Robert Planquette's *Les Cloches de Corneville* (1877) and Franz Lehár's *The Merry Widow* (1905) offered an element of the fantastic and were popular with the more socially ambitious groups. Perhaps they also offered to a war-tired England in the 1920s another dream of a peaceful and lost Europe, even though elaborately uniformed soldiers figured in many such works. Here again, there were often confusions. The variety of works on offer outside the heavier operatic tradition had seen careful attempts by music critics to classify them – opera comique, opera bouffe, light opera and so on – and the range was extended by the musical comedies and musical plays of interwar composers. But these usually remained the distinctions of the critics, and the societies were often far less precise in their choices, although local rivalries could lead to a specialisation which was frequently more apparent than real. Societies borrowed or poached good singers and producers from one minor tradition to another with no sense of incongruity and only occasional grumbles.[30]

The dominant productions and, therefore, the defining element remained the Gilbert and Sullivan works (or, rather, some eight of them, most noticeably *Mikado* and *Gondoliers*), but their hegemony slipped from 90 per cent of all productions in 1923 to 40 per cent by the later 1930s. If they represented the epitome of British musical humour, particularly laughter at self, many of the values they offered were already being transferred to rival works. What they did provide was a central, national canon against which almost all newcomers, as well as the older European imports, were judged. David Cannadine has offered a useful, but by no means exhaustive, analysis of their appeal: especially, the understated Englishness, the wry humour and the reinforcement of existing social codes by their temporary inversion during performances.[31] By the 1920s they had become highly stylised, with the words fixed and almost every stage movement part of a preordained ritual; almost an English version of the Japanese *Noh* drama. Control of performances remained in the hands of the D'Oyly Carte family, who licensed amateur productions so that they did not conflict with their touring company's annual cycle. One result of their increasingly tight control was that the formerly mobile and adaptable humour of Gilbert's librettos was fixed in an increasingly anachronistic Edwardian mould. There was some paradox in that the family's company changed both its set and costume designs during the period but demanded, on pain of prosecution and licence withdrawal, that amateurs retain the fixed language and stage gestures and movement (the 'business') which had coagulated after the authors' deaths. Although some societies complained about these restrictions, demand remained high for these near-sacred shows and audiences, many of whom knew the works virtually by heart, protested if the absolute forms of the ritual were not followed.[32] In some towns, the more ambitious societies mounted an annual Gilbert and Sullivan show to underwrite financially a second, less popular production. In others, there were parallel societies, one devoted to Gilbert and Sullivan entirely and the other to newer works. One fairly sure way of raising money for charity remained a concert performance of favourite Gilbert and Sullivan pieces, a re-iteration of the Victorian secular choral concert.

By comparison the minor European operettas which remained popular were augmented by new interwar productions with plots set largely overseas. One of the best received of these was Sigmund Romberg's *The Student Prince* (1924), imported from America but set in Heidelberg in the 1860s. It was an exercise in pure nostalgia, about the romance of love lost for duty, replacing tragedy with a mild heartache whilst remaining deeply rooted in an exotic *Mittel Europ* vaguely remembered from the days before German imperial ambitions erupted. There was much of the Ruritanian in such works and much room for enjoyment of the slightly dotty, elaborately uniformed world of students, duelling societies, hussars and make-believe revelry. Ever since Anthony Hope published his romantic and swashbuckling novel *The Prisoner of Zenda* in 1894 this mythical world, based on English fascination for and distrust of the Balkans, has had a cultural influence whose ramifications remain largely unexplored by scholars.[33] Another of Romberg's New York originated works, *The Desert Song* (1926), proved even more popular. For a Britain happily deluded by the well-publicised mythology of Lawrence of Arabia and Rudolf Valentino's cinematic Sheikh, the story of a dashing desert horseman offered a very successful formula for amateur staging, whatever the actual shortcomings of local voices and productions. There had also been an influential flirtation with the 'other' of Orientalism in the wake of *The Mikado* (1885), with *The Geisha* (1896) and *Chu Chin Chow* (1916). These were often performed between the wars but rarely augmented by significant new works in the genre.[34] The relative speed of releasing new shows after their West End debuts for amateur performance indicated the growing power of the movement in providing an input to the music market on which amateurs were singularly dependent.

Set in paradox against this was the claim that the very nature of such operatics meant that they were often seen as higher-grade alternatives to the noise of jazz and the repetitive lyrics of crooners, and therefore they could be identified more readily with the assumptions of elite than mass culture. At the same time there was a steady trickle of newer works based on an excited presentation of Noel Coward's studied languor and on the images of a Ritzy life style often reinforced by the new sound movies and middlebrow novels. Musical plays, another sub-type, offered their participants the chance to dress as lounge lizards and stroll around such representations of grand hotels and ocean liners as could be constructed on small local stages. Coward's *Bitter Sweet* (1929) and Ivor Novello's *Careless Rapture* (1936) brought a slightly daring touch of the modern to many societies cautious about the moral propriety of what they offered.

Although Romberg's works were transplanted happily from the United States, the new Broadway-derived cinema musicals offered a glamorous model which few societies could emulate but which their audiences used as ideals. The key text in a change which accelerated after the Second World War was Hammerstein's and Kern's *Showboat* (1926, filmed 1929 and 1936), which was mildly critical of racism whilst reinforcing a nostalgia for a glamorous South well before *Gone with the Wind* appeared on cinema screens in 1939. Whilst its reception was generally favourable, there were increasing warnings that Americanisation would destroy the gentler themes of the combined Anglo-European tradition. By the time Rock and Roll appeared in the mid-1950s, many American musicals were regarded very ambivalently by quite a number of older society members and the few music critics who devoted any attention to amateur productions.[35] The western folksiness of *Oklahoma* (1943), one of the first great challenges for British societies to try to emulate the cinema's glamour, soon gave way to the 'tendency to shock your audience rather than to charm them' deplored by one critic, who warned that the singularly randy *South Pacific* was 'not exactly suited to the family type of education which amateur operatics provide'. This was a year before its appearance as a film in 1958 gave it a major boost as a possibility for amateur production.[36] Yet the attraction of the transatlantic imports was their vitality when set against what could be seen as a stultifyingly limited traditionalism. They appealed to many of the younger members whom the societies were keen to attract and they were also seen as essential if amateur operatics were to maintain their public appeal against competition from more overtly glamorous forms of entertainment. By taking up and modifying them for the resources of amateur performance, the movement ensured its continued survival.

These strands were supplemented occasionally by a few exercises in local history set to music by clergy and schoolteachers. One such, mounted by the Eastbourne society in 1926, was *Dacre of the South*, whose librettist was Arthur Beckett, a prolific writer of Sussex nature mysticism. In it, he took major liberties with an actual historical event, Henry VIII's imprisonment and eventual execution of Lord Dacre, to turn it into an improbable romance festooned with Merrie England doggerel:

> In sweet springtime, when winter's gone,
> And Nature wakes from sleep,
> We ramble o'er the fallows green
> To where the lambkins leap;
> Then take I Prue,
> And John takes Sue,
> And Will takes little Mollee,
> We dance and we trip it,
> We jump and we skip it,
> Under the greenwood tree.[37]

Such works as this thankfully near-forgotten 'First Sussex Opera', together with much of Gilbert and Sullivan and the *Merrie England* (1902) of Edward German, added considerably to the construction of Georgina Boyes's 'Imagined Village' of the popular mind, a rural half-timbered world of tudorised rustics who embodied the 'real' spirit of England.[38] NODA and others produced guides to the loosely constructed canon of amateur operatic taste, analysing the staging demands and the quality of most available works.[39] What they had largely in common formed the essentials of middlebrow music. They were 'light', low in intellectual and emotional demands, and offered a collection of easily memorised tunes and lyrics. They were largely happy, romantic and nostalgic with a strong emphasis on humour rather than irony. Although they required considerable efforts to produce, offering to their active members various useful bonding devices, including a role as marriage marts, they were relatively undemanding to watch.

Audiences were expected to leave happier than when they entered and many participants claimed that they were a means of finding their true selves or of escaping into wonder from a grimmer daily environment. Writing of another middlebrow event, the Festival of Britain of 1951, the satirist Michael Frayn claimed that: 'For a few hours people stepped out of the squalid compromises of the everyday urban scene into a world where everything was made to please.'[40] This is a fitting characterisation of amateur operatics as well. Whatever their setting in time or country, they offered a reinforcement of British stereotypes both of selves and foreigners, often at odds with the portrayals of press, radio and newsreels as the country drew towards the Second World War. Frayn was wrong, however, when he also claimed that this world of the 'Herbivores' (mild-mannered optimists, such as the readers of the *News Chronicle*, for whom middlebrow entertainment was an essential prop of their existence) lost out entirely to a much more predatory world in the 1950s. One remarkable feature of amateur operatics is that, having faced the onslaught of popular cinema, they also survived its decline and the threats from television with a remarkable tenacity.

Yet considerable difficulty has remained in accepting them as occupying a separate category in their own right. Most professional music critics at any level beyond an adulatory local press either ignored them altogether or were remarkably condescending when they turned their attention to Gilbert and Sullivan.[41] The BBC, with its preferred emphasis on the classical, could only lump them together with the necessary but uneasily accepted mass culture it found itself feeding.[42] In his history of the Third Programme, which was born with the welfare state of the 1940s, Humphrey Carpenter has outlined the way in which marketing executives weakened its purist early stance with middlebrow dilutions, much to the despair of such traditionalists as the historian Peter Laslett.[43] Most histories of music and encyclopaedic works on opera still continue to ignore the light majority. Oxford University Press lists the key composers of the genre and their works in its *Companion to Popular Music* together with Rock and Roll, Punk and the Pop world in general.[44] Of course, that is exactly what they were, popular, but even many of their proponents still found it difficult to accept the description as they tried to distance themselves from most other categories covered by the adjective. But they have remained uncertain about where they would like to be placed in the canons of taste. Instead, amateur operatics continue to occupy the uneasy ground of the middlebrow, still with a largely middle-class following, a peculiarly strong British form of allodoxia.

NOTES

Earlier versions of this chapter were read at the Manchester conference on the 'British Middle Classes' in 1996 and at the History Work-in-Progress seminar of the University of Sussex. I am grateful for the encouragement and insights offered there and for the unstinted time and help of a number of activists from various societies mentioned here. The research for this and for the much fuller book-length treatment which will follow was made possible by the generous support of the British Academy and the University of Sussex.

1 G. W. H. Lampe, *A Patristic Greek Lexicon* (Oxford, Clarendon, 1961), p. 76.

2 Pierre Bourdieu, *Distinction: A Social Critique of the Judgement of Taste* (Paris, 1979; English trans. London, Routledge and Kegan Paul, 1986), pp. 323 ff.

3 F. M. L.Thompson, *The Rise of Respectable Society: A Social History of Victorian Britain, 1830–1900* (London, Fontana, 1988).

4 For example, see John Frow, *Cultural Studies and Cultural Value* (Oxford, Clarendon, 1995), especially pp. 24–5; it is worth comparing the gloom of Richard Hoggart, *The Uses of Literacy* (London, Chatto and Windus, 1957), with his more relaxed and almost celebratory *The Way We Live Now* (London, Chatto and Windus, 1995), at least as far as the latter's discussion of middle-class participation in the arts is concerned. See also Graham Vulliamy, 'Music and the mass culture debate', in John Shepherd et al., *Whose Music?: A Sociology of Musical Languages* (New Brunswick, Transaction Books, 1977), pp. 179 ff.

5 See Simon Frith, 'The good, the bad and the indifferent: defending popular culture from the populists', *Diacritics*, Winter 1991, 102 ff; Frith, *Music for Pleasure: Essays in the Sociology of Pop* (Cambridge, Polity Press in association with Blackwell, 1988); Frith and A. Goodwin (eds), *On Record: Rock, Pop and the Written Word* (London, Routledge, 1990), especially the essays by Adorno and Riesmann.

6 *Oxford English Dictionary*, 2nd edition, 1989, gives the various derivations.

7 *Radio Times Music Handbook* (Oxford, Oxford University Press, 1935 and 1950), Introduction.

8 Joan M. Rubin, *The Making of Middlebrow Culture* (Chapel Hill, University of North Carolina Press, 1992) is a typical example of this approach. See also Russell Lynes, *The Tastemakers* (New York, Harper, 1954), chapter 27, ' Highbrow, Lowbrow, Middlebrow', pp.310 ff.

9 Ruth Finnegan, *The Hidden Musicians* (Cambridge, Cambridge University Press, 1989).

10 See, for example, John Rosselli, *Music and Musicians in Nineteenth Century Italy* (London, Batsford, 1991), and John Dizikes, *Opera in America; a Cultural History* (New Haven, Yale University Press, 1993).

11 For country house performances, see Sybil Rosenfeld, *The Temples of Thespis: Some Private Theatres and Theatricals in England and Wales, 1700–1820* (London, The Society for Theatre Research, 1978); for the origins of societies, see George Taylor, *History of the Amateur Theatre* (Melksham, Venton, 1976), pp. 38, 46; for Manchester, Manchester Central Library, Manchester Athenaeum Dramatic Society, *Jubilee Commemoration*, April 1897, *passim*. and Manchester Athenaeum, *Centenary Celebrations*, 1835–1935, *passim*.

12 *NODA Bulletin*, Summer 1976, 64.

13 These data and most subsequent listings of societies are culled from various editions of NODA, *Directory, Yearbook, Bulletin*.

14 Dumayne Warne, *Fifty Years of Amateur Theatre* (London, National Operatic and

Dramatic Association, 1949), was the official Golden Jubilee history; another is in preparation for its centenary.

15 Frank Clarke, *Rossington Remembered*, Book 3 (Rossington, self-published, 1994), pp. 83–5.

16 *NODA Bulletin*, December 1937.

17 For a discussion of earlier popular forms, see Dave Russell, *Popular Music in England, 1840–1914* (Manchester, Manchester University Press, 2nd edn, 1987).

18 Dina Mira Copelman, *Women in the Classroom Struggle: Elementary Schoolteachers in London, 1870–1914* (Ann Arbor, University of Michigan Press, 1987), p. 201; I owe this reference to Carol Dyhouse of the University of Sussex.

19 See Peter Bailey, *Music Hall: the Basics of Pleasure* (Milton Keynes, Open University Press, 1986).

20 A. A. Jackson, *Semi-detached London* (London, Allen and Unwin 1973), p. 184.

21 Alan Ayckbourn, *A Chorus of Disapproval* (London, Faber, 1986).

22 Peter Bailey, '"Naughty but nice": musical comedy and the rhetoric of the girl, 1892–1914', in Michael R. Booth and Joel H. Kaplan (eds), *The Edwardian Theatre* (Cambridge, Cambridge University Press, 1996).

23 For a discussion of the sporting divide, see John Lowerson, *Sport and the English Middle Classes, 1870–1914* (Manchester, Manchester University Press, 1993), ch. 6, pp.154 ff.

24 Alan P. Herbert, *No Fine on Fun* (London, Methuen, 1957).

25 Preston Reference Library, Preston and District Amateur Operatic Society, Programmes, *Hit the Deck*, 1936.

26 Croydon Public Library, 'Croydon Operatic Society'; Bristol Public Library, Bristol Opera, miscellaneous papers; *Rotherham Advertiser*, 14 March 1925.

27 Birmingham Central Library, Midland Music Makers Grand Opera Society, various programmes.

28 W. Blunt, *John Christie of Glyndebourne* (London, Geoffrey Bles, 1968), and S. Hughes, *Glyndebourne* (London, David and Charles, 1981).

29 Arts Council of Great Britain, *A Report on Opera and Ballet in the UK, 1966–69* (London, Arts Council, 1969), pp. 15–16; Conrad Wilson, *Scottish Opera: The First Ten Years* (London, Collins, 1972).

30 For outlines of individual works see Kurt Ganzl and Alan Lamb, *Ganzl's Book of the Musical Theatre* (London, Bodley Head, 1988). For operetta see Paul H. Lang, *The Experience of Opera* (London, Faber and Faber, 1973), ch. 21, pp. 316 ff.

31 David Cannadine, 'Gilbert and Sullivan: the making and un-making of a "British Tradition"', in Roy Porter (ed.), *Myths of the English* (Cambridge, Polity Press, 1992), pp.12 ff.

32 Arthur Jacobs, *Gilbert and Sullivan* (London, Max Parrish, 1951), pp. 58 ff., and Tony Joseph, *The D'Oyly Carte Opera Company 1875–1982* (Bristol, Bunthorne, 1984).

33 Anthony Hope, *The Prisoner of Zenda* (London 1894 and many subsequent editions). The decades of scholarly neglect have been rectified by Vesna Goldsworthy, *Inventing Ruritania: The Imperialism of the Imagination* (New Haven, Conn., Yale University Press, 1998), which deals very well with literature, film and press but very thinly with operetta.

34 John M. Mackenzie, *Orientalism : History, Theory and the Arts* (Manchester, Manchester University Press, 1995), pp. 189 ff.

35 *Amateur Stage*, February 1959.

36 A.Mcleod, 'Amateur Operatics', *NODA Bulletin*, September 1957, 21.

37 H. Daintree, ' The first Sussex opera', *Sussex County Magazine*, 1927, 30 ff., and Arthur Beckett, 'Dacre of the South', *Sussex County Magazine*, 1931, 32 ff.

38 Georgina Boyes, *The Imagined Village* (Manchester, Manchester University Press, 1993).

39 For instance, D. S. Page and D. R. Billings, *Operas Old and New* (London, Simpson, Marshall, 1929), as an early example.

40 Michael Frayn, 'Festival', in Michael Sissons and Philip French (eds), *Age of Austerity, 1945–1951* (London, Hodder and Stoughton, 1963), p. 334; I am very grateful to Nannette Aldred of the University of Sussex for this reference.

41 For example, see Wilfred Mellers, *Music and Society: England and the European Tradition* (London, Dobson, 1946), pp.102–3.

42 Paddy Scannell, 'Music for the Multitude', *Media, Culture and Society*, 3 (1981), 243 ff.

43 Humphrey Carpenter, *The Envy of the World: Fifty Years of the Third Programme and Radio 3* (London, Weidenfield and Nicholson, 1996), pp. 181 ff.

44 Peter Gammond, *The Oxford Companion to Popular Music* (Oxford, Oxford University Press, 1993).

FURTHER READING

PART ONE: GENDER, IDENTITY AND CIVIC CULTURE

Abercrombie, N., *et al.*, *Sovereign Individuals of Capitalism*, London, Allen & Unwin, 1986.

Belk, R., *Collecting in a Consumer Society*, London, Routledge, 1995.

Bennett, T., *The Birth of the Museum: History, Theory, Politics*, London, Routledge, 1995.

Bourdieu, P., *The Field of Cultural Production*, Cambridge, Polity Press, 1993.

Bunn, J. H., 'The aesthetics of British mercantilism', *New Literary History*, 11 (1980), 303–21.

Burton, A., 'Rules of thumb: British history and "imperial culture" in nineteenth and twentieth-century Britain', *Women's History Review*, 3 (1994), 483–500.

Coleman, B. I. (ed.), *The Idea of the City in Nineteenth-Century Britain*, London, Routledge & Kegan Paul, 1973.

Comaroff, J. and Comaroff, J., *Ethnography and the Historical Imagination*, Oxford, Westview Press, 1992.

Connerton, P., *How Societies Remember*, Cambridge, Cambridge University Press, 1989.

Corbin, A., *Time, Desire and Horror: Towards a History of the Senses*, Cambridge, Polity Press, 1995.

Darcy, C. P., *The Encouragement of Fine Arts in Lancashire 1760–1860*, Manchester, Chetham Society, 1976.

Davidoff, L., '"Adam spoke first and named the orders of the the world": masculine and feminine domains in history and sociology', in H. Corr and L. Jamieson (eds), *Continuity and Change in Work and the Family*, London, Macmillan, 1988.

Davison, G., 'The city as a natural system: theories of urban space in early nineteenth-century Britain', in D. Fraser and A. Sutcliffe (eds), *The Pursuit of Urban History*, London, Edward Arnold, 1983.

Dellheim, C., *The Face of the Past: The Preservation of the Medieval Inheritance in Victorian England*, Cambridge, Cambridge University Press, 1982.

Dennis, R., *English Industrial Cities of the Nineteenth Century*, Cambridge, Cambridge University Press.

Fraser, D., *Power and Authority in the Victorian City*, Oxford, Basil Blackwell, 1979.

Garrard, J., 'Urban elites, 1850–1914: the rule and decline of a new squirearchy?', *Albion*, 27 (1995) 583–621.

Girouard, M., *The English Town*, London, Yale University Press, 1990.

Gunson, N., *Messengers of Grace: Evangelical Missionaries in the South Seas, 1797–1860*, Oxford, Oxford University Press, 1978.

Hall, C., *White, Male and Middle Class: Explorations in Feminism and History*, Oxford, Polity Press, 1992.

Hennock, E. P., *Fit and Proper Persons: Ideal and Reality in Nineteenth-century Urban Government*, London, Edward Arnold, 1973.

Howe, A., *The Cotton Masters 1830–1860*, Oxford, Clarendon, 1984.

Inkster, I., and Morrell, J., *Metropolis and Province: Science in British Culture 1780–1850*, London, Hutchinson, 1983.

Joyce, P., *Democratic Subjects: The Self and the Social in Nineteenth-Century England*, Cambridge, Cambridge University Press, 1994.

Kestener, J., *Masculinities in Victorian Painting*, Aldershot, Scolar Press, 1995.

Kidd, A. J., and Nicholls, D. (eds), *The Making of the British Middle Class? Studies of Regional and Cultural Diversity since the Eighteenth Century*, Stroud, Sutton, 1998.

Lane, T., *Liverpool: City of the Sea*, Liverpool, Liverpool University Press, 1997.

McCracken, G., *Culture and Consumption: New Approaches to the Symbolic Character of Consumer Goods and Activities*, Bloomington, Indiana, University of Indiana Press, 1988.

Macleod, D. S., *Art and the Victorian Middle Class: Money and the Making of Cultural Identity*, Cambridge, Cambridge University Press, 1996.

Mangan, J. A., and Walvin, J. (eds), *Manliness and Morality: Middle-Class Masculinity in Britain and America 1800–1940*, Manchester, Manchester University Press, 1987.

Melman, B., *Women's Orients: English Women and the Middle East, 1718–1918*, London, Macmillan, 1992.

Moore, A., and Crawley, C., *Family and Friends: A Regional Survey of British Portraiture*, London, HMSO, 1992.

Morris, R. J., *The Victorian City: A Reader in British Urban History 1820–1914*, Harlow, Longman, 1993.

Pearce, S. M., *Museums, Objects and Collections: A Cultural Study*, Leicester, Leicester University Press, 1992.

Pratt, M. L., *Imperial Eyes: Travel Writing and Transculturation*, London, Routledge, 1992.

Poovey, M., *Making a Social Body: British Cultural Formation, 1830–1864*, Chicago, University of Chicago Press, 1995.

Savage, M., and Warde, D., *Urban Sociology, Capitalism and Modernity*, London, Macmillan, 1993.

Sedgwick, E. K., *Between Men: English Literature and Homosocial Desire*, New York, Columbia University Press, 1985.

Seed, J., 'Unitarianism, political economy and the antinomies of liberal culture in Manchester 1830–1850', *Social History*, 7 (1982), 1–25.

Sennett, R., *The Fall of Public Man*, London, Faber & Faber, 1993.

—— *Flesh and Stone: The Body and the City in Western Civilisation*, London, Faber & Faber, 1996.

Shires, L. (ed.), *Rewriting the Victorians: Theory, History and the Politics of Gender*, London, Routledge, 1992.

Soloman-Godeau, A., *Male Trouble: A Crisis in Representation*, London, Thames & Hudson, 1997.

Smail, J., *The Origins of Middle-Class Culture: Halifax, Yorkshire, 1660–1780*, London, Cornell University Press, 1994.

Sussman, H., *Victorian Masculinities: Manhood and Masculine Poetics in Early Victorian Literature and Art*, Cambridge, Cambridge University Press, 1995.

Thomas, N., *Colonialism's Culture: Anthropology, Travel and Government*, Oxford, Polity Press, 1994.

Vernon, J., *Politics and the People: A Study in English Political Culture c. 1815–1867*, Cambridge, Cambridge University Press, 1993.

Walkowitz, J., *City of Dreadful Delight: Narratives of Sexual Danger in Later Victorian London*, London, Virago, 1992.

Wolff, J., *Feminine Sentences: Essays on Women and Culture*, Oxford, Polity Press, 1990.

Wolff, J., and Seed, J. (eds), *The Culture of Capital: Art, Power and the Nineteenth-Century Middle Class*, Manchester, Manchester University Press, 1988.

Ware, V., *Beyond the Pale: White Women, Racism and History*, London, Verso, 1992.

Yeo, E. J., *The Contest for Social Science: Relations and Representations of Gender and Class*, London, Rivers Oram Press, 1996.

PART TWO: GENDER, IDENTITY AND CONSUMER CULTURE

Anderson, G., *Victorian Clerks*, Manchester, Manchester University Press, 1976.

Beetham, M., *A Magazine of her Own? Domesticity and Desire in the Woman's Magazine 1800–1914*, London, Routledge, 1996.

Benson, J., *The Rise of Consumer Society in Britain: 1880–1980*, London, Longman, 1994.

Blomley, N. K., *Law, Space and the Geographies of Power*, London, Guildford Press, 1994.

Booth, M. R., and Kaplan, J. H. (eds), *The Edwardian Theatre*, Cambridge, Cambridge University Press, 1996.

Bourdieu, P., *Distinction: A Social Critique of the Judgement of Taste*, London, Routledge & Kegan Paul, 1986.

Boyes, G., *The Imagined Village: Culture, Ideology and the English Folk Revival*, Manchester, Manchester University Press, 1993.

Carey, J., *The Intellectuals and the Masses*, London, Faber & Faber, 1992.

Chouinard, V., 'Geography, law and legal struggles: which ways ahead?', *Progress in Human Geography*, 18 (1994), 415–40.

Copelman, D. M., *London's Women Teachers: Gender, Class and Feminism, 1870–1930*, London, Routledge, 1996.

Craik, E. (ed.), *Marriage and Property: Women and Marital Customs in History*, Aberdeen, Aberdeen University Press, 1984.

Crossick, G. (ed.), *The Lower Middle Class in Britain, 1870–1914*, London, Croom Helm, 1977.

—— and Gerhaud-Haupt, H. (eds), *Shopkeepers and Master Artisans in Nineteeth-century Europe*, London, Methuen, 1984.

—— and Gerhaud-Haupt, H. (eds), *The Petite Bourgeoisie in Europe 1780–1914*, London, Routledge, 1995.

—— and Jaumain S. (eds), *Cathedrals of Consumption: The European Department Store, 1850–1939*, Aldershot, Scolar Press, 1998.

Davidoff, L. & Hall, C., *Family Fortunes: Men and Women of the English Middle Class, 1780–1850*, London, Hutchinson, 1987.

Finnegan, R., *The Hidden Musicians: Music Making in an English Town*, Cambridge, Cambridge University Press, 1989.

Frost, G. S., *Promises Broken: Courtship, Class and Gender in Victorian England*, Charlottesville, University of Virginia Press, 1995.

Gammond, P., *The Oxford Companion to Popular Music*, Oxford, Oxford University Press, 1993.

Goldsworthy, V., *Inventing Ruritania: The Imperialism of the Imagination*, New Haven, 1998.

Goransson, 'Gender and property rights: capital, kin and owner influence in nineteenth and twentieth century Sweden', *Business History*, 35 (1993), 11–32.

Grazia, V. de, and Furlough, E. (eds), *The Sex of Things: Gender and Consumption in Historical Perspective*, Berkeley, University of California Press, 1996.

Grossmith, G. and W. *The Diary of A Nobody*, [1892,] London, Penguin, 1965.

Holcombe, L., *Wives and Property: Reform of the Married Women's Property Law in Nineteenth Century England*, Oxford, Martin Robertson, 1983.

Holmes, A. S., 'The double standard in the English divorce laws, 1857–1923', *Law and Social Enquiry*, 20 (1995), 601–20.

Hosgood, C., '"The knights of the road": commercial travellers and the culture of the commercial room in late Victorian and Edwardian England', *Victorian Studies*, 37 (1994), 519–47.

Kidd, A. J., and Nicholls, D. (eds), *The Making of the British Middle Class? Studies of Regional and Cultural Diversity since the Eighteenth Century*, Stroud, Sutton, 1998.

Light, A., *Forever England: Femininity, Literature and Conservatism between the Wars*, London, Routledge, 1991.

Lockwood, D., *The Blackcoated Worker: A Study in Class Consciousness*, 2nd edn, Oxford, Clarendon Press, 1989.

Loeb, L., *Consuming Angels: Advertising and the Victorian Woman*, Oxford, Oxford University Press, 1994.

Lowerson, J., *Sport and the English Middle Classes: 1880–1914*, Manchester, Manchester University Press, 1993.

McKibbin, R., *Classes and Culture, England 1918–1951*, Oxford, Oxford University Press, 1998.

McLaren, A., *The Trials of Masculinity: Policing Sexual Boundaries, 1870–1930*, Chicago, Chicago University Press.

Mayer, A. J., 'The lower middle class as a historical problem', *Journal of Modern History*, 47 (1975), 409–36.

Miller, D., *Acknowledging Consumption: A Review of New Studies*, London, Routledge, 1995.

Mort, F., *Cultures of Consumption, Masculinities and Social Space in Late Twentieth Century Britain*, London, Routledge, 1996.

Nixon, S., *Hard Looks: Masculinities, Spectatorship and Contemporary Consumption*, London, UCL Press, 1996.

Pennybacker, S., *A Vision for London, 1889–1914: Labour and Everyday Life and the LCC Experiment*, London, Routledge, 1995.

Porter, R. (ed.), *Myths of the English*, Cambridge, Polity Press, 1992.

Pugh, M., *Women and the Women's Movement in Britain 1914–1959*, London, Macmillan, 1992.

Richards, T., *The Commodity Culture of Victorian England: Advertising and Spectacle, 1851–1914*, London, Verso, 1990.

Robson, J. M., *Marriage or Celibacy? The Daily Telegraph on a Victorian Dilemma*, Toronto, University of Toronto Press, 1995.

Roper, M., and Tosh, J., *Manful Assertions: Masculinities in Britain Since 1800*, London, Routledge, 1991.

Russell, D., *Popular Music in England, 1840–1914: A Social History*, Manchester, Manchester University Press, 2nd edn, 1997.

Shanley, M. L., *Feminism, Marriage and the Law in Victorian England*, Princeton, Princeton University Press, 1989.

Smith, C. (ed.), *Regulating Womanhood: Historical Essays on Marriage, Motherhood and Sexuality*, London, Routledge, 1992.

White, C., *Women's Magazines 1693–1968*, London, Michael Joseph, 1970.

Winstanley, M., *The Shopkeeper's World, 1830–1914*, Manchester, Manchester University Press, 1983.

INDEX